Instructor's Manual to Accompany

WESTERN CIVILIZATION

Volume 2 • Since 1300 • Second Edition

JACKSON J. SPIELVOGEL
PENNSYLVANIA STATE UNIVERSITY

PREPARED BY
JAMES W. ERMATINGER
UNIVERSITY OF NEBRASKA–KEARNEY

WEST PUBLISHING COMPANY
MINNEAPOLIS/ST. PAUL   NEW YORK   LOS ANGELES   SAN FRANCISCO

 *TEXT IS PRINTED ON 10% POST CONSUMER RECYCLED PAPER*

COPYRIGHT © 1994 by WEST PUBLISHING CO.
610 Opperman Drive
P.O. Box 64526
St. Paul, MN 55164–0526

ISBN 0–314–03417–X

TABLE OF CONTENTS

PREFACE

2nd Edition

Each chapter of this manual contains six main sections. A *Chapter Outline* provides a quick overview of the materials from <u>Western Civilization</u>. Suggested *Lecture Topics* offers ideas for class presentations. A *Map and Artwork* section includes suggestions for the discussion of geographical and artistic concepts. *Discussion Questions for the Primary Sources (Boxed Documents)*, with page numbers, suggests questions for generating classroom discussion of the primary sources and for integrating them more fully with the text material. *Examination Questions* includes essays, identifications, and multiple-choice questions to meet a variety of testing needs. Each chapter contains about seven to ten essay questions, twenty identifications, and fifty multiple-choice questions. Although some of the multiple-choice questions test students' knowledge of facts and concepts, many have been written to evaluate students' understanding of the material rather than the memorization of facts. Included with the questions are the answers, level of difficulty (easy, medium, difficult) and page number where the material is discussed. The essay questions are meant to foster students' analytical skills in handling historical materials. Finally, each chapter of the manual provides suggestions for *Documentary Films and Musical Selections* that would enhance the presentation of the material covered in the text. At the end of the volume is a set of *Map Identifications* similar to the map exercises in the accompanying Study Guide to facilitate specific geographical points.

-- James W. Ermatinger
1993

CHAPTER 13: RECOVERY AND REBIRTH: THE AGE OF THE RENAISSANCE

CHAPTER OUTLINE

The Impact of Printing

THE ARTISTIC RENAISSANCE
The Artist and Social Status
The Northern Artistic Renaissance
Music in the Renaissance

THE EUROPEAN STATE IN THE RENAISSANCE
The "New Monarchies"
France
England
Spain
The Holy Roman Empire
Eastern Europe
The Ottoman Turks and the End of Byzantium

THE CHURCH IN THE RENAISSANCE
The Problems of Heresy and Reform
The Renaissance Papacy

SUGGESTED LECTURE TOPICS

1. "The Development of Printing and Its Impact on the Development of Western Civilization"

2. "The Role of Women in the Renaissance: Was Rebirth Only for Men?"

3. "The Art of the Renaissance" [a slide lecture]

4. "Were the New Monarchs Really New?"

5. "The Church and the Renaissance"

MAPS AND ARTWORK

1. How Renaissance Italy was an outgrowth of her political separatism.

2. The new national kingdoms of Europe after the Middle Ages, Maps 13.2 and 13.3.

3. The decline of Byzantium and the rise of the Ottomans, Map 13.4.

DISCUSSION QUESTIONS FOR THE PRIMARY SOURCES (BOXED DOCUMENTS)

"Florence, 'Queen City of the Renaissance'": From the viewpoint of Benedetto Dei, what were the characteristics of Florence that made the city so outstanding? Do you think Benedetto was an objective observer? Why or why not? (page 409)

"A Renaissance Banquet": Describe the kinds of people who would be present at a banquet where the foods listed on this menu would be served. (page 411)

"Marriage Negotiations": What were the most important considerations in marriage negotiations? Why were they so important? (page 414)

"A Renaissance Prince": Based on their description, what kind of characteristics did Federigo da Montefeltro display as a ruler? Do you think these were typical of Italian Renaissance princes? (page 418)

"Machiavelli: How Princes Should Honor their Word": What does Machiavelli have to say about being truthful and honest? Compare his ideas with modern politics. (page 420)

"Petrarch: Mountain Climbing and the Search for Spiritual Contentment": What bothers Petrarch about his own intellectual pursuits? How does the conflict within himself reflect the historical debate about the nature of the Renaissance? (page 422)

"A Humanist's Enthusiasm for Greek": Why was Bruni so enthusiastic about the study of Greek? (page 423)

"Pico della Mirandola and the Dignity of Man": What does Pico mean by the "dignity of man?" Why would Pico be regarded as one of the Renaissance Magi? (page 425)

EXAMINATION QUESTIONS

Essays

1. What does the term "Renaissance" mean in the context of Italy in the fourteenth and fifteenth century?

2. Discuss Italian Renaissance humanism: What does the word humanism mean? Who were the humanists? What were their goals? Did they achieve them?

3. Assume that you are a pupil in a Renaissance school. Discuss the curriculum of your school and explain what kind of education you plan to receive. For what occupations will you be prepared?

4. How does the art of the Renaissance reflect the political and social events of the period?

5. In what ways did the European world experience an economic recovery in the fifteenth century? Did the revived economy differ greatly from what it had been?

6. Discuss the major social changes of the Renaissance era. Were these changes actually a rejection of medieval trends? Why or why not?

7. "The major characteristic in the development of the "new monarchies" was the expansion of central government authority in the areas of economic, political, judicial, military, and religious policy." Is this a valid statement in regard to England, Spain, and France? Was the pattern of political development the same in eastern Europe?

8. What was the pattern of political development in Italy? What new political practices (statecraft) did the Italians contribute to Europe? How are these new political practices reflected in the work of Machiavelli?

9. Discuss the major characteristics of the Renaissance papacy. What impact did the policies of the Renaissance popes have on the Catholic church?

Identifications

10. Hanseatic League
11. Monte della Doti
12. Isabella d'Este
13. Petrarch

14. <u>New Cicero</u>
15. Lorenzo Valla
16. civic humanism
17. <u>Corpus Hermeticum</u>
18. Francesco Guicciardini
19. Johannes Gutenberg
20. Raphael
21. Jan van Eyck
22. <u>hermandades</u>
23. Louis XI the Spider
24. Habsburgs
25. Ivan III
26. John Wyclif
27. <u>Sacrosancta</u>
28. Julius II
29. nepotism

Multiple Choice

30. The Italian Renaissance was:
    a. a mass movement of the peasants
    b. characterized by a preoccupation with religion
    c. largely a product of rural Italy
    d. above all a recovery from the "calamitous fourteenth century"

Answer: d, medium, page 408

31. The word Renaissance means:
    a. rebirth
    b. new world
    c. maturation
    d. escape

Answer: a, easy, page 407

32. Economic developments in the Renaissance included:
    a. the growing concentration of more wealth in fewer hands
    b. increased employment due to the change from wool to luxury manufacturing
    c. a boom rivaling that of the High Middle Ages
    d. new trade routes made possible by the Ottoman Turks

Answer: a, difficult, page 408

33. According to Jacob Burckhardt, the Renaissance began in:
     a. France
     b. Switzerland
     c. Italy
     d. Germany

Answer: c, easy, page 407

34. The _____ controlled the finances of Florence.
     a. Fugger
     b. Hansa
     c. Medici
     d. none of the above

Answer: c, easy, page 408

35. The _____ was a commercial and military league set up off the north coast of Germany.
     a. Delian League
     b. Prussian Confederation
     c. Hanseatic League
     d. League of German Cities

Answer: c, easy, page 408

36. The "Queen City of the Renaissance" was:
     a. London
     b. Florence
     c. Rome
     d. Paris

Answer: b, medium, page 409

37. Castiglione's The Courtier described the aristocracy in the sixteenth century through its:
     a. rejection of military training for a classical education
     b. praising of the courtly life
     c. advocating humanism strictly for one's individualistic pleasures
     d. disapproval of the political life

Answer: b, difficult, page 410

38. The aristocracy of the sixteenth century was:
    a. to dominate society as it had done in the Middle Ages
    b. largely surpassed by the upcoming merchant class
    c. still powerful, but with little new blood to keep it vital
    d. extremely uneducated compared to the nobility of the Middle Ages

Answer: a, medium, page 410

39. Banquets during the Renaissance:
    a. expressed the simplicity of the life idealized in courtly society
    b. were not held on Holy Days and on such celebrations as weddings
    c. used used to express wealth and power
    d. were banned by the papacy

Answer: c, medium, page 411 + DOC 2

40. The Third Estate of the fifteenth century was:
    a. predominantly urban
    b. essentially free from the manorial system, especially in eastern Europe
    c. relatively free from violence and disease in urban areas
    d. highly stratified socially and economically in the cities

Answer: d, medium, page 412

41. Slavery in Renaissance Italy:
    a. reached its height in the early sixteenth century
    b. was universally condemned by the Catholic church
    c. saw black slaves from Africa used mostly as courtly domestic servants
    d. all of the above

Answer: c, easy, page 412

42. The reintroduction of slavery in the fourteenth century occurred largely as a result of:
    a. continued warfare and the capture of prisoners
    b. the shortage of labor created by the Black Death
    c. papal decrees encouraging a paternal relationship with heathens
    d. movements for Italian supremacy

Answer: b, medium, page 412

43. Which of the following statements was <u>not</u> true of marriage and family life in Renaissance Italy?
   a. A strong family bond provided political and economic security in a violent world.
   b. Prostitution and homosexuality were condemned as evils that threatened the family structure.
   c. The <u>Monte della Doti</u> was a Florentine investment fund providing dowries for girls in poor families.
   d. Women held autonomy in the household, though the husband made all decisions concerning children.

Answer: b, easy, page 414

44. Marriages in Renaissance Italy were:
   a. based on love and mutual affection
   b. easy to dissolve or annul
   c. an economic necessity of life
   d. often worked out hastily with little thought

Answer: c, medium, page 413 + DOC 3

45. The Medici family in the fifteenth century dominated:
   a. Venice
   b. Florence
   c. Naples
   d. Papal States

Answer: b, easy, page 415

46. By the fifteenth century, Italy was:
   a. a centralized state
   b. dominated by the Papal States exclusively
   c. dominated by five major regional independent powers
   d. the foremost European power

Answer: c, medium, page 415

47. Italy's decline into a battleground for the French and Spanish forces was due to all of the following <u>except</u>:
   a. the political failings of Federico da Montefeltro of Urbino
   b. the failure of Italy's balance of power system
   c. the Italians' fierce loyalty to their own city-states
   d. the lack of a confederation system

Answer: a, difficult, page 417

48.   Federigo da Montefeltro of Urbino was:
      a.   an example of a self-willed, independent Italian prince
      b.   an outspoken advocate of Italian unification
      c.   a callous, disloyal prince, loathed by the papacy
      d.   strictly opposed to the proliferation of <u>condottieri</u> in Italy

Answer: a, difficult, page 416

49.   The idea of a permanent diplomatic ambassador first developed in:
      a.   Russia
      b.   England
      c.   Germany
      d.   Italy

Answer: d, easy, page 418

50.   Machiavelli's ideas as expressed in <u>The Prince</u> achieved:
      a.   a republican state in Italy
      b.   a new attitude of moral responsibility among politicians
      c.   a modern secular concept of power politics
      d.   little in the way of lasting influence

Answer: c, medium, page 419

51.   Humanism in the early fifteenth century:
      a.   increasingly became alienated from political life
      b.   became a self-conscious movement
      c.   rejected the church and Christianity in general
      d.   helped revive Greek as a "living" language

Answer: b, medium, page 421

52.   With the Roman statesman and intellectual Cicero as their model, Florentine humanists defined the role of intellectuals as:
      a.   a passive role, reserving judgment for themselves
      b.   living an active civil life to stimulate intellectual activities
      c.   advisors to great heads of state and politicians
      d.   living a life of leisure and self-gratification to arouse the higher functions of intellect

Answer: b, medium, page 421

53.   Neoplatonism in mid-fifteenth century Italy:
      a.   rejected a hierarchy of substances
      b.   was revived when Marsilio Ficino translated Plato's dialogues
      c.   postulated that humanity's highest duty was obedience to God
      d.   logically denied the previously held belief in the idea of Platonic love

Answer: b, difficult, page 424

54.   Neoplatonism was based on two primary ideas:
      a.   a hierarchy of substances and spiritual love
      b.   dualism of nature and stress on the feminine side
      c.   love of God and order of the universe
      d.   knowledge of the mind and knowledge of the spirit

Answer: a, medium, page 424

55.   The Corpus Hermeticum:
      a.   contained nothing about the occult
      b.   radically conflicted with the ideas of Pico della Mirandola's Oration on the Dignity of Man
      c.   postulated that humanity's highest duty was obedience to God
      d.   logically denied the previously held belief in the idea of Platonic love

Answer: c, difficult, page 424

56.   Pico della Mirandola's Oration on the Dignity of Man stated that:
      a.   humans were fallen creatures, but regain their place by following God's will
      b.   human beings were nothing more than undifferentiated animals
      c.   humans were divine and destined to spiritual life
      d.   humans could choose to be earthly or spiritual creatures

Answer: d, medium, page 425 + DOC 8

57.   The liberal education taught by Vittorino da Feltre:
      a.   contained as its primary goal the creation of well-rounded citizens
      b.   was for all segments of society, rich and poor
      c.   advocated concentration on science and research, not rhetoric and verbal skills
      d.   almost entirely excluded Christian teachings

Answer: a, medium, page 425

58. Liberal education in the Renaissance included all of the following except:
    a. the mastery of Greek and Latin
    b. a stress on physical education
    c. the study of military theory
    d. the study of music

Answer: c, easy, page 426

59. Humanism's effect on the writing of history included:
    a. a stress on God's influence on human events
    b. an emphasis on political, economic, and other social forces
    c. anti-Christian attacks on medieval historians and non-humanists
    d. an increasing reliance on archaeological evidence

Answer: b, difficult, page 426

60. _____ played a leading role in perfecting reusable, movable type for printing:
    a. Johannes Gutenberg
    b. François Rabelais
    c. Francesco Guicciardini
    d. Lorenzo Valla

Answer: a, easy, page 426

61. The development of printing in the fifteenth century:
    a. pertained predominantly to secular works, as theological works were still done by hand
    b. saw the invention of movable type by Nicholas Fabian
    c. ensured that literacy would spread rapidly in European society
    d. all of the above

Answer: c, medium, page 427

62. Italian artists in the fifteenth century began to:
    a. ignore nature and paint for expression
    b. experiment in areas of perspective
    c. copy the works of previous artists
    d. move away from the study of anatomical structure

Answer: b, difficult, page 428

63.   The shift to the High Renaissance saw _____ as a new cultural center of
       the Italian Renaissance.
      a.   Rome
      b.   Venice
      c.   Naples
      d.   Milan

Answer: a, medium, page 429

64.   During the Renaissance, artists emerged as heroes.
      a.   True
      b.   False

Answer: a, easy, page 431

65.   Choose the correct relationship between artist and his work:
      a.   Leonardo da Vinci--<u>Last Supper</u>
      b.   Raphael--<u>The Martyrdom of St. Sebastian</u>
      c.   Michelangelo--<u>Alba Madonna</u>
      d.   Antonio Pollaiuolo--<u>Mona Lisa</u>

Answer: a, easy, page 430

66.   Which of the following is <u>not</u> true of Northern Renaissance artists?
      a.   They had an incredible mastery of the laws of perspective.
      b.   The most influential artist was Jan van Eyck.
      c.   There was an emphasis on illuminated manuscripts and wooden
          panel painting.
      d.   They valued the human form as the primary vehicle of expression.

Answer: d, difficult, page 433

67.   The "new monarchs" of the late fifteenth century in Europe:
      a.   continued the trend toward decentralization
      b.   were often obsessed with the acquisition and expansion of power
      c.   attempted to build up the nobility for support
      d.   accepted the domination of the church as a matter of course

Answer: b, medium, page 434

68.   The result of the Hundred Years' War:
      a.   reinvigorated France
      b.   caused economic turmoil in England

    c.   factionalized England
    d.   all of the above

Answer: d, easy, page 435

69.   Under Ferdinand and Isabella, Spain:
    a.   became increasingly corrupt and inefficient
    b.   saw society become more secular
    c.   saw Muslim power vanish from the peninsula
    d.   had little remaining dissension and was thoroughly unified

Answer: c, medium, page 436

70.   All of the following monarchs were successful in continuing the centralization of their "new monarchies" except:
    a.   Maximilian I of the Holy Roman Empire
    b.   Henry VII of England
    c.   Ferdinand of Aragon in Spain
    d.   Louis XI the Spider of France

Answer: a, medium, page 438

71.   The most centralized state of eastern Europe by the early sixteenth century was:
    a.   Hungary
    b.   Russia
    c.   Poland
    d.   the Byzantine Empire

Answer: b, easy, page 439

72.   The Habsburg dynasty ruled in:
    a.   Poland
    b.   Italy
    c.   Holy Roman Empire
    d.   Russia

Answer: c, medium, page 439

73.   The Byzantine Empire was finally destroyed by_____in 1453.
    a.   the crusaders
    b.   the Persians
    c.   the Russians

    d.   the Turks

Answer: d, easy, page 440

74.   Religious unrest in the fifteenth century saw:
        a.   John Wyclif start the Lollard movement in Germany
        b.   the conciliar movement greatly weaken papal power
        c.   John Hus burned at the stake as a heretic
        d.   church decrees of <u>Sacrosancta</u> and <u>Frequens</u> work to great effect

Answer: c, medium, page 441

75.   John Wyclif did all of the following <u>except</u>:
        a.   claim the pope was the Antichrist
        b.   claim faith alone was the Christian's sole source of authority
        c.   claim there was no scriptural basis for papal claims of temporal
              authority
        d.   condemn the printing of the Bible in the vernacular

Answer: b, difficult, page 441

76.   The Renaissance popes did all of the following <u>except</u>:
        a.   patronize Renaissance culture
        b.   participate in temporal authority and interests
        c.   attempt to return the papacy to more humble times
        d.   all of the above

Answer: c, easy, page 442

77.   The Renaissance papacy:
        a.   was exemplified by the spartan existence of Leo X
        b.   saw popes build dynasties over several generations to maintain
              power
        c.   was little concerned with war and politics, as shown by Julius II
        d.   was often seen as debauched, especially under Pope Alexander VI

Answer: d, medium, page 443

SUGGESTED FILMS

The Spirit of the Renaissance. Encyclopedia Britannica, 31 min. (color).

Renaissance: Its Beginnings in Italy. Encyclopedia Britannica, 26 min. (color).

Civilisation: Man--The Measure of All Things. Time-Life Films, 52 min. (color).

Civilisation: The Hero as Artist. Time-Life Films, 52 min. (color).

Once Upon a Wall. The Great Age of Fresco. BFA Educational Media, 18 min. (color).

Michelangelo. Encyclopedia Britannica, 32 min. (color).

Michelangelo: The Last Giant. McGraw-Hill, 68 min. (color).

I, Leonardo da Vinci. McGraw-Hill, 52 min. (color).

Tell Me If Anything Ever Was Done: Leonardo da Vinci. Time-Life Films, 50 min. (color).

Flanders in the Fifteenth Century--The First Oil Paintings. Radim Films, 25 min. (color).

Dürer and the Renaissance. McGraw-Hill, 15 min. (color).

Music in the Arts of the Renaissance. CC Films, 28 min. (color).

Hanseatic League. Association-Sterling Films, 10 min. (color).

1492: Queen Isabel and Her Spain. International Film Bureau, 32 min. (color).

Venice: The Great Renaissance Merchant State. Benckmark Films, Inc., 20 min. (color).

The Fall of Constantinople. Time-Life Films, 34 min. (color).

The Christians: Princes and Prelates. McGraw-Hill Films, 41 min. (color).

SUGGESTIONS FOR MUSIC

Songs, Gaillardes and Dances of the Renaissance (Musical Heritage Society-3594)

<u>Secular Music of the Renaissance</u> (Musical Heritage Society-713)

<u>Lute Music of the German Renaissance</u> (Musical Heritage Society-1188)

<u>Fifteenth Century Netherlands Masters</u> (Decca-DL9413)

Palestrina, <u>Stabat Mater</u> (Vox-PL9740)

<u>A Renaissance Christmas</u> (Nonesuch-9-79134-1 F)

CHAPTER 14: THE AGE OF REFORMATION

CHAPTER OUTLINE

PRELUDE TO REFORMATION: THE NORTHERN RENAISSANCE
Christian or Northern Renaissance Humanism
Erasmus
Thomas More

PRELUDE TO REFORMATION: CHURCH AND RELIGION ON THE EVE OF THE REFORMATION
The Clergy
Popular Religion

MARTIN LUTHER AND THE REFORMATION IN GERMANY
The Early Luther
The Development of Lutheranism
Church and State

GERMANY AND THE REFORMATION: RELIGION AND POLITICS

THE SPREAD OF THE PROTESTANT REFORMATION
Lutheranism in Scandinavia
The Zwinglian Reformation
The Radical Reformation: The Anabaptists
The Reformation in England
The Brief Reign of Edward
Queen Mary and the Catholic Revival

John Calvin and the Development of Calvinism
Calvin's Geneva
The Spread of Calvinism

THE SOCIAL IMPACT OF THE PROTESTANT REFORMATION
The Family
Education
Religious Practices and Popular Culture

THE CATHOLIC REFORMATION
The Society of Jesus
A Revived Papacy
The Council of Trent

SUGGESTED LECTURE TOPICS

1. "Reformers in Profile: Luther, Calvin, and Henry"

2. "Politics and the Reformation: The Role of Charles V"

3. "The Social Implications of the Reformation: Was Europe Transformed by Religious Divisions?"

4. "The Church's Response: Loyola, Avila and the Inquisition"

MAPS AND ARTWORK

1. Charles V, a dissipated conglomeration of family lands, Map 14.1.

2. How quickly the Religious map of Europe changed and fragmented, Map 14.2.

DISCUSSION QUESTIONS FOR THE PRIMARY SOURCES (BOXED DOCUMENTS)

"Erasmus: In Praise of Folly": What are Erasmus's criticisms of monks? What did he hope to achieve by this satirical attack on monastic practices? (page 450)

"Luther and the Ninety-Five Theses": Summarize the major points of Luther's Ninety-Five Theses? Why did they have such a strong appeal in Germany? (page

454)

"Luther and the 'Robbing and Murdering Hordes of Peasants'": What are the three terrible sins of the peasants? Why is Luther so harsh on the peasants? (page 457)

"A Reformation Debate: The Marburg Colloquy": Based on this example, why do you think Reformation debates led to further hostility rather than compromise and unity? (page 464)

"The Trial of Michael Sattler": Based on this example, create a profile of an Anabaptist. Why were Sattler's judges so hostile? (page 466)

"The Role of Discipline in the 'Most Perfect School of Christ on Earth'": Based on the examples given here, what kinds of activities did the consistory hope to prevent? Why was Calvinism so determined to control the personal lives of citizens? (page 471)

"A Protestant Woman": What new ideas did Catherine Zell bring to the Reformation? Why did people react so strongly against them? (page 472)

"Loyola and Obedience to 'Our Holy Mother, the Hierarchical Church'": What are the fundamental assumptions that underlie Loyola's rules for "thinking with the church"? What do these assumptions tell you about the nature of the Catholic reform movement? (page 477)

EXAMINATION QUESTIONS

Essays

1. What was Christian humanism and how did it help prepare the way for the Protestant Reformation? Did Erasmus "lay the egg that Luther hatched?"

2. What were the sources of discontent among the Catholic clergy on the eve of the Reformation? What were the manifestations of popular religious piety on the eve of the Reformation?

3. What was Luther's problem and how did he solve it? How did Luther's new religious ideas differ from those of Catholicism?

4. What role did politics play in the establishment of Lutheranism? Use examples from Germany and Scandinavia.

5. Compare and contrast the chief ideas of Zwinglianism, Anabaptism, and Lutheranism. What did they have in common? How were they different?

6. Why do some historians speak of the English Reformation as an act of state?

7. Discuss the chief ideas of Calvinism and show how they were similar to the ideas of Lutheranism. How did they vary from the ideas of Lutheranism? Why did Calvinism become the major international form of Protestantism?

8. What impact did Reformation doctrines have on the family, education, and popular religious practices?

9. What were the contributions of the papacy, Council of Trent, and the Jesuits to the revival of Catholicism?

Identifications

10. Utopia
11. Erasmus
12. Johann Eck
13. "A Mighty Fortress is Our God"
14. Charles V
15. Habsburg-Valois Wars
16. Philip Melanchthon
17. Peace of Augsburg
18. Ulrich Zwingli
19. Anabaptists
20. John of Leiden
21. Anne Boleyn
22. Thomas Cromwell
23. Queen Mary
24. John Calvin
25. Ecclesiastical Ordinances
26. predestination
27. Genevan Academy
28. Pope Paul III
29. Council of Trent
30. Inquisition
31. Marburg Colloquy

Multiple Choice

32. The northern Christian humanists:
    a. felt pessimistic about the future of humanity
    b. were sophisticated and realistic in their expectations
    c. gained much support from wealthy patricians, especially in the south German cities
    d. doubted that education could solve the world's problems

Answer: c, medium, page 448

33. Erasmus aimed at reforming Christianity through all of the following except:
    a. spreading Luther's ideas on reform
    b. deemphasizing and satirizing the external forms of religion
    c. translating the Bible and works of the early church fathers
    d. emphasizing "the philosophy of Christ" as a guide for daily life

Answer: a, easy, page 449

34. Thomas More's Utopia:
    a. illustrated the northern humanists' break with the Catholic church
    b. represented the high point of northern humanist thought
    c. presented a revolutionary social order based on communal property
    d. led to his execution at the hands of Henry VIII

Answer: c, medium, page 450

35. Just prior to Luther's reform movement, Europe's clergy:
    a. ended the practice of pluralism
    b. saw the nobility dominate the highest church offices
    c. was economically prosperous at every level
    d. all of the above

Answer: b, medium, page 451

36. Popular religion in the Late Middle Ages and Renaissance:
    a. saw the popular growth of the mystical movement known as the Modern Devotion
    b. witnessed a decline in the belief in relics and indulgences
    c. never existed
    d. sought to do away with traditional beliefs and practices of the

Catholic church

Answer: a, difficult, page 452

37. The Imitation of Christ:
    a. was Luther's earliest criticism of the Catholic church
    b. is generally regarded as written by Frederick the Wise of Saxony
    c. stressed a life of religious dogma and devotion to formal theology
    d. was the great mystical classic of the Modern Devotion movement

Answer: d, difficult, page 452

38. Martin Luther's early life was characterized by:
    a. failure to follow the daily routine of monastic life
    b. an obsession with his own sins
    c. his love for the study of law
    d. his rejection of the Bible as a 'contradictory' work

Answer: b, medium, page 453

39. To Martin Luther, the question of "How can I be saved?" was answered through:
    a. the doctrine of justification by grace through faith
    b. doing good works for one's universal brotherhood
    c. a strict devotion to a monastic order, as with his own Augustinian order
    d. the sacramental system

Answer: a, difficult, page 453

40. The indulgence controversy that drove Luther to split with the Catholic church concerned:
    a. Albrecht of Brandenburg's selling of a special jubilee indulgence
    b. the archbishopric of Mainz
    c. the construction of Saint Peter's Cathedral in Rome
    d. all of the above

Answer: d, easy, page 453

41. Luther's Ninety-Five Theses were not concerned with:
    a. the financial policies of the papacy
    b. the dismantling of the sacramental system
    c. the selling of indulgences

    d.   the souls in purgatory

Answer: b, medium, page 454

42.   An important result of the Leipzig Debate of 1519 was:
        a.   Luther's conviction that he was doing God's will
        b.   Luther's defeat of the Catholic theologian Johann Eck
        c.   Pope Leo X's acceptance of Luther's stand on justification through faith alone
        d.   all of the above

Answer: a, easy, page 454

43.   Martin Luther's pamphlets of 1520 dealt with all of the following <u>except</u>:
        a.   the papal interpretation of scripture
        b.   the destructive nature of marriage
        c.   a call for German princes to overthrow the papacy
        d.   the freedoms and duties of the Christian man

Answer: d, difficult, page 454

44.   The Edict of Worms:
        a.   contained Luther's refutation of Johann Eck's accusations
        b.   expressed Luther's rejection of Pope Leo X's spiritual authority
        c.   called Luther to appear before Emperor Charles V to recant his "heresies"
        d.   made Luther an outlaw within the Holy Roman Empire

Answer: d, easy, page 455

45.   The German city that served as the center for the diffusion of Luther's ideas was:
        a.   Wittenberg
        b.   Frankenhausen
        c.   Nuremberg
        d.   Berlin

Answer: a, easy, page 456

46.   The Peasants' War of 1524-1525:
        a.   was led by a radical ex-follower of Luther, Philip Melanchthon
        b.   furthered the spread of Lutheranism throughout all of Europe
        c.   was praised by Luther as it destroyed the papal-dominated areas of

Germany
 d. was primarily a revolt by peasants against local lords

Answer: d, medium, page 457

47. All of the following were associated with Luther's new form of Protestantism <u>except</u>:
  a. a "priesthood of all believers"
  b. transubstantiation
  c. baptism
  d. musical versions of the Gospel

Answer: b, difficult, page 458

48. As Holy Roman Emperor, Charles V did all of the following <u>except</u>:
  a. ally his forces with the Ottoman Turks in attacking German Protestants
  b. fight a series of wars with Francis I of France, known as the Habsburg-Valois wars
  c. fail to stop the political fragmentation of Germany
  d. fight the Schmalkaldic Wars against an alliance of Lutheran cities

Answer: a, medium, page 458

49. The Habsburg-Valois Wars led to:
  a. the defeat of Francis I of France in 1544
  b. the solution of the Lutheran problem in Germany
  c. Charles V's sacking of Rome in 1527
  d. the final defeat of the Turks in Austria at the Battle of Mohács in 1526

Answer: c, difficult, page 459

50. The Schmalkaldic Wars fought between Charles V and German Protestant princes resulted in:
  a. the defeat of the Schmalkaldic League
  b. the defeat of Charles V at the Battle of Mühlberg
  c. Charles joining forces with Henry II of France to neutralize the Schmalkaldic League
  d. the abdication of Charles V in 1566

Answer: d, medium, page 461

51. An end to the religious warfare in Germany in the first half of the sixteenth century came in 1555 with:
    a. the Battle of Mühlberg
    b. the Battle of Mohács
    c. the Peace of Augsburg
    d. the Diet of Augsburg

Answer: c, easy, page 461

52. During the Protestant Reformation, the Scandinavian countries:
    a. remained bastions of Catholicism
    b. failed to achieve any long-lasting unification
    c. were dominated by the Norwegian king Christian II
    d. became Calvinist, especially during the rule of Gustavus Vasa

Answer: b, easy, page 461

53. Prior to the Zwinglian Reformation, Switzerland:
    a. was unified under the rule of Maximilian in 1499
    b. was composed of thirteen forest cantons ruled by oligarchies of wealthy citizens
    c. became Europe's greatest economic power under the Swiss Confederation
    d. was the principal exporter of mercenary soldiers in Europe

Answer: d, medium, page 462

54. The Swiss reform movement under Ulrich Zwingli:
    a. was largely a rural movement among the forest cantons
    b. was temporarily halted by Zwingli's death in the Swiss Civil War of 1531
    c. concurred with Luther's views on the sacraments
    d. was aided by the unity between Swiss and German reform movements

Answer: b, difficult, page 463

55. Zwinglianism was a Swiss Reformation movement that:
    a. first took hold in Zurich with the military coup led by Ulrich Zwingli
    b. was known for its elaborate church decorations and services
    c. stressed state supervision over the church
    d. kept many remnants of "papal Christianity"

Answer: c, difficult, page 463

56. The Marburg Colloquy of 1529:
     a. produced no agreement or alliance between the Lutheran and Zwinglian movements
     b. was fought over the fundamental issue of baptism
     c. pitted Martin Bucer against Landgrave Philip of Hesse over the issue of the Lord's Supper
     d. swayed Ulrich Zwingli to accept Lutheran doctrine

Answer: a, medium, page 463 + DOC 4

57. The Anabaptists:
     a. were most radical and militant under Menno Simons in Zürich
     b. were not regarded as a political threat as they preached separation between church and state
     c. were founded by Conrad Grebel, beginning as an elitist movement
     d. considered all its believers equal priests spreading the spirit of early Christianity

Answer: d, easy, page 463 + DOC 4

58. The group of Anabaptists known as the Swiss Brethren were founded in Zürich by:
     a. Heinrich Büllinger
     b. Conrad Grebel
     c. Menno Simons
     d. Gretchen Grendle

Answer: b, medium, page 465

59. Anabaptism in the German city of Münster was characterized by:
     a. a wild-eyed millenarian movement
     b. the dominant leadership of Michael Sattler
     c. conservative pacifist tendencies under the leadership of John of Leiden
     d. all of the above

Answer: a, easy, page 465

60. The Reformation in England under Henry VIII:
     a. was triggered by Henry's desire to annul his marriage
     b. witnessed the complete transformation of Catholic doctrine

    c.   nearly ended with Thomas Cromwell's mishandling of the treasury

    d.   saw Parliament's leadership over the Church of England

Answer: a, easy, page 467

61.   Prior to the Reformation, English religious life was characterized by:

    a.   the strength of the heretical Lollard movement among the aristocracy

    b.   Henry VIII's savage attacks against the pope

    c.   strong antipapal and anticlerical feelings among the populace

    d.   none of the above

Answer: c, easy, page 467

62.   The immediate cause of the Reformation in England was:

    a.   the renewed strength and dominance of the papacy in the late 1520s

    b.   the spreading of Luther's writings throughout England in the 1520s

    c.   Cardinal Wolsey's treachery against Henry VIII

    d.   Queen Catherine's failure to produce a male offspring

Answer: d, medium, page 467

63.   Identify the false description among the following officials of Henry VIII:

    a.   Thomas More--Lord Chancellor executed for not accepting the new Church of England

    b.   Thomas Cranmer--Archbishop of Canterbury executed for refusing to annul the king's marriage

    c.   Thomas Cromwell--principal secretary who confiscated monasteries to bolster the treasury

    d.   Cardinal Wolsey--Lord Chancellor who failed to gain papal annulment of the king's marriage

Answer: b, difficult, page 467

64.   After establishing the Church of England, Henry VIII:

    a.   reaffirmed many Catholic doctrines through the Six Articles Act of 1539

    b.   involved Parliament in approving church doctrine

    c.   became preoccupied with foreign affairs and finding a perfect wife

    d.   all of the above

Answer: d, easy, page 468

65.   The Edwardian Reformation:

    a.   began with the brilliant regency of the Duke of Somerset

    b.   saw King Edward strip away the powers granted to Parliament by Henry VIII

    c.   witnessed rapid changes in Protestant doctrine and liturgy

    d.   ended with the military coup of the duke of Northumberland

Answer: c, medium, page 468

66.   The reign of Queen Mary of England was most noted for:

    a.   a failed Catholic restoration

    b.   constant war with Spanish territories

    c.   temporarily ending the Protestant Reformation in England

    d.   the issuing of the Act of Supremacy and the Treason Act in 1534

Answer: a, easy, page 468

67.   Which of the following statements best applies to John Calvin's reform movement?

    a.   Calvin rejected Luther's writings for their belief in "justification by faith alone."

    b.   Predestination made Calvinism a most passive religion as its followers were ensured salvation.

    c.   The belief that humans must "obey God rather than men" opened the door for Calvinist rebellion against secular powers.

    d.   As only God possessed the power of discipline and enforcing popular behavior, the Calvinist church did little to interfere in people's lives.

Answer: c, medium, page 469

68.   John Calvin's <u>Institutes of the Christian Religion</u>:

    a.   had little popular impact as it was only written in Latin

    b.   was a masterful synthesis of Protestant thought

    c.   systematically explained the fundamental difference between Calvinist and Lutheran doctrines

    d.   led to his eviction from France by Francis I

Answer: b, difficult, page 469

69.   In Geneva, the Calvinists:

    a.   imposed strict penalties for blasphemy and immoral behavior

    b.   reformed the city with little opposition from an enthusiastic populace

    c.   saw their reforms jeopardized by the execution of Michael Servetus

    d.   withdrew the Ecclesiastical Ordinances in 1541

Answer: a, difficult, page 470

70. The Ecclesiastical Ordinances of 1541 in Geneva:
    a. eradicated the city's former church offices of pastors, teachers, elders, and deacons
    b. enabled the Consistory to oversee the moral life of the city and issue "fraternal corrections"
    c. was the Genevan nationalists' attempt to overthrow the control of John Calvin
    d. none of the above

Answer: b, easy, page 470

71. The efforts of "God's trumpet," John Knox, enabled:
    a. Calvinism to emerge victorious in Scotland
    b. the Belgic Confession to become the first confession of faith in the Netherlands
    c. the German Reformed church to dominate German and Polish lands
    d. the Genevan Academy to train leaders for the Reformed Protestant movement of Europe

Answer: a, easy, page 471

72. The Reformation changed conceptions of the family by:
    a. substantially transforming women's subordinate place in society
    b. destroying possible career avenues for women
    c. extoling the superior state of marriage over celibacy
    d. encouraging women to take more active roles in religious life, as exemplified by Catherine Zell of Germany

Answer: b, medium, page 473

73. The Reformation affected the development of education in Europe by:
    a. replacing Philip Melanchthon's long-standing educational system
    b. aiming Protestant education at only the nobility and wealthy bourgeoisie
    c. eradicating all humanist influences
    d. introducing the gymnasium into schools, especially in Germany

Answer: d, easy, page 474

74. The Reformation successfully abolished all of the following from the lives of Europe's Protestant community <u>except</u> for:

    a.   indulgences
    b.   the celebrations of religious holy days
    c.   taverns
    d.   clerical celibacy

Answer: c, difficult, page 474

75.   Teresa of Avila was a:
    a.   realist
    b.   pragmatist
    c.   mystic
    d.   none of the above

Answer: c, easy, page 475

76.   Ignatius Loyola's <u>The Spiritual Exercises</u>:
    a.   was a training manual for spiritual development
    b.   called for the putting aside of personal judgment in favor of obeying the Catholic church
    c.   praised the construction, adornment, and veneration of churches
    d.   all of the above

Answer: d, easy, page 475

77.   The efforts at reform in the Catholic Reformation were well characterized by:
    a.   Pope Paul III, who proved to be ultra-conservative in refusing possible changes within the church
    b.   the Roman Inquisition, which in 1542 ferreted out "heretics" compromising with Protestant innovations
    c.   the Council of Trent, at which moderate Catholics and Jesuits heard the Protestants proclaim their doctrines
    d.   Pope Paul IV, a moderate pope who proposed compromise in Catholic-Protestant disputes

Answer: b, difficult, page 476

78.   The pontificate of Pope Paul III witnessed:
    a.   the victory of moderate, compromising cardinals, led by Cardinal Contarini, at the colloquy at Regensburg
    b.   the creation of the Index of Forbidden Books
    c.   a study of the church's problems and corruption by the Reform Commission
    d.   the end to Cardinal Caraffa's Roman Inquisition in 1542

Answer: c, easy, page 476

79. Under Pope Paul IV,:
    a. compromise and concessions to Protestants on doctrinal issues were encouraged
    b. any hope of restoring Christian unity was lost
    c. the Jesuits were stripped of their uncontrollable powers
    d. the Council of Trent was begun and concluded in under three years

Answer: b, medium, page 477

80. Following the Council of Trent, the Catholic church:
    a. possessed a clear body of doctrine under the supremacy of the popes
    b. declared that it was the only institution that could interpret Scripture
    c. reaffirmed its belief in purgatory and indulgences
    d. all of the above

Answer: d, easy, page 478

SUGGESTIONS FOR FILMS

The Reformation: Age of Revolt. Encyclopedia Educational Corp., 24 min. (color).

The Reformation. Coronet Instructional Films, 14 min. (color).

The Reformation. McGraw-Hill Films, 52 min. (color).

Civilization: Protest and Communication. Time-Life Films, 52 min. (color).

The Christians: Protest and Reform. McGraw-Hill Films, 39 min. (color).

The World of Martin Luther. Columbia Pictures, 30 min. (black/white).

Martin Luther and the Protestant Reformation. Time-Life Films, 30 min. (black/white).

John Calvin. University of Utah, Educational Media Center, 29 min. (color).

A Matter of Conscience: Henry VIII and Thomas More. Learning Corporation of America, 30 min. (color).

<u>English History: Tudor Period</u>. Coronet Instructional Films, 11 min. (black/white).

CHAPTER 15: DISCOVERY AND CRISIS IN THE SIXTEENTH AND SEVENTEENTH CENTURIES

CHAPTER OUTLINE

Rebellions
The English Revolution

THE WITCHCRAFT CRAZE

CULTURE IN A TURBULENT WORLD
Art
Thought: The World of Montaigne
A Golden Age of Literature: England and Spain

SUGGESTED LECTURE TOPICS

1. "The Age of Discovery: The Iberian Scramble for the World"

2. "Europe, 1560-1650: Was It an Age of Crisis?"

3. "The Wars of Religion in the Sixteenth and Seventeenth Centuries: How Religious Were They?

4. "The Baroque Style" [a slide lecture]

5. "Spain: How a First Rate Power Became a Third Rate Power in Less than a Century"

MAPS AND ARTWORK

1. Coastal Exploration of the world, Map 15.1. Compare the map with the picture of the World Map of the Early 16th century.

2. The Thirty Years war, a total war, nearly all of Europe involved, Map 15.3.

3. The Northern Renaissance compared with the Italian Renaissance in art.

4. The Imperial Portraiture, showing the elegance and stature of the office.

DISCUSSION QUESTIONS FOR THE PRIMARY SOURCES (BOXED DOCUMENTS)

"The Spanish Conquistador: Cortés and the Conquest of Mexico": What does Cortés focus on in his description of an Aztec city? Why do you think he felt justified in overthrowing the Aztec Empire? (page 487)

"Las Casas and the Spanish Treatment of the American Natives": In what ways did this account help create the image of the Spaniards as "cruel and murderous fanatics?" Do you think Las Casas exaggerated in his account? How? (page 488)

"Philip II, the Most Catholic King of Spain": What did Suriano's account reveal about the personality of Philip II? Is it in agreement with the picture of the king evident in Philip's own letter? How do you explain the differences? (page 493)

"Queen Elizabeth Addresses Parliament (1601)": Summarize the arguments that Elizabeth made in her speech to Parliament. How does this speech reveal Elizabeth's shrewdness as a ruler? (page 498)

"The Face of War in the Seventeenth Century": What does this document reveal about the effect of war on ordinary Europeans? Compare this description to the descriptions of the treatment of civilians in other wars. Does Grimmelshausen exaggerate or does this description agree with the other descriptions? (page 506)

"The Execution of a King": What can you learn about the qualities of Charles I from this document? How did these same qualities help determine the outcome of the English Civil War? (page 511)

"A Witchcraft Trial in Germany": What does this document tell us about the spread of witchcraft persecutions in the seventeenth century? (page 513)

"William Shakespeare: In Praise of England": Besides patriotism, what other motives did Shakespeare have in writing this tribute to England? (page 518)

EXAMINATION QUESTIONS

Essays

1. Compare and contrast Portuguese and Spanish patterns of exploration and expansion.

2. What correlation is there between overseas expansion and economic, social, and

political developments?

3. The wars of religion in the second half of the sixteenth century were often confused conflicts that involved religious, political, economic, and social issues. Discuss the religious, economic, social, and political issues involved in the French Wars of Religion and the revolt of the Netherlands. Do you think the religious issue was the most important one? Why or why not?

4. Elizabeth of England and Philip II of Spain were two of Europe's most famous monarchs in the second half of the sixteenth century. Compare and contrast their methods of ruling and their foreign policies. Which one was a more successful ruler? Why?

5. What were the economic and social problems that troubled Europe from 1560 to 1650? Do these problems constitute a "crisis?"

6. Why have some historians labeled the Thirty Years' War as the "last of the religious wars," while others have called it the "first modern war?" Why can 1648 be seen as a true turning point in European civilization?

7. What was the military revolution and what effect did it have on warfare in the sixteenth and seventeenth centuries?

8. England in the seventeenth century witnessed a general revolutionary upheaval that involved a struggle between king and Parliament. What were the issues (causes) of this struggle? What role did the Puritans play in its course? In what ways was England changed by it?

9. What does the witchcraft craze tell us about European society in the sixteenth and seventeenth centuries?

10. How did the artistic and literary achievements of the late sixteenth and early seventeenth centuries reflect the political and social developments of that period?

Identifications

11. Ferdinand Magellan
12. Hernando Cortés
13. encomienda
14. Huguenots
15. St. Bartholomew's Day massacre

16. Edict of Nantes
17. William of Orange
18. Spanish Armada
19. Gustavus Adolphus
20. Peace of Westphalia
21. King James I
22. Charles I
23. Oliver Cromwell
24. Roundheads
25. <u>Malleus Maleficarum</u>
26. Mannerism
27. Baroque
28. Michel de Montaigne
29. William Shakespeare
30. <u>Don Quixote</u>

Multiple Choice

31. The European age of expansion into the rest of the world was <u>not</u> greatly aided by:
    a. a desire for the spices of the Far East
    b. a strong religious, crusading zeal
    c. the growth of centralized monarchies in the Renaissance period
    d. detailed map-work performed by medieval scholars from the tenth through the fourteenth centuries

Answer: d, medium, page 483

32. Written by _____, <u>The Travels</u> was a very informative and influential document describing Asia to Europeans:
    a. Marco Polo
    b. Hernando Cortés
    c. Kublai Khan
    d. Ferdinand Magellan

Answer: a, easy, page 484

33. Portugal became the early leader in European expansion largely through:
    a. direct trade policies with China
    b. defeating Muslim opposition in establishing trade opportunities with

India
    c.   sparsely spending its wealth on ships and manpower
    d.   winning the race of exploration to the New World

Answer: b, difficult, page 484

34.   What were the accomplishments of these fifteenth-century adventurers:
    a.   Prince Henry--founded a navigation school in 1419
    b.   Bartholomew Diaz--rounded the Cape of Good Hope in Africa in 1487
    c.   Vasco de Gama--began an all water route to India
    d.   all of the above

Answer: d, easy, page 485

35.   Spanish expansion and exploration of the New World was best characterized by:
    a.   the first circumnavigation of the globe by Amerigo Vespucci
    b.   the conquest of the Aztec Empire by Cortés
    c.   the conquest of the Incas by Magellan
    d.   Pizarro's rounding of South America in 1519

Answer: b, medium, page 486

36.   The first known circumnavigation of the earth was by:
    a.   Amerigo Vespucci
    b.   Ferdinand Magellan
    c.   John Cabot
    d.   Christopher Columbus

Answer: b, easy, page 486

37.   Hernando Cortés looked on the Aztecs as:
    a.   very poor people who needed western goods and services
    b.   a magnificent people who should trade with and be allied to Spain
    c.   wealthy beyond belief and ripe for Spanish exploration
    d.   a possible threat to Spain's mastery of the seas

Answer: c, medium, page 487 + DOC 1

38.   The <u>encomienda</u> in reality made the natives:
    a.   equal to the Spanish
    b.   slaves of the Spanish
    c.   masters of the spanish

      d.   none of the above

Answer: b, difficult, page 486

39.   Bartholomé de Las Casas, a Dominican monk, was known for his:
      a.   cruel and barbarous treatment of the Indians
      b.   magnificent monastery he built in Cuba
      c.   championing of the plight of the Indians under Spanish rule
      d.   conversion to a heathen religion and the start of the Native American church

Answer: c, medium, page 486

40.   European expansion:
      a.   put new varieties of foods on European tables
      b.   intensified European rivalries
      c.   fueled the growth of commercial capitalism
      d.   all of the above

Answer: d, easy, page 490

41.   The religious climate of France prior to the French Wars of Religion was best characterized by:
      a.   a nobility that was approximately 50 percent Huguenot
      b.   a population split evenly among Catholic and Huguenot affiliations
      c.   Catherine de' Medici's suppression of Calvinists
      d.   a poorly organized Huguenot opposition to the Catholic majority

Answer: a, medium, page 491

42.   The French Huguenots came from:
      a.   the lower class
      b.   the aristocracy
      c.   the merchant class
      d.   all classes

Answer: d, easy, page 491

43.   The French Wars of Religion from 1562 to 1598:
      a.   ended with Henry of Navarre's Edict of Nantes, which tolerated both Catholicism and Calvinism for France
      b.   saw the Huguenots' larger army force the Catholics to recognize them officially

    c.   witnessed the St. Bartholomew's Day massacre effectively end Huguenot resistance
    d.   were entirely French affairs with no foreign influences

Answer: a, easy, page 494

44.   The French Wars of Religion:
    a.   were primarily caused by economic factors
    b.   were fought for political as well as religious reasons
    c.   greatly strengthened the Valois kings
    d.   was really a simple slaughter of Huguenots

Answer: b, medium, page 492

45.   Philip II of Spain was most successful in:
    a.   delegating authority in establishing an efficient administrative machinery
    b.   ending the spiraling inflation caused by American gold and silver
    c.   his military actions against England
    d.   his leadership of the Holy League against Muslim, Mediterranean holdings

Answer: d, easy, page 496

46.   Philip II of Spain was:
    a.   an advocate of religious toleration
    b.   well liked by most of his subjects
    c.   a militant Catholic ruler
    d.   an ally of the Turks in the Mediterranean

Answer: c, easy, page 494

47.   One of the major goals of Philip II was to:
    a.   make Spain a dominant power in Europe
    b.   abandon the New World colonies as a drain on Spain's economy
    c.   take away power from the church, even though he was a fervent believer
    d.   establish an efficient state bureaucracy

Answer: a, medium, page 495

48.   The revolt of the Netherlands against Philip II of Spain ultimately resulted in:
    a.   the division of the Netherlands into northern and southern provinces

after 1609
    b. the formation of a Catholic kingdom ruled by the Duke of Parma
    c. military victory for the Union of Utrecht, led by William of Orange
    d. the Pacification of Ghent, in which all 17 provinces were united and respected religious differences

Answer: a, difficult, page 497

49. Which of the following was not a cause of the Netherlands' rebellion against Philip II?:
    a. taxes to support Spanish interests
    b. the privileges of nobles
    c. an influx of German workers to meet the labor shortage
    d. religious beliefs

Answer: c, difficult, page 496

50. Under Elizabeth Tudor, England:
    a. became extremely intolerant of religious dissent against the Anglican church
    b. saw Catholicism flourish alongside Puritanism
    c. suffered humiliating defeats at the hands of the Spanish Armada
    d. became the leader of Protestant Europe

Answer: d, easy, page 497

51. Queen Elizabeth's dealings with the Parliament:
    a. were crude and disrespectful
    b. reflected a cooperative and symbiotic relationship
    c. reflected a general dissatisfaction with her rule
    d. reflected her poor diplomatic skills

Answer: b, medium, page 497

52. The Catholics continued to be a majority in England after Elizabeth.
    a. True
    b. False

Answer: b, difficult, page 498

53. Elizabeth's military posture:
    a. was mainly of a covert nature and included aid to piracy and the Huguenots

    b.   was very aggressive, provoking wars on the continent

    c.   was that of a declining power

    d.   expressed her complete disinterest in continental affairs

Answer: a, easy, page 499

54.   The inflation of the sixteenth and early seventeenth centuries:

    a.   severely hampered commercial expansion

    b.   caused a shift in industry to urban centers

    c.   caused a decline in the standard of living for wage earners

    d.   was caused largely by a declining labor force

Answer: c, difficult, page 499

55.   In the sixteenth and seventeenth centuries, all of the following countries dominated world trade except:

    a.   the Netherlands

    b.   England

    c.   France

    d.   Germany

Answer: d, easy, page 501

56.   Which of the following statements best applies to the economy of sixteenth- and seventeenth-century Europe?

    a.   The joint-stock trading company made for the raising of spectacular sums of capital for world trading ventures.

    b.   The early seventeenth century saw a general stagnation in the areas of mining and metallurgy.

    c.   Technological innovations made the agricultural lives of the peasants improve dramatically.

    d.   The population expansion made for urban growth and more social equality in European cities.

Answer: a, difficult, page 501

57.   Which of the following was a factor in the population expansion in Europe in the sixteenth century?

    a.   advances in medicine

    b.   relaxation of morals

    c.   increased food supply

    d.   less warfare in Europe

Answer: c, easy, page 501

58. <u>Not</u> among the motives of the original participants of the Thirty Years' War was:
    a. French efforts to join with the Habsburgs in defeating Italy
    b. Spain's attempt to regain control of the Netherlands
    c. the Austrian Habsburgs' wish to gain real authority over the Holy Roman Empire
    d. individual German princes' desire for political and religious autonomy

Answer: a, difficult, page 502

59. The event that sparked the Thirty Years' War was:
    a. a Protestant noble rebellion against the Catholic Ferdinand in Bohemia
    b. the invasion of France by Frederick IV
    c. the Spanish conquest of the Netherlands and subsequent Inquisition
    d. the overthrow of the Spanish rule in the New World by the Dutch

Answer: a, medium, page 503

60. All of the following were phases of the Thirty Years' War <u>except</u>:
    a. the Bohemian phase
    b. the English phase
    c. the Swedish phase
    d. the Franco-Swedish phase

Answer: b, easy, page 503

61. As a result of the Thirty Years' War and the Peace of Westphalia of 1648:
    a. the German economy and population was universally destroyed
    b. all Germanic states could choose their own religions, except for Calvinism
    c. the growing gulf between religious and political motives was demonstrated
    d. the institution of the Holy Roman Empire was strengthened for another hundred years.

Answer: c, difficult, page 505

62. Following the Thirty Years' War, _____ was the dominant nation in Europe:
    a. Sweden
    b. France

       c. Germany
       d. Spain

Answer: b, difficult, page 505

63.   The Thirty Years' War:
       a.   was largely confined to agreed upon battlefields
       b.   witnessed the devastation of the German countryside
       c.   was fought according to chivalric codes
       d.   was fought mainly in Italy

Answer: b, medium, page 506

64.   The "military revolution," or changes in the science of warfare between 1560 and 1650, saw armies:
       a.   become more disciplined but less flexible
       b.   align in units of blocks rather than lines
       c.   abandon the use of cavalry
       d.   change from mercenaries to conscripts

Answer: d, medium, page 507

65.   Military changes from 1560 to 1650 included all of the following except:
       a.   the increased use of firearms
       b.   more flexible tactics
       c.   the use of more mobile artillery
       d.   the development of better armor

Answer: d, easy, page 507

66.   Some historians believe that the creation of large bureaucracies to supervise the military resources of the state led to a rise in royal absolutism.
       a.   True
       b.   False

Answer: a, easy, page 507

67.   When the Scottish king James VI became King James I of England:
       a.   Catholic expectations of sympathy from this son of Mary were largely realized
       b.   Puritan expectations of sympathy due to Scotland's Calvinist heritage were realized
       c.   the episcopal system of the Church of England was abandoned

    d.   he defended the divine right of kings in his <u>True Law of Free Monarchy</u>

Answer: d, medium, page 508

68.   King James I of England:
    a.   was a dynamic politician and statesman
    b.   was driven from his native Scotland
    c.   met much opposition from the Parliament
    d.   was deposed and executed

Answer: c, difficult, page 507

69.   Charles I's rule of England, which led to the English Civil War,:
    a.   witnessed his marriage to Henrietta Maria, the Catholic sister of Louis XIII of France
    b.   was characterized by tolerance towards Puritans
    c.   often relied on Parliament to decide national policy
    d.   was hampered by the Petition of Right, which Charles was coerced into obeying throughout his reign

Answer: a, medium, page 509

70.   The event that touched off the English Civil War in 1642 was:
    a.   the arrest of some members of Parliament by King Charles I
    b.   the secession of Wales and Cornwall
    c.   the abolition of the Parliament by Charles
    d.   the invasion of the Scots

Answer: a, easy, page 509

71.   Oliver Cromwell as head of the English government was responsible for all of the following <u>except</u>:
    a.   leading the trial and execution of Charles I in 1649
    b.   brutally suppressing revolts in Ireland and Scotland
    c.   proclaiming England a Commonwealth before abolishing the Rump Parliament
    d.   creating the Instrument of Government by which military rule was ended

Answer: d, medium, page 511

72.   Probably the most significant factor in Cromwell's victory in the English Civil

War was:
- a.   the aid of the Dutch
- b.   the creation of the New Model Army
- c.   the support of the Cavaliers
- d.   the aid of the French

Answer: b, easy, page 510

73.   The execution of Charles I was:
- a.   at his own request
- b.   not an uncommon occurrence in the seventeenth century
- c.   ordered by the Rump Parliament
- d.   preceded by most gruesome tortures

Answer: c, easy, page 510

74.   A typical witch trial in the seventeenth century consisted of:
- a.   torture to gain "confessions" from the accused
- b.   trial by the accused's peers
- c.   voluntary confession and penance
- d.   a swift declaration of guilt by a judge and execution

Answer: a, easy, page 514

75.   The witchhunts of the sixteenth and seventeenth centuries:
- a.   came out of the social unrest deriving from the shift from communalism to individualism
- b.   were generally directed at the wealthy by jealous neighbors
- c.   resulted in accusations of mainly lower-class women
- d.   were primarily restricted to rural areas

Answer: c, easy, page 514

76.   Which of the following descriptions most accurately describes the following artists of the sixteenth and seventeenth centuries?
- a.   El Greco--Greek, Baroque artist who used rich ornamentation in his works
- b.   Gian Lorenzo Bernini--his Deposition of Christ made him the greatest figure in Mannerism
- c.   Peter Paul Rubens--used dramatic effects of the Baroque to create emotional intensity
- d.   Jacopo da Pontormo--Baroque architect who created the Throne of St.Peter

Answer: d, difficult, page 515

77. The artistic movement of Mannerism was best characterized as:
    a. a continuation of High Renaissance art
    b. an attempt to find strict rules of proportion
    c. exclusively an English movement
    d. reflection of the uncertainty, suffering, and spiritual longing of the time

Answer: b, medium, page 515

78. Identify the <u>false</u> description among the following writers of the sixteenth and seventeenth centuries:
    a. Cervantes--his <u>Don Quixote</u> satirized chivalric literature while advocating both realism and idealism for the human soul
    b. Lope de Vega--Spanish playwright whose few remaining works were intended for a limited elite audience
    c. Michel de Montaigne--his <u>Essay on Experience</u> used "positive skepticism" to advocate the "middle way"
    d. William Shakespeare--"complete man of the theater" who wrote plays covering all aspects of the human condition

Answer: c, easy, page 517

79. The concept of positive skepticism is associated with:
    a. Oliver Cromwell
    b. Gustavus Adolphus
    c. Michel de Montaigne
    d. Jacopo da Pontormo

Answer: c, medium, page 517

80. The patriotic enthusiasm of the English during the Elizabethan era is best characterized by:
    a. the philosophy of John Cabot
    b. the plays of William Shakespeare
    c. the New Model Army
    d. all of the above

Answer: b, difficult, page 517 + DOC 8

81. The late 1500s and early 1600s constituted a period of:
    a. great accomplishments in English literature

     b. dramatic decline of theater
     c. a new blossoming of Latin literature
     d. a return to morality plays in Spain

Answer: a, easy, page 518

SUGGESTED FILMS

The Age of Exploration and Expansion. Centron Educational Films, 17 min., color.

Explorations of Prince Henry. McGraw-Hill Films, 15 min. (color).

Age of Discovery: English, French, and Dutch Exploration. Coronet Instructional
Films, 12 min. (color).

Age of Discovery: Spanish and Portuguese Exploration. Coronet Instructional Films,
12 min. (color).

Francisco Pizarro. Time-Life Films, 30 min. (color).

Christopher Columbus. Time-Life Films, 30 min. (color).

Cortez and the Legend. McGraw-Hill Films, 52 min. (color).

South to the Strait of Magellan. Association-Sterling Films, 12 min. (color).

The Christians: The Conquest of Souls. McGraw-Hill Films, 39 min. (color).

Age of Elizabeth. Encyclopedia Britannica, 30 min. (color).

The England of Elizabeth. International Film Bureau, 26 min. (color).

The Spanish Armada. McGraw-Hill Films, 31 min. (color).

Gunpowder and the Transformation of Europe. Houghton Mifflin, 20 min. (color).

English History: Absolutism and Civil War. Coronet Instructional Films, 11 min.
(color).

Puritan Revolution: Cromwell and the Rise of Parliamentary Democracy. Learning
Corp. of America, 33 min. (color).

<u>Civilization: Grandeur and Obedience</u>. Time-Life Films, 52 min. (color).

<u>El Greco</u>. Graphic Curriculum, 30 min. (color).

<u>Flemish Painting 1540-1640</u>. Detroit Institute of Arts, 10 min. (color).

<u>Rubens</u>. International Film Bureau, 26 min. (color).

<u>Bernini's Rome</u>. Indiana University Audio-Visual Library, 29 min. (color).

<u>Shakespeare's World and Shakespeare's London</u>, Fleetwood Films, 29 min. (black/white).

SUGGESTIONS FOR MUSIC

Giovanni Gabrieli, <u>Sacrae Symphoniae</u>, Vol. 1 (Musical Heritage Society-1737)

Claudio Monteverdi, <u>Psalm Beatus Vir</u> (Musical Heritage Society-538)

Claudio Monteverdi, <u>Orfeo</u> (Musical Heritage Society-939/40/41)

CHAPTER 16: RESPONSE TO CRISIS: ABSOLUTE AND LIMITED MONARCHY IN THE SEVENTEENTH AND EARLY EIGHTEENTH CENTURIES (1715)

CHAPTER OUTLINE

THE THEORY OF ABSOLUTISM

ABSOLUTISM IN WESTERN EUROPE
 France
  Foundations of French Absolutism
  The Reign of Louis XIV (1661-1715)
  Daily Life at the Court of Versailles
  The Wars of Louis XIV
 Spain

ABSOLUTISM IN CENTRAL, EASTERN, AND NORTHERN EUROPE

 The German States
  Brandenburg-Prussia
  The Emergence of Austria
 Italy
 From Muscovy to Russia
  The Reign of Peter the Great (1689-1725)
 Scandinavia
 The Ottoman Empire
 The Limits of Absolutism

LIMITED MONARCHY AND REPUBLICS

Poland
The United Provinces
Daily Life in Seventeenth-Century Amsterdam
England and the Emergence of Constitutional Monarchy

ECONOMIC TRENDS: MERCANTILISM AND EUROPEAN COLONIES IN THE SEVENTEENTH CENTURY
Mercantilism
Overseas Trade and Colonies

THE WORLD OF SEVENTEENTH-CENTURY CULTURE
Art
The Golden Age of Dutch Painting
The Theater: The Triumph of French Neoclassicism
International Law and Political Thought
Political Thought

SUGGESTED LECTURE TOPICS

1. "How Absolute was Absolutism?"

2. "Life at the Court of the Sun King"

3. "Life in the Urban and Rural Communities of France in the Seventeenth Century"

4. "Absolutism in Western and Eastern Europe"

5. "Economic and Political Expansion in the New World"

MAPS AND ARTWORK

1. Louis XIV's costly wars for small area, Map 16.1.

2. Austria, a national state growing into a cosmopolitan empire, Map 16.3.

3. Expansion of Russia, hemmed in in the West, glory in the East, Map 16.4.

4. Louix XIV and his impact on art and architecture.

DISCUSSION QUESTIONS FOR THE PRIMARY SOURCES (BOXED DOCUMENTS)

"Louis XIV: Kingly Advice": What general principles did Louis XIV enunciate for the guidance of his son (and heir to the throne)? To what extent did Louis follow his own advice? (page 528)

"Travels with the King": Discuss the king's personality. Would this account be biased? Why? (page 532)

"Peter the Great Deals with a Rebellion": How did Peter deal with the revolt of the streltsy? What does his approach to this problem tell us about the tsar? (page 541)

"The Economic Superiority of the Dutch": According to John Keymer, what are the "secrets" to Dutch economic success? (page 549)

"The Bill of Rights": The author states that the Bill of Rights" laid the foundation for a constitutional monarchy?" How? (page 551)

"West Meets East": How honest is Louis about the real political situation? Why would the king of Tonkin refuse Louis' request? (page 555)

"French Comedy: The Would-Be Gentleman": How does M. Jourdan appear in this scene? Who is being ridiculed? (page 558)

"Hobbes and the War of 'Every Man against Every Man'": Why, according to Hobbes, was human life "solitary, poor, nasty, brutish, and short," in the state of nature? What can be done about it? How would you refute this basic argument of Hobbes? (page 560)

EXAMINATION QUESTIONS

Essays

1. Define absolutism and determine to what extent France's government in the seventeenth century can be labeled an absolute monarchy.

2. What did Louis XIV hope to accomplish in his domestic and foreign policies? To what extent did he succeed?

3. Compare the reigns of Frederick William of Brandenburg-Prussia and Peter the Great of Russia. How are their policies similar? How are they different?

4. What role did the nobility play in Poland and England?

5. Compare and contrast developments in the United Netherlands and England. Can it be said that both states were moving in the direction of constitutional monarchy by the end of the seventeenth century? Why or why not?

6. What is the doctrine of mercantilism? How did the Dutch practice it? How is it related to European colonial expansion?

7. Assume that you are a nobleman and also a merchant. Describe your reactions to governments in England, France, Brandenburg-Prussia, and Poland. Which country would you prefer to live in? Why?

8. How did the art, literature, and political thought of the second half of the seventeenth century reflect the political and social life of that period.

Identifications

9. the Fronde
10. Cardinal Richelieu
11. Cardinal Mazarin
12. Edict of Fontainebleau
13. Jean-Baptiste Colbert
14. Peace of Utrecht
15. Versailles
16. Frederick William the Great Elector
17. cossacks
18. Great Northern War
19. Janissaries
20. Charles XII
21. Seym
22. Bill of Rights
23. Glorious Revolution
24. mercantilism
25. Dutch East India Company

26. neoclassicism
27. Rembrandt van Rijn
28. Jean-Baptiste Molière
29. Leviathan

Multiple Choice

30. Jacques Bossuet's <u>Politics Drawn from the Very Words of Holy Scripture</u>:
     a. rejected Louis XIV's system of absolute rule
     b. was the fundamental statement of seventeenth-century divine-right monarchy
     c. stressed that a limited monarchy with representative bodies was the purest form of government
     d. claimed that a king's authority and power were absolute under the law of God

Answer: b, medium, page 524

31. One result of the seventeenth-century crises in Europe was:
     a. an increased rule of the church in everyday affairs
     b. a general trend toward democratic reforms in government
     c. the disintegration of empires into smaller, feudal kingdoms
     d. a trend towards absolutism, as exemplified by Louis XIV of France

Answer: d, medium, page 524

32. Prior to the reign of Louis XIV, France witnessed:
     a. the complete collapse of the state treasury under the duke of Sully
     b. the end of the Bourbon dynasty
     c. the demise of the central government's authority under Henry IV
     d. none of the above

Answer: d, easy, page 524

33. As Louis XIII's chief minister, Cardinal Richelieu was most successful in:
     a. evicting the Huguenot presence from France after the La Rochelle rebellion
     b. strengthening the central role of the monarchy in domestic and foreign policy
     c. creating a reservoir of funds for the treasury
     d. emerging victorious in the Fronde revolts of the nobility

Answer: b, medium, page 525

34. Cardinal Richelieu was responsible for all of the following except:
     a. establishing a spy network to crush noble conspiracies
     b. eliminating the taille to cut down government expenditures
     c. subsidizing Sweden in order to help the Protestant cause against the Habsburgs
     d. creating a system of intendants to strengthen the orders of the central government

Answer: b, difficult, page 525

35. The effective ruler of France during the childhood of Louis XIV was:
     a. Cardinal Mazarin
     b. the duke of Sully
     c. Marie de' Medici
     d. the Parlement of Paris

Answer: a, easy, page 526

36. The series of noble revolts known as the Fronde resulted in:
     a. the assassination of Cardinal Mazarin in 1661
     b. renewed power for the Parlement of Paris
     c. a unified noble army securing and increasing its own power
     d. French citizens looking to the monarchy for stability

Answer: d, medium, page 526

37. Which of the following statements was not true of Louis XIV's reign?
     a. Newly created French trading companies became very competitive with the English and Dutch.
     b. The Edict of Fontainebleau provided for the destruction of Huguenot churches and schools.
     c. Attempts were made to seize control of church functions from the papacy.
     d. The French army utilized conscription to become the largest army of its time.

Answer: a, easy, page 529

38. Louis XIV restructured the policy-making machinery of the French government by:
     a. personally dominating the actions of his ministers and secretaries

b. stacking the royal council with high nobles and royal princes
c. selecting his ministers from established aristocratic families
d. all of the above

Answer: a, medium, page 527

39. Louis XIV was most successful in controlling the internal administration of his kingdom by:
    a. working through the hereditary, aristocratic officeholders
    b. using his intendants as direct royal agents
    c. employing royal patronage to "bribe" clients into executing the king's policies
    d. eliminating town councils and representative Estates in the provinces

Answer: c, medium, page 528

40. The economic policies of Jean-Baptiste Colbert, Louis XIV's controller-general of finances,:
    a. were noted for their innovation and originality
    b. used mercantilist practices to take the tax burden off the peasants
    c. did little to change the old system of tax farming and office-selling
    d. gave Louis the large surplus in the treasury needed to carry out his wars

Answer: c, easy, page 529

41. Jean-Baptiste Colbert's economic policies succeeded in:
    a. redistributing the tax burden more equally among the populace
    b. overthrowing the ancient practice of mercantilism
    c. founding new luxury industries in France
    d. lifting high tariffs on French manufactured goods

Answer: c, medium, page 529

42. Louis made the decision to transform a hunting lodge at Versailles because of:
    a. his dislike of Paris
    b. a result of his being humiliated during the Fronde
    c. humiliation by Parisian mobs
    d. all of the above

Answer: d, medium, page 529

43. Louis XVI's only clear-cut military victory was in:

    a.   the War of Devolution
    b   the War of the League of Augsburg
    c.   the War of the Spanish Succession
    d.   none of the above

Answer: d, easy, page 533

44.   The War of the Spanish Succession was effectively concluded with the Peace of Utrecht in 1713, which:
    a.   gave the French king control of Spanish territories
    b.   gave France control over the Spanish Netherlands, Naples, and Milan
    c.   greatly benefitted England, by then a strong naval power
    d.   destroyed the European balance of power

Answer: c, easy, page 533

45.   Activities at the court of Versailles included all of the following except:
    a.   gaming and gambling with enormous sums of money
    b.   noble courtiers participating in humiliating ceremonies on behalf of Louis XIV
    c.   accepted challenges to Louis XIV's authority during the holding of the appartement
    d.   an overwhelming concern with court etiquette

Answer: c, medium, page 530

46.   The overall practical purpose of the court of Versailles was:
    a.   to exclude the high nobility and royal princes from real power
    b.   to serve as Louis XIV's residence
    c.   to act as a reception hall for state affairs
    d.   to give Louis XIV a life of privacy

Answer: a, medium, page 530

47.   A continual trend in Spain during the sixteenth century was:
    a.   an economic regeneration from its New World colonies
    b.   the loss of its European possessions
    c.   the waning of the power of the Catholic church
    d.   the growth of a dominant middle class

Answer: b, easy, page 534

48.   The Duke of Lerma's most drastic decision was to:

a. provide Spain with excellent ministers
b. allow for a strong urban middle class
c. not appoint relatives
d. expel the remaining Moriscos

Answer: d, difficult, page 534

49. During the reign of Philip IV, Spain:
a. suffered under the misrule of the duke of Lerma
b. won back its European possessions in the Thirty Years' War
c. received a respite from the civil wars and internal revolts of Philip's predecessors
d. failed to make any real progress under the chief minister, the count of Olivares

Answer: d, medium, page 535

50. Frederick William the Great Elector built Brandenburg-Prussia into a significant European power by:
a. establishing religious uniformity in his kingdom, as evidenced in his eviction of the Huguenots
b. freeing the peasants from the domination of the nobles
c. using his army whenever possible to gain his ends
d. making the General War Commissarist the bureaucratic machine of his state

Answer: d, easy, page 536

51. The Austrian Empire in the seventeenth century:
a. was unified by linguistic and ethnic ties
b. was defeated at Vienna by a Turkish army in 1687
c. was a highly centralized, absolutist state under Leopold I
d. lost a German empire, but gained one in eastern Europe

Answer: d, easy, page 538

52. By the eighteenth century, the Austrian Empire's possessions did not include:
a. Bohemia
b. the Spanish Netherlands
c. Hungary
d. Venice

Answer: d, medium, page 538

53.   Russian society in the seventeenth century:
       a.   witnessed the reign of Ivan the Stern
       b.   witnessed profound religious reforms in the Russian Orthodox church
       c.   was characterized by a highly oppressive system of serfdom
       d.   saw the rise of the merchant class to power

  Answer: c, medium, page 539

54.   The "Time of Troubles" describes:
       a.   an anarchic period in Russian history before the rise of the Romanov
             dynasty
       b.   the religious turmoil in Russia in which thousands of Old Believers
             killed themselves in religious protests
       c.   the period of revolt led by the Russian peasant Stenka Razin
       d.   the reign of Tsar Alexis, who made serfdom legal in the Russian state

  Answer: a, medium, page 539

55.   Which of the following statements best applies to Peter the Great of Russia?
       a.   His program of Europeanization was predominantly technical and
             aimed at modernizing the military.
       b.   His respect for western governments led to increased powers for the
             Duma and consultative bodies.
       c.   His traditional, conservative attitudes stripped away all previous social
             gains for women.
       d.   His desire to teach Russians western customs could not be enforced
             among the old-fashioned nobles.

  Answer: a, medium, page 539

56.   Peter demanded that all members of the landholders class serve in either
       military or civil offices.
       a.   True
       b.   False

  Answer: a, easy, page 540

57.   In his efforts to Europeanize Russia, Peter the Great:
       a.   used conscription to build a standing army of 30,000 men
       b.   reorganized the central government so that the Duma and consultative
             bodies played a dominant role
       c.   adopted mercantilistic policies to stimulate economic growth
       d.   achieved his goal of a "police state" with the aid of his bureaucrats

Answer: c, difficult, page 540

58. Peter the Great's cultural reforms:
    a. failed to change the nobles' habits of dress and grooming
    b. did not touch the Russian Orthodox church
    c. required Russian men to wear lengthy beards
    d. allowed Russian women many new freedoms

Answer: d, medium, page 541

59. Peter the Great's foreign policy had as its primary goal:
    a. the opening of a warm-water port accessible to Europe
    b. the destruction of the Ottoman Empire
    c. the capture of the Scandinavian countries
    d. all of the above

Answer: a, difficult, page 542

60. Scandinavia in the seventeenth and eighteenth centuries witnessed:
    a. Denmark expand so as to dominate the Baltic
    b. Sweden become a second-rate northern power after the Great Northern War
    c. Sweden and Denmark join forces to defeat and occupy Poland in 1660
    d. the economic dominance of Sweden over the rest of northern Europe

Answer: b, medium, page 544

61. The Ottoman Empire in the seventeenth century:
    a. declined in strength due to the lack of a well organized military system
    b. conquered much of central Europe as well as southern Italy
    c. was treated much like any European nation by European rulers seeking trade concessions
    d. developed an orderly method of succession to the throne to allow internal stability

Answer: c, easy, page 544

62. The political institution known as the <u>Seym</u> made seventeenth-century Poland:
    a. an absolutist, monarchical state dominated by King Sigismund III
    b. a powerful militaristic machine that controlled Russian, Austrian, and Swedish lands
    c. a land without powerful nobles
    d. an impotent, decentralized state

Answer: d, easy, page 546

63. Characteristic of the power of the United Provinces of the Netherlands in the seventeenth century was:
   a. religious intolerance under the Calvinist church
   b. equal political powers between monarchical and republican factions
   c. the great influence of Holland and the House of Orange
   d. economic prosperity caused by an avoidance of military entanglements

Answer: c, medium, page 547

64. The "Golden Age" of the Dutch Republic in the seventeenth century witnessed:
   a. William become the first in a line of hereditary monarchs
   b. the economic prosperity of the United Provinces ruined by a series of wars late in the century
   c. the weakness of the States General
   d. all of the above

Answer: d, medium, page 547

65. Despite Amsterdam's enormous financial success in the seventeenth century:
   a. it had huge social differences and was a very class conscious society
   b. its merchant marine was hopelessly outdated by European standards
   c. it did not extend its prosperity to persecuted minorities like the Jews
   d. the city's size and population grew little

Answer: a, medium, page 549

66. The restoration of Charles II to the throne of England meant:
   a. the end of parliamentary power
   b. a renewed series of civil wars
   c. the division of Parliament into two political groupings, the Whigs and the Tories
   d. the resurgence of Catholics to the highest government positions

Answer: c, difficult, page 550

67. The devout Catholic English monarch who instigated a constitutional crisis for England in 1687-1688 was:
   a. Charles II
   b. James II
   c. William I
   d. Charles IV

Answer: b, easy, page 550

68. The "Glorious Revolution" of 1688 in England was significant for:
    a. restoring Charles II and the Stuart dynasty to power
    b. deposing James II in favor of William of Orange
    c. returning England to a Catholic commonwealth
    d. Parliament's establishment of a new monarch through a series of bloody wars

Answer: b, medium, page 552

69. The incident that prompted the nobles to depose James II was:
    a. his marriage to the Duchess of Orange
    b. the death of his first wife
    c. the birth of a Catholic son
    d. all of the above

Answer: c, medium, page 552

70. The Declaration of Rights and the Bill of Rights of 1688:
    a. laid the foundation for a future constitutional monarchy
    b. resolved England's seventeenth-century religious questions
    c. reaffirmed the divine-right theory of kingship while limiting the king's power
    d. confirmed the king's right to raise standing armies without parliamentary consent

Answer: a, difficult, page 552

71. Europe's seventeenth-century economy was affected by all of the following except:
    a. a doubling of population figures
    b. high rates of taxation
    c. worsening climatic patterns
    d. major outbursts of the bubonic plague

Answer: a, medium, page 552

72. The mercantilist policies that dominated Europe's seventeenth-century economy:
    a. concerned the ever-changing volume of trade
    b. stressed co-prosperity among nations through fair trading practices
    c. were responsible for the economic and population growths of the

century
d.   focused on the role of the state in conducting economic affairs

Answer: d, difficult, page 553

73.   The flowering of culture in the seventeenth century witnessed all of the
following except:
a.   France replacing Italy as Europe's cultural leader
b.   France's neoclassical theater break away from royal patronage, as
demonstrated by Molière
c.   the Golden Age of Dutch painting, best exemplified by Rembrandt
d.   the neoclassic emphasis on the clever and polished over the emotional
and imaginative

Answer: b, difficult, page 556

74.   The Dutch painter Rembrandt van Rijn was most noted for:
a.   his formation of the French Academy of Painting and Sculptors
b.   reflecting the values of the Dutch aristocracy in his works
c.   being the great Protestant painter of the seventeenth century
d.   rejecting the Dutch preoccupation with realism for the Baroque style
of French classicism

Answer: c, medium, page 556

75.   The French playwright Moliére was regarded for all of the following except:
a.   Tartuffe
b.   The Misanthrope
c.   satirizing French religious and social customs
d.   perfecting neoclassical tragedy

Answer: d, difficult, page 558

76.   Political thought in the seventeenth century was best characterized by:
a.   the influence of Thomas Hobbes and his idea of absolute authority
invested in the state
b.   Hugo Grotius's political work Two Treatises of Government
c.   John Locke's work, On the Law of War and Peace
d.   the revival of "corpus Christianum," a plan for a common European,
Christian community

Answer: a, medium, page 559

77. As stated in <u>Leviathan</u>, the political ideas of Thomas Hobbes stressed:
    a. the need for a strong spiritual foundation in government
    b. the need for an absolute ruler to possess unlimited power
    c. constant revolution by the people to ensure obedient forms of government
    d. that the wisdom and reason of humans ensured that republican forms of government were the most stable

Answer: b, difficult, page 559

78. John Locke was responsible for:
    a. synthesizing previous doctrines on international law in his <u>On The Law of War and Peace</u>
    b. the idea of society as being in a constant state of war
    c. advocating political democracy for the entire populace
    d. The <u>Two Treatises of Government</u>, which emphasized the natural contract between the people and government

Answer: d, medium, page 559

SUGGESTED FILMS

<u>The Age of Absolute Monarchs in Europe</u>. Coronet Instructional Films, 14 min. (color).

<u>The Rise of Nations in Europe</u>. Coronet Instructional Films, 14 min. (black/white).

<u>The Sun King</u>. National Education TV, 30 min. (black/white).

<u>The Stuarts Restored</u>. Films Inc., 60 min. (color).

<u>The Restoration and the Glorious Revolution</u>. Coronet Instructional Films, 11 min. (color).

<u>The Colonial Expansion of European Nations</u>. Coronet Instructional Films, 13 min. (black/white).

<u>Colonial Expansion</u>. Encyclopedia Britannica, 11 min. (color).

<u>The Pilgrim Adventure</u>. McGraw-Hill Films, 54 min. (color).

Civilization: The Light of Experience. Time-Life Films, 52 min. (color).

The Age of Rembrandt. Perennial Education Films, 26 min. (color).

Rembrandt Van Rijn: Self Portrait. Lutheran Church in America, 27 min. (color).

The Comedy of Manners. Moliére: The Misanthrope. Films for the Humanities, 49 min. (color).

SUGGESTIONS FOR MUSIC:

Henry Purcell, King Arthur (Musical Heritage Society-4188/89)

Johann Pachelbel, Canon in D Major (Musical Heritage Society-7267H)

Ceremonial Music from the Court of Louis XIV (Musical Heritage Society-1624)

Marc-Antoine Charpentier, Midnight Mass (Musical Heritage Society-522)

Michel-Richard Delalande, Simphonies for the King's Supper (Musical Heritage Society-1661)

CHAPTER 17: TOWARD A NEW HEAVEN AND A NEW EARTH: THE SCIENTIFIC REVOLUTION AND THE EMERGENCE OF MODERN SCIENCE

CHAPTER OUTLINE

BACKGROUND TO THE SCIENTIFIC REVOLUTION

TOWARD A NEW HEAVEN: A REVOLUTION IN ASTRONOMY
Copernicus
Brahe and Kepler
Galileo
Newton

ADVANCES IN MEDICINE

WOMEN IN THE ORIGINS OF MODERN SCIENCE

TOWARD A NEW EARTH: DESCARTES, RATIONALISM, AND A NEW VIEW OF HUMANKIND

THE SCIENTIFIC METHOD

SCIENCE AND RELIGION IN THE SEVENTEENTH CENTURY

THE SPREAD OF SCIENTIFIC KNOWLEDGE
The Scientific Societies
Science and Society

SUGGESTED LECTURE TOPICS

1. "The Significance of the Scientific Revolution for the Development of Western Civilization"

2. "Did the Hermetic Tradition Have an Impact on the Emergence of the Scientific Revolution?"

3. "The Role of Isaac Newton in the Scientific Revolution"

4. "Why Religions Vehemently Supported Ptolemy and Galen's System"

MAPS AND ARTWORK

1. Comparison of Medieval Universe with Copernican model.

DISCUSSION QUESTIONS FOR THE PRIMARY SOURCES (BOXED DOCUMENTS)

"Magic and Science: The Case of Girolamo Cardano": How would we evaluate the unusual experiences of Cardano? (page 567)

"On the Revolutions of the Heavenly Spheres": What major new ideas did Copernicus discuss in this selection? What was the source of these ideas? (page 570)

"Kepler and the Emerging Scientific Community": What did the correspondence between Galileo and Kepler reveal about an emerging spirit of scientific inquiry? (page 573)

"The Starry Messenger": What was the significance of Galileo's invention? What impressions did he receive of the moon? (page 575)

"Newton's Rules of Reasoning": What are Newton's rules of reasoning? How important were they to the development of the Scientific Revolution? (page 577)

"The 'Natural Inferiority' of Women": What arguments did Spinoza use to support the idea of female inferiority? How would you refute these arguments? What was the effect of his line of reasoning upon the roles women could play? (page 583)

"The Father of Modern Rationalism": Describe Descartes's principles and compare them to Newton's rules of reasoning. What are their limitations? (pae 585)

"Pascal: 'What is a Man in the Infinite?'": Why did Pascal question whether human beings could achieve scientific certainty? What is the significance of Pascal's thoughts for modern science? (page 589)

EXAMINATION QUESTIONS

Essays

1. How do you explain the emergence of the Scientific Revolution?

2. One of the major aspects of the Scientific Revolution was the advance in astronomy that led to a new conception of the universe. What was the old Ptolemaic conception of the universe and what did Copernicus, Kepler, and Galileo contribute to the development of a new conception?

3. What do we mean by the Newtonian world-machine? How did Newton arrive at this conception?

4. What did Paracelsus, Vesalius, and Harvey contribute to a scientific view of medicine?

5. How did women contribute to the beginnings of modern science? How did male scientists view women and female scientists?

6. Why is Descartes considered the "founder of modern rationalism?"

7. Compare the methods used by Bacon and Descartes. Would Pascal agree with the methods and interests of these men? Why or why not?

8. How was the new scientific knowledge spread in the seventeenth century?

Identifications

9. Ptolemaic universe
10. heliocentric/geocentric
11. On the Revolutions of the Heavenly Spheres
12. Tycho Brahe
13. The Starry Messenger
14. Principia
15. Paracelsus
16. Andreas Vesalius
17. William Harvey
18. Margaret Cavendish
19. Maria Winkelmann
20. querrelles des femmes
21. Discourse on Method
22. Cartesian dualism
23. Francis Bacon
24. Benedict de Spinoza
25. Johann Comenius
26. pansophia
27. Penseés
28. The English Royal Society

Multiple Choice

29.   The Scientific Revolution of the seventeenth century was:
      a.   stimulated by a revived interest in Galen and Aristotle
      b.   directly a result of reaction and revolt against the social and historical conditions of the Middle Ages
      c.   largely due to a monastic revolution
      d.   a graduate building on the accomplishments of previous centuries, not a sudden shift in thought

Answer: d, medium, page 565

30.   Which of the following did not contribute to the Scientific Revolution?
      a.   the breakdown of Christian unity
      b.   warfare and rejection of traditional authority
      c.   the advent of the internal combustion engine
      d.   a desire to break away from the classical ideas and explore new ones

Answer: c, easy, page 566

31. All of the following are considered possible influences and causes of the Scientific Revolution <u>except</u>:
    a.   the practical knowledge and technical skills emphasized by sixteenth-century universities
    b.   mathematical and naturalistic skills of Renaissance artists
    c.   the Hermetic belief in magic and alchemy
    d.   the humanists' rediscovery of Greek mathematicians and thinkers

Answer: a, medium, page 566

32. Which ancient authority was not relied on by medieval scholars?
    a.   Aristotle
    b.   Galen
    c.   Ptolemy
    d.   Galileo

Answer: d, easy, page 566

33. According to Leonardo da Vinci, _____was the key to understanding the nature of things:
    a.   astronomy
    b.   art
    c.   mathematics
    d.   the Bible

Answer: c, medium, page 566

34. Girolamo Cardano was:
    a.   physician and professor of medicine
    b.   an important figure in mathematics
    c.   a pupil of magic and astrology
    d.   all of the above

Answer: d, medium + DOC 1

35. The general conception of the universe before Copernicus was that:
    a.   it was orderly with heaven at the center and the earth circling around it
    b.   the earth was the stationary center and perfect crystalline spheres orbited it
    c.   the earth rested on the shell of a giant tortoise
    d.   it could not be revealed according to God's will

Answer: b, easy, page 568

36.   The greatest achievements in science during the sixteenth and seventeenth
      centuries came in what three areas?
         a.   astronomy, mechanics, and medicine
         b.   astronomy, biology, and chemistry
         c.   biology, mechanics, and ballistics
         d.   engineering, physics, and dentistry

Answer: a, medium, page 568

37.   The Ptolemaic conception of the universe was also known as:
         a.   God's master plan
         b.   the geocentric conception
         c.   the lunacentric conception
         d.   the expanding universe

Answer: b, easy, page 568

38.   Copernicus's heliocentric theory was:
         a.   based on the observations of several ancient astronomers and his own
              computations
         b.   published without fear of scorn or reprisal
         c.   derived from a vision he'd had
         d.   a hoax he thought up to win an award in science

Answer: a, medium, page 570

39.   The universal theories proposed by Nicholas Copernicus:
         a.   led to his persecution at the hands of the Catholic church
         b.   were supported by Protestant reformers in order to oppose the church
         c.   made the universe less complicated by rejecting Ptolemy's epicycles
         d.   explained the appearance of the sun's rotation as caused by the
              earth's axial rotation

Answer: d, medium, page 570

40.   The ideas of Copernicus were:
         a.   radically different from Aristotle's principle of the existence of
              heavenly spheres
         b.   nearly as complicated as those of Ptolemy
         c.   not too different from the ideas of today
         d.   quite consistent with Biblical ideas

Answer: b, difficult, page 570

41. Following upon Copernicus's heliocentric theories,:
    a. Johannes Kepler produced three laws of planetary motion, destroying the Ptolemaic system
    b. Kepler proved that planetary motion was circular
    c. Tycho Brahe proved that the earth was in motion, but remained unconvinced of his own discoveries
    d. Brahe and Kepler demonstrated that the motion of the planets is steady and unchanging

Answer: a, medium, page 572

42. Tycho Brahe:
    a. was a major supporter in the scientific community for Copernicus's theory
    b. did most of his work in Italy
    c. recorded astronomical data from the observatory he built at Uraniborg castle
    d. was a Protestant minister who attacked Copernicus

Answer: c, easy, page 571

43. Kepler and Galileo were:
    a. fierce and bitter rivals
    b. both from Italy
    c. both burned at the stake
    d. friends and part of the new "scientific community"

Answer: d, medium + DOC 3

44. Kepler's laws of planetary motion:
    a. solved the riddle of what planets are made of
    b. addressed the issue of motion in the universe
    c. were beginning to be accepted toward the end of his life
    d. showed that planets are constantly gaining speed

Answer: c, difficult, page 572

45. Which of the following statements concerning Galileo is false?
    a. The recognition of his proposals by Europe's scientific community made Italy a center for scientific innovation.
    b. His telescopic observations of the planets destroyed the conception of

their ethereal composition.

    c.   His theories of dynamics did not unite theories of universal motion with the Copernican universe.

    d.   As it threatened its conception of the universe, the Catholic church forced his recantation of the Copernican system in 1633.

Answer: a, medium, page 574

46.   The first European to make systematic observations of the heavens by telescope was:
    a.   Galileo
    b.   Copernicus
    c.   Kepler
    d.   Aristotle

Answer: a, easy, page 574

47.   Galileo's <u>Dialogue</u> was really an attempt to:
    a.   embarrass Copernicus
    b.   support Copernicus
    c.   attack Luther
    d.   none of the above

Answer: b, medium, page 575

47.   Galileo proposed that the planets were:
    a.   composed of material substances like the earth
    b.   reflections of the divine
    c.   spheres composed of pure energy
    d.   merely mirages like images in the "desert" of space

Answer: a, medium + DOC 4

48.   Galileo's ideas on motion included:
    a.   the idea that a rush of air behind a projectile kept it in motion
    b.   the principle of inertia
    c.   the law of force
    d.   the spring-reaction model

Answer: b, medium, page 576

49.   Isaac Newton's scientific discoveries:
    a.   were resisted more in his own country, England, than in the rest of

Europe

    b.   provided the basis for an understanding of the universe until the twentieth century

    c.   were modern in their removal of God from universal laws

    d.   were among the first to be printed in a language other than Latin

Answer: b, medium, page 578

50.   In Newton's <u>Principia</u>, he demonstrated through his rules of reasoning that the universe was:

    a.   a chaotic, unpredictable place

    b.   in fact, a mathematical impossibility

    c.   a regulated machine operating according to universal laws

    d.   finite and its boundaries are clearly defined

Answer: c, difficult, page 577

51.   Newton's mathematical discoveries include:

    a.   the invention of algebra

    b.   the invention of geometry

    c.   the invention of calculus

    d.   the invention of the whole number system

Answer: c, easy, page 576

52.   Newton's universal law of gravity proved that:

    a.   through its mathematical proof it could explain all motion in the universe

    b.   motion in the universe operated on a series of distinct universal laws

    c.   people could never comprehend why the planets moved the way they did

    d.   the universe began with the "big bang"

Answer: a, medium, page 578

53.   Identify the correct relationship between astronomer and major work:

    a.   Kepler--<u>The Starry Messenger</u>

    b.   Copernicus--<u>On the Revolutions of the Heavenly Spheres</u>

    c.   Newton--<u>Dialogue on the Two Chief World Systems</u>

    d.   Galileo--<u>Principia</u>

Answer: b, medium, page 578

54.   Paracelsus revolutionized the world of medicine in the sixteenth century by:
    a.   disproving Galen's ancient theory of two separate blood systems
    b.   dissecting human rather than animals cadavers
    c.   effectively curing diseases through a "like cures like" philosophy
    d.   rejecting the medieval Christian chemical philosophy of the universities

Answer: c, medium, page 579

55.   Which of the following is not associated with changes in medicine in the sixteenth and seventeenth centuries?
    a.   Andreas Vesalius
    b.   William Harvey
    c.   Paracelsus
    d.   Galen

Answer: d, easy, page 578

56.   <u>On the Fabric of the Human Body</u>:
    a.   was Andreas Vesalius's masterpiece on anatomical structure
    b.   contained William Harvey's theories on blood circulation
    c.   contained Paracelsus's theories on a macrocosm-microcosm universe
    d.   none of the above

Answer: a, easy, page 580

57.   William Harvey's <u>On the Motion of the Heart and Blood</u> refuted the ideas of:
    a.   the immune system being associated with the pancreas
    b.   the liver as the beginning point of circulation of blood
    c.   the independent functioning of the lymph system
    d.   herbal healing

Answer: b, medium, page 580

58.   The role of women in the Scientific Revolution was characterized by:
    a.   the scientific community's growing acceptance of female members
    b.   Maria Merian's breakthrough in astronomy
    c.   Margaret Cavendish, who participated with men in her day's scientific debates
    d.   Maria Winkelmann, an entomologist accepted into the Berlin Academy of Sciences

Answer: c, medium, page 581

59. The overall effect of the Scientific Revolution on the <u>querrelles des femmes</u>, arguments about women, was to:
    a.   dispel traditional myths of female inferiority
    b.   increase the role of women in the child-bearing process
    c.   further justify male dominance
    d.   demonstrate that there was no inherent skeletal differences between the sexes

Answer: c, difficult, page 582

60. Most women involved in the Scientific Revolution were from:
    a.   the lower class
    b.   Russia
    c.   the middle class
    d.   the aristocracy

Answer: d, medium, page 581

61. Margaret Cavendish attacked the belief:
    a.   that humans through science were masters of nature
    b.   that science was for the benefit of all humanity
    c.   in women being equal to men, despite her position
    d.   of a Newtonian world-machine

Answer: a, difficult, page 581

62. Benedict de Spinoza believed that women:
    a.   were equal to men
    b.   were little more than soulless animals
    c.   were meant to be ruled by men
    d.   could stand on their own, but society functioned better when men were allowed to rule

Answer: c, medium + DOC 6

63. The philosophy of René Descartes:
    a.   is exemplified by the phrase, "I think, therefore I am"
    b.   stressed a holistic universe of mind and matter devoid of a creator-God
    c.   saw the material world as a living thing containing the human essence
    d.   would not have a wide influence upon Western thought until the nineteenth century

Answer: a, easy, page 584

64.   The "father of modern rationalism" is recognized as being:
      a.   Plato
      b.   Hegel
      c.   Lingus
      d.   Descartes

Answer: d, easy, page 585

65.   Descartes believed that the world could be understood by:
      a.   the same principles inherent in mathematical thinking
      b.   quiet contemplation and following of the Scriptures
      c.   mystical experiences
      d.   interpreting dreams and applying that knowledge to our everyday lives

Answer: a, difficult, page 585

66.   Francis Bacon was important to the Scientific Revolution for his emphasis on:
      a.   empirical, experimental observation
      b.   pure, theoretical science
      c.   reaching deductive conclusions by moving from general to particular principles
      d.   science's urgent need to work with nature

Answer: a, difficult, page 586

67.   Francis Bacon rejected:
      a.   the ideas of Copernicus and Kepler
      b.   the betterment of human beings through scientific learning
      c.   Jesus Christ
      d.   all of the above

Answer: a, easy, page 585

68.   Organized religions in the seventeenth century:
      a.   conceded the accomplishments of science and separated theology from science proper
      b.   rejected scientific discoveries that conflicted with the Christian view of the world
      c.   contributed greatly to scientific research
      d.   largely ignored science as merely a "toy for the minds of God's

children"

Answer: b, medium, page 587

69. Benedict de Spinoza:
    a. believed humans were created separate from nature in order to rule the earth
    b. saw his complex synthesis of God and the universe adopted as Catholic doctrine
    c. was influenced by Descartes, but saw no separation between mind and matter
    d. rejected all forms of pantheistic belief

Answer: c, medium, page 587

70. For Spinoza, the failure to understand God led to:
    a. a false worship of nature
    b. all people concerned only with their own self-interest
    c. a lack of moral judgment of others
    d. sexual permissiveness

Answer: b, difficult, page 587

71. Both Johann Comenius and Blaise Pascal:
    a. were greatly influenced by pansophism
    b. could be labeled "utopian Hermeticists"
    c. collaborated on the philosophical work <u>Penseés</u>
    d. believed that Christianity and science were not mutually exclusive

Answer: d, medium, page 588

72. Choose the correct relationship between the seventeenth-century intellectual and his work:
    a. Johann Comenius--<u>The Thoughts</u>
    b. Blaise Pascal--<u>Ethics Demonstrated in the Geometrical Manner</u>
    c. René Descartes--<u>Discourse on Method</u>
    d. Benedict de Spinoza--<u>The Way of Light</u>

Answer: c, medium + DOC 6

73. For Blaise Pascal, humans:
    a. could know infinity through reason
    b. were the summation of all things

    c.   could only understand that which is revealed to them by the Bible
    d.   could not understand infinity; only God could

Answer: d, medium, page 588 + DOC 7

74.   Concerning the first important scientific societies, the French Academy differed from the English Royal Society in the former's:
    a.   government support and support
    b.   publication of scientific journals
    c.   focus on theoretical work in mechanics and astronomy
    d.   belief that science should proceed along the lines of a cooperative venture

Answer: a, easy, page 590

75.   During the seventeenth century, royal and princely patronage of science:
    a.   declined greatly
    b.   was common only in Italy
    c.   became an international phenomenon
    d.   replaced funding by the church

Answer: c, medium, page 591

76.   The first of the scientific societies appeared in _____ and included the Academy of Experiments:
    a.   Italy
    b.   Russia
    c.   Poland
    d.   Scotland

Answer: a, medium, page 590

77.   The scientific societies established the first:
    a.   fundraising events for medicine
    b.   scientific journals
    c.   code of ethics for experimentation on animals
    d.   all of the above

Answer: b, easy, page 591

78.   Science became an integral part of Western culture in the eighteenth century because:
    a.   people perceived it to be rationally superior

b. its mechanistic nature was popular with the lower classes
c. of the victory of radical political groups, such as the Levellers, following the Puritan Revolution
d. it offered a new means to make profit and maintain social order

Answer: d, medium, page 592

SUGGESTED FILMS

<u>Ascent of Man: The Starry Messenger</u>. Time-Life Films, 52 min. (color).

<u>Ascent of Man: The Majestic Clock-Work</u>. Time-Life Films, 52 min. (color).

<u>Nicolas Copernicus</u>. Pyramid Film Production, 10 min. (color).

<u>Galileo, the Challenge of Reason</u>. Learning Corporation of America, 26 min. (color)

<u>Newton: The Mind that Found the Future</u>. Learning Corporation of America, 21 min. (color).

<u>Paracelsus</u>. Indiana University Audio-Visual Center, 30 min. (black/white).

<u>William Harvey</u>. University of California Extension Media Center, 19 min. (color).

<u>William Harvey and the Circulation of the Blood</u>. International Film Bureau, 33 min. (color).

<u>Vesalius: Founder of Modern Anatomy</u>. Yale Medical School, 13 min. (color).

<u>Science and Society</u>. McGraw-Hill Films, 18 min. (color).

CHAPTER 18: THE EIGHTEENTH CENTURY: AN AGE OF ENLIGHTENMENT

CHAPTER OUTLINE

THE ENLIGHTENMENT
 The Paths to Enlightenment
  The Popularization of Science
  Skepticism
  The Impact of Travel Literature
  The Legacy of Locke and Newton
 The Philosophes and Their Ideas
  Montesquieu
  Voltaire
  Diderot
  Toward a New "Science of Man"
  The Later Enlightenment
 The Social Environment of the Philosophes

CULTURE AND SOCIETY IN AN AGE OF ENLIGHTENMENT
 Innovations in Art, Music, and Literature
  Rococo
  The Development of Music
  The Development of the Novel
  The Writing of History
 High Culture
  Education and Universities
 Law, Crime, and Punishment
 Medicine

Popular Culture

RELIGION AND THE CHURCHES
The Institutional Church
Church-State Relations
Toleration and Religious Minorities
Toleration and the Jews
Popular Religion in the Eighteenth Century
Catholic Piety
Protestant Revivalism

SUGGESTED LECTURE TOPICS

1. "The Ideas of the Philosophes"

2. "Women and the Enlightenment"

3. "Religion in the Enlightenment: The Intellectuals and the Masses"

4. "The New Forms of Entertainment and Enlightenment"

MAPS AND ARTWORK

1. Intellectual achievements, why Italy and northern Europe? Map 18.1.

2. Representation of Cathedrals in art and architecture.

3. Engraving vs. Paintings: Which are more "realistic?"

DISCUSSION QUESTIONS FOR THE PRIMARY SOURCES (BOXED DOCUMENTS)

"The Separation of Powers": As seen in this selection, what is Montesquieu's doctrine of the separation of powers? How was this doctrine incorporated into the American constitution? (page 602)

"The Attack on Religious Intolerance": Compare the two approaches of Voltaire to the problem of religious intolerance. Do you think one is more effective than the other? Why? (page 604)

"Diderot Questions Christian Sexual Standards": What attack does Diderot make on Christian sexual standards? Would you characterize his position as a modern one? Why? (page 606)

"A Social Contract": What is Rousseau's concept of the social contract? What implications did it contain for political thought, especially in regard to the development of democratic ideas? (page 609)

"The Salon: Can Men and Women Be Friends without Sex?": What did Mlle. de Scudery think of the relations between men and women? Why was she opposed to the institution of marriage? (page 611)

"Gibbon and the Idea of Progress": What is Gibbon's view of progress? How does this idea compare with our times? (page 617)

"The Punishment of Crime": What does this selection reveal about the punishment of crime in the eighteenth century? What impact did such descriptions have on the philosophes' attitudes toward justice? (page 621)

"The Conversion Experience in Wesley's Methodism": Describe a conversion experience. What would you compare it to in today's world? Why? (page 627)

EXAMINATION QUESTIONS

Essays

1. Discuss the major intellectual changes that led to the Enlightenment.

2. What contributions did Montesquieu, Voltaire, and Diderot make to the age of the Enlightenment? What did they have in common? How did they differ?

3. What new ideas did the philosophes contribute on the following subjects: politics, the "new science of man," economics, education, and religion?

4. What were the major ideas of Jean-Jacques Rousseau? In what ways were Rousseau's ideas different from those of his predecessors?

5. What role did women play in the development of the Enlightenment?

6. How do the art and literature of the eighteenth century reflect the political and social life of the period?

7. What is high culture and in what ways was high culture expressed in the eighteenth century?

8. What is popular culture and how was it expressed in the eighteenth century? How do you explain the differences between high and popular culture?

9. What kinds of experiences would you associate with the popular religion of the eighteenth century? How do you explain the continuing growth of this popular religious devotion?

Identifications

10. philosophes
11. Plurality of Worlds
12. Pierre Bayle
13. Montesquieu
14. deism
15. Encyclopedia
16. David Hume
17. Physiocrats
18. Adam Smith
19. Cesare Beccaria
20. The Social Contract
21. Marie-Thérèse de Geoffrin
22. salons
23. Rococo
24. Balthasar Neumann
25. Johann Sebastian Bach
26. Pamela; or Virtue Rewarded
27. Spectator
28. Carnival
29. John Wesley
30. Gibbon

Multiple Choice

31. The Enlightenment of the eighteenth century was characterized by the philosophes'
    a. naive optimism that they could change society
    b. rejection of traditional Christianity
    c. emphasis on the spiritual as opposed to the rational
    d. revival of medieval thought

Answer: b, easy, page 597

32. European intellectual life in the eighteenth century was marked by the emergence of:
    a. anti-Semitism
    b. secularization
    c. sophism
    d. monastic schools

Answer: b, medium, page 597

33. Bernard de Fontenelle was best known for his:
    a. Historical and Critical Dictionary
    b. support of the churches as an aid to scientific progress
    c. original scientific experiments and discoveries
    d. Plurality of Worlds, which praised the new ideas of a mechanistic universe

Answer: d, medium, page 598

34. Which of the following was not a positive influence on the thinking of the Enlightenment?
    a. the Middle Ages
    b. Italian humanists of the Renaissance
    c. thinkers of the seventeenth century
    d. the pagan philosophies of antiquity

Answer: a, medium, page 599

35. All of the following were influences on the Enlightenment except:
    a. the cultural relativism inspired by Europeans' contact with foreign civilizations
    b. the Newtonian idea of a world-machine
    c. the growing religious skepticism of the eighteenth century
    d. Locke's philosophy stressing the importance of innate knowledge

Answer: d, difficult, page 599

36. The French philosophes:
    a. created a grand, rational system of thought to explain all things
    b. flourished in an atmosphere of government support
    c. were the leaders in spreading the Enlightenment through the entire Western world
    d. supported state censorship of ideas contrary to their own

Answer: a, medium, page 599

37. Who was responsible for the quote, "Dare to know! Have the courage to use your own intelligence"?
    a. Immanuel Kant
    b. Bernard de Fontenelle
    c. John Locke
    d. St. Augustine

Answer: a, easy, page 597

38. Isaac Newton and _____ provided the intellectual inspiration for the enlightenment.
    a. Charles de Secondat
    b. Montesquieu
    c. John Locke
    d. Immanuel Kant

Answer: c, difficult, page 600

39. The French philosophes included people from:
    a. the nobility and the middle class
    b. the lower class and the lower middle class
    c. both a and b
    d. neither a or b

Answer: a, medium, page 601

40. Montesquieu's most famous work, The Spirit of the Laws,
    a. revealed a relativism that distinguished him from many other philosophes
    b. was a political treatise ridiculing England's form of government
    c. claimed the republic was the form of government most suitable for all states
    d. rejected a checks and balance system as ineffective for controlling the

nobility

Answer: a, medium, page 601 + DOC 1

41. Above all, Montesquieu's <u>The Spirit of the Laws</u> was concerned with:
    a. the superior position of executive leadership
    b. the importance of the legislature
    c. the judiciary being the most important element of government
    d. maintaining balances among the various branches of government

Answer: d, medium, page 601 + DOC 1

42. <u>Not</u> central to the formation of Voltaire's philosophy was:
    a. the Calas affair
    b. religious toleration
    c. disgust for the English way of life
    d. deism

Answer: c, difficult, page 602

43. Voltaire's works included all of the following except:
    a. <u>Philosophic Letters</u>
    b. <u>Essay Concerning Human Understanding</u>
    c. <u>Treatise on Toleration</u>
    d. <u>Henriade</u>

Answer: b, difficult, page 603

44. Voltaire was best known for his criticism of:
    a. the German monarchical system
    b. the separation of church and state
    c. religious intolerance
    d. Plato and the Greeks

Answer: c, medium, page 603

45. Deism was based on:
    a. the Newtonian world-machine with God as mechanic
    b. God answering prayers
    c. the divinity of Jesus
    d. the denial of the existence of a Supreme Being

Answer: a, easy, page 603

46. Voltaire feared _____ believing that it might create social disorder among the common people.
    a. deism
    b. atheism
    c. philosophes
    d. socialism

Answer: b, difficult, page 603

47. Which of the following statements best applies to Denis Diderot?
    a. His materialistic, atheistic beliefs became tempered by his adoption of deism.
    b. His various artistic endeavors were united by his desire to teach moral lessons.
    c. His Encyclopedia had little impact due to its limited elitist appeal.
    d. The core of his educational beliefs was based on his belief in sexual monogamy and chastity.

Answer: b, medium, page 605

48. Diderot's views on sexuality included:
    a. the belief in the intellectual advantages of homosexuality
    b. the importance of ritual and tradition in marriage
    c. the belief in strict monogamy
    d. the renunciation of chastity for the unwed

Answer: d, medium, DOC 3

49. Identify the correct relationship between the Enlightenment "social scientist" and his beliefs:
    a. Cesare Beccaria-advocated capital punishment as the most effective deterrent to crime
    b. François Quesnay-leading Physiocrat who tried to discover the natural economic laws governing society
    c. Adam Smith-his Wealth of Nations advocated a state-controlled, mercantilistic economy
    d. David Hume-Physiocrat who tried to discover the natural economic laws governing society

Answer: b, difficult, page 606

50. The belief in natural laws underlying all areas of human life led to:
    a. the social sciences

b. an abandonment of the scientific method
c. intellectual stagnation
d. the formation of the Church of Latter-Day Saints

Answer: a, medium, page 605

51. The best statement of laissez-faire was made in 1776 by:
    a. Thomas Jefferson
    b. John Locke
    c. John Adams
    d. Adam Smith

Answer: d, difficult, page 607

52. Which of the following works expressed Rousseau's political ideas on the "general will"?
    a. The Progress of the Human Mind
    b. Emile
    c. The Social Contract
    d. Discourse on the Origins of the Inequality of Mankind

Answer: c, medium, DOC 4

53. Which philosophe expressed the idea that human perfectability is limitless before taking his own life to avoid execution?
    a. Baron Paul d'Holbach
    b. Marie-Jean de Condorcet
    c. Denis Diderot
    d. François Quesnay

Answer: b, difficult, page 608

54. For Rousseau, _____ was the source of inequality and the cause of crimes.
    a. private property
    b. marriage
    c. religion
    d. philosophy

Answer: a, medium, page 608

55. In Rousseau's The Social Contract, he expressed his belief that:
    a. government was an evil that should be eliminated
    b. the individual's will is the most important

    c. freedom is achieved by being forced to follow what is best for all people

    d. a child was a small adult with all the same abilities and obligations

Answer: c, medium, page 609

56. Of great importance to the Enlightenment were the salons, which:
    a. gave social mobility to both men and women
    b. were usually run by women but for male guests
    c. provided a forum for the serious discussion of the ideas of the philosophes
    d. all of the above

Answer: d, medium, page 610

57. By the eighteenth century, it was recognized that in salons:
    a. no men could be admitted whatsoever
    b. sexual relations were more important than intellectual stimulation
    c. only men would be admitted
    d. relations between men and women would be purely platonic

Answer: d, medium, page 611 + DOC 5

58. The Rococo artistic style of the eighteenth century was:
    a. largely confined to France
    b. best expressed in the architectural works of Baron d'Holbach
    c. evident in the masterpieces of Balthasar Neumann
    d. characterized by strict geometric patterns and an emphasis on power

Answer: c, medium, page 613

59. Choose the correct relationship between the Rococo artist and his work:
    a. Antoine Watteau-Bishop's Palace at Würzburg
    b. Giovanni Battista Tiepolo-<u>Plurality of Worlds</u>
    c. Balthasar Neumann-pilgrimage church of the Vierzehnheiligen
    d. Domenikus Zimmermann-the salon

Answer: c, easy, page 613

60. Bach also developed the _____, an intricate form of the round in which each voice begins the tune in turn while the other voices repeat and elaborate it.
    a. quartet
    b. concert
    c. fugue

    d. none of the above

Answer: c, difficult, page 615

61. European music in the eighteenth century was well characterized by:
    a. Mozart, who caused a shift in the musical center from Italy to Austria
    b. Handel, the most religiously inspired of the period's composers
    c. the strictly elitist, aristocratic works of Haydn
    d. the innovative, secular compositions of Bach

Answer: a, medium, page 615

62. Which eighteenth-century composer was considered most innovative and wrote the opera, <u>The Marriage of Figaro</u>?
    a. Bach
    b. Handel
    c. Haydn
    d. Mozart

Answer: d, easy, page 615

63. All of the following were true of eighteenth-century literary developments <u>except</u>:
    a. the removal of God from history
    b. the popularization of the novel by English authors, such as Henry Fielding
    c. the broadening of historical scope, as shown in Voltaire's <u>The Age of Louis XIV</u>
    d. the establishment of strict rules for the writing of novels

Answer: d, difficult, page 616

64. The establishment of the modern novel as a vehicle for fiction writing is generally attributed to:
    a. the French
    b. the English
    c. the Germans
    d. the Italians

Answer: b, easy, page 616

65. Which of the following trends is true of historical literature of the eighteenth century?

   a. a growing preoccupation with politics
   b. it was more of a social science than literature
   c. more attention was paid to economic and social elements of history
   d. it generally looked favorably on the Middle Ages

Answer: b, medium, page 616

66. Great Britain led the way in the eighteenth century in producing the literary form of:
   a. magazines
   b. newspapers
   c. novels
   d. all of the above

Answer: d, medium, page 618

67. High culture in eighteenth-century Europe was characterized by:
   a. the enormous impact of the book publishing industry
   b. the decline of French as an international language
   c. the decline of the magazine with the rise of the novel
   d. the increased dependency of authors on wealthy patrons

Answer: a, medium, page 618

68. Most universities in eighteenth-century Europe were:
   a. centers of innovation and intellectual growth
   b. secular institutions
   c. elitist and designed for the needs of the upper class
   d. concentrating on practical and vocational education

Answer: c, medium, page 618

69. An important development in education in Europe in the eighteenth century was:
   a. increased social mobility made possible by secondary schools
   b. a boom in university enrollment
   c. a broader and more practical university curriculum by the end of the century
   d. the universities' leadership in scientific innovation

Answer: c, medium, page 619

70. Concerning the European legal system, by the end of the eighteenth century:
   a. a trend away from imprisonment and toward capital punishment began

   b. English attorneys gained prestige and respect
   c. criminal punishments became more cruel as violent crimes increased
   d. all of the above

Answer: b, easy, page 619

71. By the beginning of the eighteenth century, most European states:
   a. had a hierarchy of courts to deal with civil and criminal cases
   b. had abandoned the use of judicial torture to obtain evidence
   c. still had no separate judicial system
   d. lacked barristers and attorneys

Answer: a, easy, page 619

72. The punishment of crime in the eighteenth century was often:
   a. public and very gruesome
   b. carried out by mobs after the criminals were charged in court
   c. less severe than the crime would merit
   d. the responsibility of the army

Answer: a, medium, page 619

73. A most noticeable trend in eighteenth-century medicine was:
   a. dramatic improvements in hospital care
   b. a decline in needless surgical practices like bleeding
   c. a lessening in the distinction between surgeons and physicians
   d. the eradication of traditional faith healing

Answer: c, medium, page 620

74. The Carnival of the Mediterranean world was:
   a. a period of intense sexual activity and gross excesses
   b. strictly a secular event with no spiritual function
   c. a popular, lower-class event seldom characterized by acts of violence or aggression
   d. none of the above

Answer: a, medium, page 621

75. Drinking habits of the rich and poor expressed:
   a. a common practice that lessed social differences
   b. the growing separation between the classes
   c. the desire for abstinence

d. the need for cheaper drinks for the lower classes

Answer: b, medium, page 622

76. Literacy rates in eighteenth-century Europe:
    a. were about equal for men and women
    b. were distributed evenly across class lines
    c. were closely related to primary education
    d. actually declined from the seventeenth century

Answer: c, medium, page 623

77. The "nationalization" of Catholic churches in European states resulted in all of the following <u>except</u>:
    a. the dissolution of the Jesuit order
    b. the destruction of the church's hierarchical structure
    c. the suppression of monastic orders, especially in the Austrian Empire
    d. the papacy's loss of power in appointing high clerical officials

Answer: b, difficult, page 624

78. In the Protestant states, the problem of church and state relations was solved by:
    a. keeping each completely autonomous
    b. making the church the ultimate authority
    c. designing special "church districts" like the Papal States
    d. establishing the principle of state control over churches

Answer: d, medium, page 623

79. The Jews of eighteenth-century Europe:
    a. were assimilated into French society through the unanimous calls of the philosophes for toleration
    b. were least persecuted in Poland and Lithuania
    c. were most free in participating in banking and commercial activities in tolerant cities
    d. won the right to public religous practice in Austria with Joseph II's Toleration Patent of 1781

Answer: c, medium, page 625

80. What philosophe is most known for his hostility toward Jewish customs?
    a. Holbach
    b. Rousseau

      c. Adam Smith
      d. Montesquieu

Answer: a, difficult, page 625

81. John Wesley:
      a. was responsible for the resurgence of Catholic piety
      b. supported a rationalistic approach to Protestantism
      c. spread the teachings of pietism through his Moravian Brethren
      d. created and controlled his evangelical Methodist church

Answer: d, medium, DOC 8

82. A movement called_____was a response to the stagnation of Protestantism in Germany during the eighteenth century.
      a. Confucianism
      b. Pietism
      c. Anglicanism
      d. New Catholicism

Answer: b, difficult, page 626

83. John Wesley described his "conversion" experiences as:
      a. blissful and joyous occasions
      b. the work of the devil
      c. violent and uncontrollable
      d. reassuring and gentle

Answer: c, medium, page 627

SUGGESTED FILMS

Age of Enlightenment in Europe. Coronet Instructional Films, 14 min. (black/white).

Civilization: The Pursuit of Happiness. Time-Life Films, 52 min. (color).

Civilization: The Smile of Reason. Time-Life Films, 52 min. (color).

Voltaire Presents Candide: An Introduction to the Age of Enlightenment. Encyclopedia Britannica, 34 min. (color).

Dinner at Baron d'Holbach's. Open University, 24 min. (color).

Johann Sebastian Bach. International Film Bureau, 27 min. (color).

The Christians: Politeness and Enthusiasm (1689-1791). McGraw-Hill, 45 min. (color).

SUGGESTIONS FOR MUSIC

Johann Sebastian Bach, Cantata No. 80, Ein Feste Burg (Philips-6514097)

Johann Sebastian Bach, The Well-Tempered Clavier (RCA-LM-6801)

Johann Sebastian Bach, Four Orchestral Suites (Musical Heritage Society-827276Z)

Johann Sebastian Bach, Mass in B Minor (Musical Heritage Society-1708/9/10)

George Frederick Handel, Messiah (Philips-PH53-992)

George Frederick Handel, Water Music (Philips-420354-2)

Wolfgang Amadeus Mozart, The Magic Flute (Angel-SCL-3807)

Wolfgang Amadeus Mozart, Don Giovanni (DG-419635-2)

Wolfgang Amadeus Mozart, Requiem (Philips-420772-2)

Wolfgang Amadeus Mozart, Eine Kleine Nachtmusik (Musical Heritage Society-7077W)

Franz Joseph Haydn, The Creation (Philips-416449-2)

Franz Joseph Haydn, Symphony No. 94 (DG-419233-2)

CHAPTER 19: THE EIGHTEENTH CENTURY: EUROPEAN STATES, INTERNATIONAL WARS, AND SOCIAL CHANGE

CHAPTER OUTLINE

THE EUROPEAN STATES
    Enlightened Politics?
    The Atlantic Seaboard States
        France
        Great Britain
        The Dutch Republic
    Absolutism in Central and Eastern Europe
        Prussia
        The Austrian Empire
        Russia
        Poland
    The Mediterranean World
    Scandinavia
    Enlightened Politics Revisited

WARS AND DIPLOMACY
    The War of the Austrian Succession (1740-1748)
    The Seven Years' War (1756-1763)
    European Armies and Warfare

ECONOMIC AND SOCIAL CHANGE

Growth of the European Population
Family, Marriage, and Birthrate Patterns
An Agricultural Revolution?
Finance and Industry
Mercantile Empires and Worldwide Trade
     Colonial Empires
     Global Trade

THE SOCIAL ORDER OF THE EIGHTEENTH CENTURY
The Peasants
The Nobility
     The Aristocratic Way of Life: The Country House
     The Aristocratic Way of Life: The Grand Tour
The Inhabitants of Towns and Cities
     The Problem of Poverty

SUGGESTED LECTURE TOPICS

1. "Enlightened Politics: Myth and Reality"

2. "Catherine the Great and Frederick the Great: What Constitutes Greatness?"

3. "The Role of the Nobility in the Eighteenth Century"

4. "The Palace and the Country House in the Eighteenth Century" [a slide lecture]

5. "The Scramble for Empire"

MAPS AND ARTWORK

1. The dismemberment of a nation, Poland, Map 19.2.

2. Worldwide conflict, the first world war. Map 19.3.

3. The art collection and a modern museum, page 662.

DISCUSSION QUESTIONS FOR THE PRIMARY SOURCES (BOXED

DOCUMENTS)

"The French King's Bedtime": What does this document reveal about the condition of the French monarchy during the reign of Louis XVI? (page 634)

"Frederick the Great and His Father": Based on these documents, why was the relationship between Frederick the Great and his father such a difficult one? How do you think Frederick would describe his father to friends his own age? (page 638)

"The Proposals of Catherine II for a New Law Code": How do the proposals of Catherine II for a new law code illustrate the influence of the philosophes? (page 641)

"British Victory in India": How do you account for Clive's victory at Plassey? (page 647)

"Propaganda for the New Agriculture": In Young's eyes, how did French agricultural practices compare to those of the English? Was this an unbiased account? Why or why not? (page 653)

"The Beginnings of Mechanized Industry: The Attack on New Machines": What arguments did the Leeds woolen workers use against the new machines? What does the petition reveal about the concept of "progress" at the end of the eighteenth century? Compare the argument of the Leeds woolen workers to those used by today's industrial workers against industrial robotic machines. (page 656)

"The Atlantic Slave Trade": What does this account reveal about the nature of slave trade practices and white attitudes toward blacks in the eighteenth century? (page 658)

"Poverty in France": What does this document reveal about the nature of poverty in France in the eighteenth century? What similarities and differences do you see with the problem of poverty in the United States today? (page 665)

EXAMINATION QUESTIONS

Essays

1. Imagine that you are a philosophe serving Joseph II or Catherine the Great. What

advice would you give him or her on the best way to rule Austria or Russia?

2. Compare the development of the two Atlantic seaboard states, France and Great Britain? How were they alike? How were they different?

3. Compare the development of absolutism in Prussia, the Austrian Empire, and Russia. What are the similarities and dissimilarities? What did the rulers achieve? How did they fail? How important was the character of the ruler in each case? How did Poland fit in the system and what was her impact on the three?

4. What do we mean by the phrase "enlightened politics" and to what extent was politics "enlightened" in the European states of the eighteenth century?

5. What was the nature of war and diplomacy in the eighteenth century? How would you compare the nature of war and diplomacy in the eighteenth century with that of the seventeenth century? How can Balance of Power be seen as Balance of Terror?

6. What important changes occurred in population, family and birthrate patterns, finance, and industry in the eighteenth century?

7. Some historians speak of an agricultural revolution in the eighteenth century? Why?

8. What changes did the European social order experience in the eighteenth century?

9. How and why did the nobility play a dominating role in the European society of the eighteenth century?

Identifications

10. Louis XV
11. Louis XVI
12. Robert Walpole
13. "Wilkes and liberty"
14. Frederick William I
15. General Directory
16. Junkers
17. Joseph II of Austria
18. <u>Instruction</u>

19. Emelyan Pugachev
20. "balance of power"
21. The War of the Austrian Succession
22. The Seven Years' War
23. Treaty of Paris
24. the Bank of England
25. infanticide
26. Jethro Tull
27. cottage industry
28. Atlantic slave trade
29. the Grand Tour
30. Sisters of Charity

Multiple Choice

31. Politically, the period from 1715 to 1789 witnessed:
    a. the rise of the masses in politics as advocated by the philosophes
    b. the waning of monarchical power
    c. the continuing process of centralization in the development of nation-states
    d. "enlightened absolutism" take its deepest roots in France

Answer: c, medium, page 631

32. The American Declaration of Independence summarized the concept of natural rights of the Enlightenment.
    a. True
    b. False

Answer: a, easy, page 632

33. France in the eighteenth century:
    a. prospered under the philosophe-inspired reforms of Louis XV
    b. suffered from severe economic depression throughout the century
    c. was torn apart by a series of civil wars
    d. lost an empire while acquiring a huge public debt

Answer: d, difficult, page 633

34. The reign of Louis XVI was predominantly concerned with:
    a. a ludicrous attention to court etiquette

    b.   solving the government's debt

    c.   establishing a strict code of moral behavior throughout France

    d.   regaining the empire lost in the Seven Years' War

Answer: a, medium, DOC 1

35.   Political developments in eighteenth-century Great Britain included:

    a.   the monarchy losing its few remaining powers to Parliament

    b.   the redistribution of boroughs to make the electoral system for the House of Commons more fair

    c.   William Pitt the Younger's corrupt power leading to calls for popular reform

    d.   the increasing influence of the king's ministers

Answer: d, difficult, page 633

36.   The British aristocracy during the eighteenth century:

    a.   was split into two two sharply divided groups in the House of Commons and House of Lords

    b.   allowed the monarchy to maintain some power because of its factional struggles

    c.   lost many seats in Parliament to the growing merchant class

    d.   was elected to the House of Commons through an equitable system of popular voting

Answer: b, medium, page 634

37.   As prime minister of Great Britain, Robert Walpole:

    a.   used the military to further Britain's world empire

    b.   was forced to follow closely the policies of George I and George II

    c.   pursued a peaceful foreign policy to avoid new land taxes

    d.   none of the above

Answer: c, easy, page 635

38.   The call for political reform in Great Britain during the reign of George III became symbolized in the person of:

    a.   John Wilkes

    b.   Geoffrey Camphire

    c.   William Pitt the Elder

    d.   William Pitt the Younger

Answer: a, easy, page 635

39. Political turmoil in the Dutch Republic was resolved in the eighteenth century through:
    a. the democratic reforms of the Patriots
    b. Prussian military intervention
    c. the overthrow of the House of Orange
    d. all of the above

Answer: b, medium, page 636

40. A continuing trend throughout eighteenth-century Prussia was:
    a. the out-of-control nature of the bureaucracy
    b. the social and military dominance of the Junker nobility
    c. an avoidance of military entanglements, especially under Frederick the Great
    d. social mobility for the peasants through the civil service

Answer: b, easy, page 637

41. Under the reign of Frederick William I, Prussia:
    a. saw the size of its army diminish
    b. became a disciplined militaristic state
    c. witnessed nobles dominate important administrative posts
    d. failed to establish an efficient civil bureaucracy

Answer: b, medium, page 637

42. Frederick the Great of Prussia succeeded in:
    a. imposing his stringent Protestantism on the populace
    b. crushing the power of the Prussian nobility
    c. devotedly carrying out all of the philosophes' recommendations for reform
    d. creating greater unity for Prussia's scattered lands

Answer: d, easy, page 639

43. The Austrian Empire under Joseph II:
    a. reversed the enlightened reforms of Joseph's mother, Maria Theresa
    b. rescinded all of Hungary's privileges
    c. saw the nobility's power permanently stripped away
    d. witnessed the general discontent of the people due to Joseph's drastic reforms

Answer: d, easy, page 640

44. Joseph II's program of Enlightenment-inspired reforms included all of the
     following <u>except</u>:
     a.   complete religious toleration
     b.   the abolition of serfdom
     c.   the construction of internal trade barriers
     d.   the establishment of the principle of equality of all before the law

   Answer: c, medium, page 639

45. The enlightened legal reforms expressed by Catherine the Great in her
     <u>Instruction</u>:
     a.   succeeded in abolishing serfdom in all of Russia
     b.   succeeded in establishing an equal system of law for all Russian
          citizens
     c.   instigated changes in Russian government that sapped power from the
          nobility
     d.   accomplished nothing and were quickly forgotten

   Answer: d, easy, page 640 + DOC 3

46. Catherine the Great of Russia:
     a.   followed a successful policy of expansion against the Turks
     b.   instigated enlightened reforms for the peasantry after the revolt of
          Emelyan Pugachev
     c.   alienated the nobility with her extensive enlightened reforms
     d.   all of the above

   Answer: a, medium, page 641

47. Emelyan Pugachev is noted in Russian history for:
     a.   leading a successful rebellion among the peasantry
     b.   causing greater repression of the peasantry
     c.   leading the Russian army in its capture of Turkish lands
     d.   the assassination of Catherine the Great

   Answer: b, difficult, page 640

48. Which of the following countries did not participate in the partition of Poland:
     a.   Austria
     b.   Prussia
     c.   France
     d.   Russia

Answer: c, easy, page 641

49. The partitioning of Poland in the late eighteenth century:
    a. occurred after decades of warfare between its neighbors
    b. was overturned by the successful rebellion of General Thaddeus Kosciuszko
    c. showed the necessity of a strong monarchy in the eighteenth century
    d. all of the above

Answer: c, medium, page 642

50. The Bourbon ruler who established a uniform system of laws and administrative institutions in Spain was:
    a. Philip V
    b. the marquis of Pombal
    c. Charles III
    d. Christian VII

Answer: a, difficult, page 642

51. Labelled "one of the most successful enlightened monarchs of his age" and among the most successful in wresting power from the nobility was:
    a. Charles III of Spain
    b. Maria Theresa of Austria
    c. Gustavus III of Sweden
    d. Frederick William I of Prussia

Answer: c, easy, page 644

52. Enlightened absolutism in the eighteenth century:
    a. could never overcome the political and social realities of the time
    b. was most successful in the strengthening of administrative systems
    c. was limited to policies that did not undermine the interests of the European nobility
    d. all of the above

Answer: a, medium, page 644

53. International relations in the eighteenth century were determined by all of the following except:
    a. cooperative international agreements
    b. a "balance of power" system
    c. international congresses that temporarily kept the peace

d.   the modern diplomatic system of ambassadors

Answer: a, easy, page 645

54.   The War of the Austrian Succession:
     a.   was limited only to Habsburg territory
     b.   made the Prussian king ruler of Austria
     c.   was fought between Austria and France, with France gaining Silesia
     d.   was resolved with the peace treaty of Aix-la-Chapelle

Answer: d, easy, page 646

55.   Maria Theresa refused to accept the loss of _____ which led to a diplomatic revolution.
     a.   Galicia
     b.   Bosnia
     c.   Hungary
     d.   Silesia

Answer: d, difficult, page 646

56.   Which of the following statements concerning the Seven Years' War is correct?
     a.   Its immediate origins can be traced to the failure of Frederick II's Pragmatic Sanction.
     b.   The French defeated the British in India due to their superior forces.
     c.   With the defeat of the French navy and the Treaty of Paris, Britain became the world's greatest colonial power.
     d.   The continuation of rivalries from the War of the Austrian Succession led to Prussia's victory in the European theater.

Answer: c, medium, page 648

57.   The European theater of the Seven Years's War witnessed:
     a.   a combined force of Austrian, Russian, and French troops defeated by Prussia
     b.   Frederick the Great's victory at the Battle of Rossbach in Saxony
     c.   the permanent end to Europe's balance of power
     d.   the recognition of Russian territorial gains under the Peace of Hubertusburg

Answer: b, difficult, page 647

58.   Fighting in India in the Seven Years' War saw:

    a. Robert Clive defeat the French at the Battle of Plassey
    b. native Indian soldiers unable to compete with superior European forces
    c. Great Britain emerge victorious due to persistence and superior troops
    d. all of the above

Answer: d, easy, page 667 + DOC 4

59. The Treaty of Paris, which concluded the Seven Years' War,:
    a. forced France to withdraw from India, leaving it to Great Britain
    b. left France with the strongest navy in the world
    c. forced William Pitt the Elder to remove British troops from the western half of North America
    d. left France in control of Canada

Answer: a, medium, page 647

60. European warfare in the eighteenth century was characterized by:
    a. the continued reliance on mercenary armies on the mainland
    b. ideological fervor leading to bloody battles
    c. limited objectives and elaborate maneuvers
    d. massive direct confrontations and pitched battles

Answer: c, difficult, page 649

61. Of the great European powers, the only one not to possess a standing army and to rely on mercenaries by the eighteenth century was:
    a. Prussia
    b. Great Britain
    c. Russia
    d. France

Answer: b, easy, page 649

62. The European population growth in the second half of the eighteenth century:
    a. saw all of the great powers grow in population except Russia
    b. occurred despite increased death and infant mortality rates
    c. was due to the absence of famines and elimination of most major diseases
    d. was nearly double the rate of the first half of the century

Answer: d, medium, page 649

63. All of the following were continuing trends in the upper-class,

eighteenth-century European family <u>except</u>:
   a.   childhood being viewed more and more as a phase in human development
   b.   the use of wet nurses
   c.   the decline in children per family due to birth control techniques
   d.   children being increasingly placed in foundling homes

Answer: d, difficult, page 651

64.   European society in the eighteenth century witnessed:
   a.   earlier marriage patterns
   b.   the continued dominance of the nuclear family
   c.   the declining importance of the woman in the "family economy"
   d.   the end of infanticide and illegitimate children due to tough laws prohibiting both

Answer: b, medium, page 652

65.   The "agricultural revolution" of the eighteenth century:
   a.   depended upon the emergence of the open field system
   b.   occurred despite a lack of new crops
   c.   was best suited to large-scale farmers who could make use of the new agricultural techniques
   d.   was resisted by traditional aristocrats like Jethro Tull

Answer: c, difficult, page 653 + DOC 5

66.   The improvements in agricultural practices and methods in eighteenth-century Europe pertained primarily to:
   a.   France
   b.   the Netherlands
   c.   Britain
   d.   Russia

Answer: c, medium, page 653

67.   Despite Britain's growing importance in finance in the eighteenth century:
   a.   its textile production suffered due to industrial innovations
   b.   its cottage industries continued to suffer
   c.   the Dutch remained Europe's banking leader
   d.   all of the above

Answer: a, medium, DOC 6

68. The rise of new financial institutions in France and Britain in the eighteenth century resulted in:
   a. a paper substitute for gold and silver currency
   b. the collapse of many speculation companies, as with John Law's investment company in France
   c. creation of "national" debts, enabling increased financing for government undertakings
   d. all of the above

Answer: d, easy, page 654

69. Textile production in eighteenth-century Europe witnessed:
   a. urban guilds maintain their monopoly on its production throughout the century
   b. the "cottage industry" take over antiquated forms of machine-produced textiles
   c. workers work amicably alongside mechanized looms
   d. none of the above

Answer: d, easy, page 654

70. The colonial empires of France and Britain in the eighteenth century:
   a. supported those countries' mercantilist activities
   b. were structured along similar autocratic guidelines
   c. avoided becoming involved with Spain's and Portugal's empires
   d. were both thinly populated due to the governments' failure to promote emigration

Answer: a, difficult, page 656

71. Europe's overseas slave trade in the eighteenth century:
   a. declined from its high point in the seventeenth century
   b. was perhaps the most profitable part of the international trade
   c. was gradually phased out due to its unprofitability
   d. was primarily used to supply colonies with domestic slaves

Answer: b, medium, page 657

72. Which of the following statements best applies to Europe's eighteenth-century social order?
   a. It differed from the Middle Ages in that wealth was the sole determinant of social standing.
   b. The nobility was homogeneous as it served the same social function

throughout Europe.
  c. The peasants were still hindered by a variety of feudal-type services and fees imposed by nobles.
  d. Peasants and nobles were most equal in eastern Europe, where serfdom was eradicated.

Answer: c, difficult, page 659

73. Europe's unequal social organization in the eighteenth century:
  a. was determined by the division of society into traditional orders
  b. was contrary to Christian teaching
  c. was least apparent in Prussia
  d. all of the above

Answer: a, medium, page 659

74. The European peasantry in the eighteenth century:
  a. comprised nearly half of Europe's population
  b. was free from serfdom in all countries by 1789
  c. often owed extensive compulsory services to aristocratic landowners
  d. benefitted the most in southern Italy and eastern Germany

Answer: c, difficult, page 659

75. The diet of the European peasantry in the eighteenth century:
  a. differed little from the Middle Ages
  b. was quite nutritious as dark bread was the basic staple
  c. found peas and beans to be quite popular
  d. all of the above

Answer: d, medium, page 660

76. The European nobility in the eighteenth century:
  a. played a significant role in the administrative machinery of European states
  b. lost its former dominance in military affairs
  c. composed twenty percent of Europe's population
  d. differed little in wealth and political power from state to state

Answer: a, medium, page 660

77. The country house of the English noble:
  a. was secondary in importance to the London townhouse

b. contained an architectural layout that reflected individualistic trends
c. reflected the growing male dominance of the eighteenth century
d. replaced the Grand Tour as the center for educating the young in noble manners

Answer: b, difficult, page 661

78. The Grand Tour:
    a. saw French aristocrats travel throughout Britain to learn noble manners
    b. avoided Italy as it diverted the young men from the tour's educational goals
    c. was facilitated by the convenient forms of travel in the eighteenth century
    d. often completed the education of an aristocrat's son

Answer: d, easy, page 662

79. All of the following were characteristic of eighteenth-century city life except:
    a. high death rates
    b. a charitable Christian attitude toward the poor
    c. a strict hierarchy dominated by the patricians and nobles
    d. overcrowding caused an influx of rural immigrants

Answer: b, medium, page 664

80. By the eighteenth century, the largest European city in terms of population was:
    a. London
    b. Paris
    c. St. Petersburg
    d. Amsterdam

Answer: a, easy, page 663

81. The problem of poverty in eighteenth-century Europe:
    a. was most chnonic in Great Britain, which lacked a system of public-supported poor relief
    b. was solved largely through the efforts of private, religious institutions
    c. was exacerbated by the hostile feelings of government officials toward the poor
    d. was solved in France in the 1770s through massive public works projects

Answer: c, difficult, page 664

SUGGESTED FILMS

Catherine the Great-A Profile in Power. Learning Corporation of America, 26 min. (color).

French and Indian War. Encyclopedia Britannica, 16 min. (color).

The Agrarian Revolution. Films Inc., 56 min. (color).

The Chateau and the Cottage. Open University Films, 24 min. (color).

The Colonial Idea. Films Inc., 56 min. (color).

Colonial Expansion. Encyclopedia Britannica, 11 min. (black/white).

The Colonial Expansion of European Nations. Coronet Instructional Films, 15 min. (color).

The Slave Trade Begins. Holt, Rinehart and Winston, 30 min. (black/white).

The Old African Blasphemer. Time-Life Films, 55 min. (color). [Atlantic slave trade]

CHAPTER 20: A REVOLUTION IN POLITICS: THE ERA OF THE FRENCH REVOLUTION AND NAPOLEON

CHAPTER OUTLINE

THE BEGINNINGS OF THE REVOLUTIONARY ERA: THE AMERICAN REVOLUTION
Reorganization, Resistance, and Rebellion
The War for Independence
Toward a New Nation
The Impact of the American Revolution on Europe

THE FRENCH REVOLUTION
Background to the French Revolution
The Destruction of the Old Regime
The Radical Revolution
      The Levy-in-Mass
      The Committee of Public Safety and the Reign of Terror
      The Reordering of Daily Lives: The Revolutionary Calendar
The Role of Women in the French Revolution
Reaction and the Directory

THE AGE OF NAPOLEON
The Rise of Napoleon
Domestic Policies
Napoleon's Empire and the European Response

SUGGESTED LECTURE TOPICS

1. "The Causes of the French Revolution"

2. "Personalities and Politics: The Role of Individuals in the French Revolution"

3. "The Origins of Total War in the Era of the French Revolution and Napoleon"

4. "Napoleon: The Man, the General, the Leader, and the Myth"

5. "The American Revolution and The Enlightenment"

MAPS AND ARTWORK

1. The attempt to regain Charlemagne's empire, Map 20.2.

2. Napoleon's empire: Political or military? Map 20.3.

3. The representation of commoners and women in art.

4. The representation of royalty.

DISCUSSION QUESTIONS FOR THE PRIMARY SOURCES (BOXED DOCUMENTS)

"The Argument for Independence": What influence did John Locke's theory of revolution have on the American Declaration of Independence? How would a member of the British Parliament respond to this declaration? (page 672)

"The Fall of the Bastille": Discuss the fall of the Bastille and indicate why its fall came to mark the triumph of French "liberty" over despotism? (page 680)

"Declaration of the Rights of Man and the Citizen": What "natural rights" does this document proclaim? To what extent was the document influenced by the writings of the philosophes? (page 684)

"The Declaration of the Rights of Woman and the Female Citizen": What rights for women does this document enunciate? To what extent have women in the Western world achieved these rights as of today? (page 685)

"Robespierre and Revolutionary Government": How did Robespierre justify the violent activities of the French revolutionaries? What criticism would you make of his argument? (page 690)

"Dechristianization": Based on this selection, what was dechristianization? What did revolutionaries hope to achieve by dechristianization? (page 692)

"Napoleon and Psychological Warfare": What themes did Napoleon use to play upon the emotions of his troops and inspire them to greater efforts? Do you think Napoleon believed any of these words? Why or why not? (page 696)

"The Man of Destiny": According to Napoleon, what is a man of destiny? What role did Napoleon's belief in himself as a man of destiny play in his successes and failures? (page 697)

EXAMINATION QUESTIONS

Essays

1. What impact did the American Revolution have on Europe?

2. Discuss the causes of the French Revolution? Do you think there is one cause that is more important than the others? Why or why not?

3. How was France changed by the revolutionary events of 1789-1792? Who benefitted most from these changes?

4. Why did the French Revolution enter a radical phase? What did that radical phase accomplish? What role did the Reign of Terror play in the Revolution?

5. What role did women play in the French Revolution?

6. Discuss the major events of the French Revolution from 1789 to 1799. Can you construct a "pattern of revolution" from these events?

7. In what ways did Napoleon's policies reject the accomplishments of the French Revolution? In what ways did his policies strengthen the accomplishments of the French Revolution?

8. Was Napoleon a great man? Defend your answer.

Identifications

9. French and Indian War
10. Tea Act
11. <u>Common Sense</u>
12. Loyalists
13. Articles of Confederation
14. Estates-General
15. "What is the Third Estate?"
16. Bastille
17. "Declaration of the Rights of Man and the Citizen"
18. "Declaration of the Rights of Woman and the Female Citizen"
19. Jacobins
20. the Mountain
21. Committee of Public Safety
22. Paris Commune
23. Reign of Terror
24. <u>décades</u>
25. the Directory
26. first consul
27. Concordat
28. Grand Empire

Multiple Choice

29.   From the Americans' point of view, the British colonies:
   a.   were merely an extension of the motherland
   b.   owed no allegiance to the king or parliamentary laws
   c.   were only a temporary residence to make economic gains
   d.   were young and vibrant compared to the old and decadent British society

Answer: d, medium, page 671

30.   After 1763, the British authorities and colonists came into conflict over:
   a.   expansion west of the Appalachians
   b.   the area south of the Rio Grande
   c.   freedom of religion
   d.   the treatment of French prisoners of war

Answer: a, easy, page 670

31. Which of the following statements is <u>not</u> true of the American colonists?
    a. They boycotted British goods after the Stamp Act in 1765.
    b. Fewer adult males could vote than in Britain.
    c. They believed in direct political representation.
    d. They resented paying for the French and Indian War.

Answer: b, medium, page 670

32. The Tea Act was devised by the British to:
    a. reduce the American economy
    b. provoke the Americans to war
    c. bail out the British East India Company
    d. standardize the quality of tea

Answer: c, easy, page 671

33. Which of the following acts of the British Parliament was a response to the colonists' Boston Tea Party?
    a. Tea Act
    b. Coercive Acts
    c. Townshend Acts
    d. Stamp Act

Answer: b, medium, page 671

34. The Coercive Acts had the effect of:
    a. causing the First Continental Congress to meet in 1774
    b. delaying the inevitable war
    c. minimizing the damage done by the Tea Act
    d. all of the above

Answer: a, difficult, page 671

35. The first shots of the American revolution occurred in:
    a. New York
    b. Pennsylvania
    c. Massachusetts
    d. Virginia

Answer: c, easy, page 671

36. The British forces during the Revolutionary War were:
    a. less well equipped than the Americans

    b.   never more than a token force
    c.   forced to fight an entirely defensive war throughout the conflict
    d.   augmented by German mercenaries

Answer: d, medium, page 672

37.   At the beginning of the Revolutionary War, the majority of the colonists were:
    a.   patriots
    b.   Loyalists
    c.   indifferent or apathetic
    d.   still recovering from the French and Indian War

Answer: c, medium, page 673

38.   The British were forced to surrender largely because of:
    a.   popular discontent at home
    b.   the intervention of other European nations and the threat of war with
         them
    c.   the overwhelming military superiority of the Americans by 1781
    d.   an outbreak of the plague in Britain in 1779

Answer: b, difficult, page 673

39.   The constitution of the United States of 1789:
    a.   was a revision of the Articles of Confederation with its provision for a
         strong central government
    b.   was seen by European liberals as a utopian document that would never
         last
    c.   was largely based on the political ideas of Montesquieu
    d.   had no real impact on the French Revolution

Answer: c, difficult, page 675

40.   The Constitution of 1789 was:
    a.   overwhelmingly rejected by the Continental Congress
    b.   overwhelmingly approved by the Continental Congress
    c.   barely passed by the Continental Congress
    d.   overturned in favor of the Articles of Confederation

Answer: c, medium, page 675

41.   The American Revolution affected Europeans by:
    a.   proving that military force was the final diplomatic authority

    b.   ending colonial expansion around the world

    c.   proving that the new United States was the most powerful nation

    d.   proving that the ideas of the Enlightenment could be realized politically

Answer: d, medium, page 675

42.   Which of the following statements concerning France's social orders on the eve of the French Revolution is <u>false</u>?

    a.   The Revolution was not a result of a battle between a unified nobility and unified bourgeoisie.

    b.   Stable bread prices meant that the urban working forces played little role in the Revolution.

    c.   Along with urban craftsmen, the peasants of the Third Estate constituted a majority of the three estates.

    d.   The nobility, frustrated by the old monarchical system, resisted the king's growing powers.

Answer: b, difficult, page 677

43.   The most immediate cause of the French Revolution was:

    a.   the government's failure to resolve its debts

    b.   the blocking of attempted reforms by the French Parliaments

    c.   the radical calls of the philosophes for reform

    d.   Louis XVI's rejection of the <u>cahiers de doléances</u>

Answer: a, easy, page 678

44.   The French economy of the eighteenth century was:

    a.   growing due to increased trade and industrial production

    b.   stagnant due to foreign competition in industry and trade

    c.   declining rapidly due to overuse of arable land

    d.   based largely on the silk industry

Answer: a, medium, page 676

45.   The third estate was composed of all of the following <u>except</u>:

    a.   shopkeepers

    b.   peasants

    c.   clergy

    d.   skilled craftsmen

Answer: c, easy, page 676

46.   By the eighteenth century, the bourgeoise and nobility were:
       a.   growing further apart in social status
       b.   increasingly less distinguishable from each other
       c.   rapidly losing social status to the third estate
       d.   openly hostile and frequently involved in street battles

Answer: b, medium, page 677

47.   The Estates-General consisted of representatives of the three orders: the Third Estate (people), the First Estate (clergy) and the Second Estate, representing the:
       a.   towns
       b.   pope
       c.   nobility
       d.   army

Answer: c, easy, page 678

48.   The Estates-General was:
       a.   Louis XVI's often consulted parliamentary body
       b.   in unanimous agreement that only radical changes could solve France's problems
       c.   dominated by the first estate composed mostly of urban lawyers
       d.   divided over the issue of voting by orders or by head

Answer: d, medium, page 678

49.   The cahiers de doléances called for:
       a.   abolishing the fiscal privileges of the church and nobility
       b.   the abolition of the Estates-General
       c.   the execution of all liberals
       d.   a graduated income tax

Answer: a, easy, page 678

50.   The Third Estate's "National Assembly" only survived because of:
       a.   Louis XVI's support
       b.   popular uprisings, especially the fall of the Bastille
       c.   the suppression of the Great Fear
       d.   the popularity of the pamphlet, "What is the Third Estate?"

Answer: b, easy, page 679

51. The controversy over voting by order versus voting by head in the Estates-General saw:
    a. the nobles of the robe advocate voting by head
    b. the "lovers of liberty" effectively block voting by head
    c. Abbé Sieyès's call for the expulsion of the Third Estate from the Estates-General
    d. the Third Estate respond by forming a "National Assembly"

Answer: d, medium, page 679

52. All of the following were actions of the Constituent Assembly except:
    a. the Declaration of the Rights of Man and the Citizen
    b. the Civil Constitution of the Clergy
    c. the Declaration of Pillnitz
    d. the administrative restructuring of France

Answer: c, medium, page 682

53. The Bastille was:
    a. the king's castle
    b. an arsenal and prison
    c. the place where most state executions took place
    d. a monastery

Answer: b, medium, page 679 + DOC 2

54. The Declaration of the Rights of Man and the Citizen:
    a. was drawn up by the monarchy to limit freedoms
    b. was rejected by those influenced by the Enlightenment
    c. owed much to the American Declaraton of Independence
    d. allowed for aristocratic privileges

Answer: c, easy, page 682 + DOC 3

55. Which of the following is not true of the National Assembly's dealings with the Catholic church?
    a. church lands were confiscated
    b. the church was secularized
    c. the pope was against the Civil Constitution of the Clergy
    d. almost all the clergy went along with the reforms

Answer: d, easy, page 683

56.   The most important act propagated by the new Legislative Assembly of 1791 was:
    a.   the abolition of all seigneurial rights and aristocratic privileges
    b.   the destruction of the radical Jacobin clubs that threatened its power
    c.   declaration of war on Austria in April of 1792
    d.   ensuring that clerics and nobles continued to play a large role in government

Answer: c, difficult, page 686

57.   At the beginning of the French Revolution, the _____ emerged as the most important radical element in French politics.
    a.   Jacobins
    b.   Papists
    c.   Communists
    d.   Loyalists

Answer: a, easy, page 683

58.   During the early stages of the "Radical Revolution," the National Convention:
    a.   was controlled by the Mountain, which defeated the less radical Girondins
    b.   successfully resisted the sansculottes' radical attempts to control the Convention
    c.   favored ending the unwinnable European war
    d.   failed to create any kind of large standing army

Answer: a, easy, page 687

59.   In September of 1792, the National Convention:
    a.   established a constitutional monarchy
    b.   abolished the monarchy and established a republic
    c.   voted to preserve the life of Louis XVI
    d.   was dismantled by Louis XVI

Answer: b, medium, page 687

60.   The Committee of Public Safety during the Reign of Terror:
    a.   was headed by Maximilien Robespierre
    b.   implemented a successful series of economic and price controls through France
    c.   attempted to reinstitute the church's influence over politics
    d.   all of the above

Answer: a, easy, page 688

61. The French Republic's army in the 1790s:
    a. received little backing from the home front
    b. was small, but efficient
    c. brought nationalism and total war to European warfare
    d. was totally defeated by 1795

Answer: c, difficult, page 688

62. In the Reign of Terror's "preservation" of the revolution from its internal enemies:
    a. the nobility was singled out as the most dangerous social group
    b. rebellious cities were brutally defeated by the Revolutionary Armies
    c. no more than 5,000 people were killed by the guillotine
    d. the Committee of Public Safety played an insignificant role

Answer: b, medium, page 690

63. During the Reign of Terror, the majority of the victims were:
    a. nobles
    b. clergy
    c. middle classes
    d. peasant and laboring classes

Answer: d, medium, page 690

64. The National Convention pursued a policy of dechristianization.
    a. True
    b. False

Answer: a, easy, page 691

65. Which of the following is not true of the revolutionary republic calendar:
    a. each month consisted of three ten-day weeks
    b. Christian holidays were kept
    c. it was largely ignored
    d. it served as a symbol of a new beginning

Answer: b, easy, page 692

66. The republican calendar created by the revolutionary government in 1793:
    a. contained new names for days and months that reflected the new

urban, bourgeois society
b. was part of the government's dechristianization efforts
c. was well received by most of the populace
d. was not abandoned by the French until Napoleon's defeat

Answer: b, medium, page 692

67. The role of French women in the Revolution:
    a. was minimal and without precedent
    b. was on the whole encouraged by their male counterparts
    c. was limited only to participation in bread riots
    d. was outside the political realm, as male leaders felt that a woman's place was still in the home

Answer: d, difficult, page 694

68. Which of the following is not true of women in revolutionary France?
    a. They participated in the "October days."
    b. They often forced additional action by revolutionary military forces.
    c. They were allowed to attend meetings of the Paris Commune.
    d. Their clubs were outlawed in the radical phase of the Revolution.

Answer: c, medium, page 694

69. The Thermidorean Reaction occurred after:
    a. the death of Louis XVI
    b. the invasion of Paris by the Prussians
    c. Napoleon came to power
    d. the death of Robespierre

Answer: d, easy, page 694

70. The government of the Directory in the period of the Thermidorean Reaction:
    a. primarily relied on the support of the royalists
    b. was unicameral and directly elected by active citizens
    c. was characterized by honest leadership and wise economic plans
    d. had to rely on military support for its survival

Answer: d, difficult, page 695

71. The Directory gathered most of its support from:
    a. Loyalists
    b. Jacobins

    c.   clergy
    d.   none of the above

Answer: d, easy, page 695

72.   Napoleon's rise to power was aided by all of the following <u>except</u>:
    a.   his tremendous intellectual capacities
    b.   his defeat of the British in Egypt in 1799
    c.   his own overwhelming sense of importance and destiny
    d.   the coup d'etat of 1799 in which the Directory was overthrown

Answer: b, medium, page 696

73.   Which of the following statements best applies to Napoleon?
    a.   He was a child of the Enlightenment and the French Revolution.
    b.   He had a sense of moral responsibility to the people of France.
    c.   He advocated an invasion of Britain in the 1790s.
    d.   He was born the son of a Parisian merchant.

Answer: a, difficult, page 695

74.   Which of the following statements best applies to Napoleon's domestic policies:
    a.   Much autonomy was given to the provincial departments as the previous system of prefects was overhauled.
    b.   His "new aristocracy" was actually little different from the old, as it was based on privilege and wealth.
    c.   His Civil Code reaffirmed the ideals of the Revolution while creating a uniform legal system.
    d.   As a devout Catholic, he reestablished Catholicism as the official state religion.

Answer: c, difficult, page 698

75.   The Concordat allowed all of the following <u>except</u>:
    a.   the church to have processions and seminaries
    b.   the pope being able to depose bishops
    c.   the pope being able to nominate bishops
    d.   the clergy being paid by the state

Answer: c, medium, page 697

76.   Napoleon's Grand Empire:

    a.   was composed of three different parts but united under the rule of Napoleon
    b.   revived the power of the nobility and clergy in all its states
    c.   included all of Europe with the defeat of Britain in 1805
    d.   had no long-lasting impact on the conquered countries

Answer: a, medium, page 699

77. Napoleon's Grand Empire included all of the following states except:
    a.   Italy
    b.   Spain
    c.   Holland
    d.   Great Britain

Answer: d, easy, page 699

78. Not among the factors in the defeat of Napoleon was:
    a.   the failure of the Continental System
    b.   the defeat of the French navy at the Battle of Trafalgar
    c.   mass reactions to his brutal suppression of local customs in the conquered countries
    d.   the spread of nationalism in the conquered countries

Answer: c, difficult, page 700

79. The Continental System tried to defeat the British by:
    a.   a massive invasion of Britain
    b.   preventing British trade
    c.   causing political unrest in Britain
    d.   none of the above

Answer: b, medium, page 700

SUGGESTED FILMS

Seeds of the Revolution: Colonial America 1763-75. Graphic Curriculum, 24 min. (color).

George Washington: The Making of a Rebel. National Geographic Society, 29 min. (color).

The French Revolution. Coronet Instructional Films, 17 min. (color).

French Revolution: The Bastille. Learning Corporation of America, 22 min. (color).

The French Revolution: The Terror. Learning Corporation of America, 29 min. (color).

Terror. The Open University, 25 min. (color).

The Napoleonic Era. Coronet Instructional Films, 15 min. (color).

Napoleon: The Making of a Dictator. Learning Corporation of America, 27 min. (color).

Napoleon: The End of a Dictator. Learning Corporation of America, 27 min. (color).

The Hundred Days: Napoleon from Elba to Waterloo. Time-Life Films, 40 min. (color).

CHAPTER 21: THE INDUSTRIAL REVOLUTION AND ITS IMPACT ON EUROPEAN SOCIETY

CHAPTER OUTLINE

Efforts at Change: The Workers
Efforts at Change: Reformers and Government

SUGGESTED LECTURE TOPICS:

1. "The Emergence of the Modern Industrial System and Its Impact on the European Way of Life"

2. "The Impact of Early Factories on Women and Children and the Development of Labor Laws"

3. "The Impact of the Industrial Revolution on the Standard of Living of the Masses"

MAPS AND ARTWORK

1. Countries with resources who succeeded or failed. Why? Map 21.2.

2. The economic union of England, railroads, industry and coalfields. Map 21.2.

3. The view of the Industrial Revolution in art.

DISCUSSION QUESTIONS FOR THE PRIMARY SOURCES (BOXED DOCUMENTS)

"The Traits of the British Industrial Entrepreneur": As seen in the life of Richard Arkwright, what traits did Edward Baines think were crucial to be a successful entrepreneur? To what extent are these still considered the necessary traits for a successful entrepreneur? (page 707)

"Discipline in the New Factories": As seen in this document, what impact did factories have on the lives of workers? To what extent have such "rules" determined much of modern industrial life? (page 713)

"S-t-e-a-m-boat a-coming'!": How does this document illustrate the impact of the transportation revolution on daily life in the United States? (page 718)

"The Great Irish Famine": Discuss the impact of the Great Irish Famine on the Irish people. Are there any contemporary parallels to this disaster? (page 720)

"Child Labor: Discipline in the Textile Mills" and "Child Labor: The Mines": What kind of working conditions did children face in the mills and mines during the early Industrial Revolution? Why did entrepreneurs permit such conditions and such treatment of children? (pages 726 and 727)

"The Political Demands of the Chartist Movement": What political demands did the Chartists make? How would these changes have benefitted them? (page 731)

EXAMINATION QUESTIONS

Essays

1. Why did the Industrial Revolution begin in Great Britain?

2. Discuss the role of the factory in the early Industrial Revolution: What made the factory system possible? Why was it such an important part of the early industrial system? What impact did it have on the lives of workers?

3. Compare the patterns of industrialization in continental Europe and the United States with Great Britain.

4. Discuss the role of government in the industrial development of the Western world. How did government encourage industrialization and how did it attempt to check its excesses?

5. How are changes in population growth and the development of urbanization related to the Industrial Revolution?

6. Discuss the basic characteristics of the new industrial system. What role did it begin to play in European society?

7. How did the early Industrial Revolution affect the family, the role of women, and the living and working conditions of the industrial workers?

8. What efforts did workers make to ameliorate the harsh working conditions of the early Industrial Revolution? How successful were they?

9. Assume that you are a small landowner who lost his lands due to economic

changes in the British countryside. In a brief essay, explain your changed position and lifestyle as you and your family move to Manchester to gain employment in one of the new factories.

Identifications

10. Industrial Revolution
11. Richard Arkwright
12. Newcomen engine
13. James Watt
14. Rocket
15. The Great Exhibition
16. John Cockerill
17. National System of Political Economy
18. Crédit Mobilier
19. "American system"
20. Great Irish Famine
21. Edwin Chadwick
22. Public Health Act
23. the report of Sadler's Committee
24. Combination Acts
25. Robert Owen
26. Amalgamated Society of Engineers
27. Luddites
28. Chartist movement
29. factory acts

Multiple Choice

30.   The Industrial Revolution had its beginnings in:
    a.   France
    b.   Belgium
    c.   Great Britain
    d.   the United States

Answer: c, easy, page 706

31.   Britain's emergence as the first industrial power was aided by all of the following except:

    a.   a rapid population growth and a surplus pool of labor
    b.   the agricultural revolution of the eighteenth century
    c.   a ready supply of domestic and colonial markets
    d.   Parliament's heavy involvement in private enterprise

Answer: d, medium, page 706

32.   The Industrial Revolution in Britain was largely inspired by:
    a.   the urgent need to solve the great poverty in the eighteenth century
    b.   the failure of the cottage industry
    c.   entrepreneurs who sought and accepted the new manufacturing methods and inventions
    d.   the industrialization of the Dutch and French

Answer: c, medium, page 706

33.   Britain's Industrial Revolution occurred despite the lack of:
    a.   an effective central bank
    b.   important mineral resources
    c.   an accessible transportation system
    d.   none of the above

Answer: d, medium, page 706

34.   The British industrial entrepreneur Richard Arkwright:
    a.   typified the highly educated and mannered entrepreneur of the Industrial Revolution
    b.   invented the water frame spinning machine
    c.   perfect the Crompton's mule
    d.   all of the above

Answer: b, easy, page 708

35.   The first step toward the Industrial Revolution in Britain occurred within its:
    a.   cotton textile industry
    b.   mining industry
    c.   iron industry
    d.   railroad industry

Answer: a, medium, page 708

36.   Britain's cotton industry in the late eighteenth century:
    a.   could not keep up with French textile production

b. was responsible for the creation of the first modern factories
c. declined due to the lack of technical innovation
d. immediately fell apart with the success of the Industrial Revolution

Answer: b, easy, page 708

37. The invention of the steam engine in Britain was initially triggered by:
    a. the textile industry's demand for new sources of power
    b. problems in the mining industry
    c. the railroad industry's call for a more efficient source of power
    d. none of the above

Answer: b, medium, page 708

38. James Watt was vital to the Industrial Revolution for his invention of:
    a. the spinning jenny
    b. the mule-powered Newcomen engine
    c. a rotary engine that could spin and weave cotton
    d. the first steam-powered locomotive

Answer: c, difficult, page 709

39. The development of the steam engine during the Industrial Revolution:
    a. was the work of Edmund Cartwright
    b. proved disastrous to Britain's mining industry
    c. made factories dependent upon the location of rivers
    d. made Britain's cotton goods the cheapest and most popular in the world

Answer: d, medium, page 709

40. The success of the steam engine in the Industrial Revolution made Britain dependent upon:
    a. timber
    b. coal
    c. water power
    d. electricity

Answer: b, easy, page 709

41. Steam power led to the demise of which of the following industries?
    a. iron
    b. mining

    c. cottage
    d. textile

Answer: c, difficult, page 709

42. The development of such superior locomotives as the Rocket, used on the first public railway lines, is attributed to:
    a. Timothy Faulkner
    b. George Stephenson
    c. Richard Trevithick
    d. Walter Zofcin

Answer: b, medium, page 711

43. The development of the railroads in the Industrial Revolution was important in:
    a. increasing British supremacy in civil and mechanical engineering
    b. increasing the size of markets and the price of goods
    c. bringing about the demise of joint-stock companies
    d. all of the above

Answer: a, difficult, page 711

44. The new set of values established by factory owners during the Industrial Revolution:
    a. was rejected by evangelical religions as being "unchristian"
    b. was basically a continuation from the cottage industry system
    c. was never adopted by the working classes
    d. relegated the worker to a life of harsh discipline

Answer: d, medium, page 711

45. The Great Exhibition of 1851:
    a. showed how the Industrial Revolution achieved human domination over nature
    b. displayed Great Britain's industrial wealth to the world
    c. was housed in the Crystal Palace, a tribute to British engineering skills
    d. all of the above

Answer: d, easy, page 712

46. Continental Europe's early inferiority to Britain in industrial production was due to all of the following except:
    a. the destruction of the Napoleonic wars

b.   a chronic lack of technical knowledge
c.   government non-interference in economic affairs
d.   guild restrictions and transportation difficulties

Answer: c, medium, page 714

47.   Prior to the Industrial Revolution, continental Europe's economy was marked by:
a.   the destruction of textile manufacturing under Napoleon's Continental system
b.   a spirit of entrepreneurial innovation
c.   an unwillingness to take risks in investment
d.   an absence of agricultural improvements and cottage industry

Answer: c, difficult, page 715

48.   John Cockerill was most noted for:
a.   creating a system of railroad lines throughout the Continent in the 1840s
b.   his National System of Political Economy
c.   spreading British technical knowledge to Belgium
d.   establishing the Banque de Belgique in Belgium

Answer: c, medium, page 716

49.   Friedrich List's National System of Political Economy:
a.   advocated protective tariffs to protect industrialization in Germany
b.   paved the way for joint-stock investment banks on the Continent
c.   blasted the investment policies of the Crédit Mobilier
d.   encouraged British technical advice in industrializing the Continent

Answer: a, easy, page 716

50.   Continental industrialization differed from Great Britain's in that the Continent:
a.   industrialized through the private capital of rich individuals like John Cockerill
b.   was dependent upon joint-stock investment banks like the Crédit Mobilier
c.   invested in the latest equipment and most productive mills
d.   never established technical schools to train engineers and mechanics

Answer: b, medium, page 716

51. By 1850, all of the following countries were close to Britain in industrial output <u>except</u>:
    a. Russia
    b. Belgium
    c. the United States
    d. France

Answer: a, medium, page 717

52. The Industrial Revolution on the Continent:
    a. was a generation behind Great Britain in cotton manufacturing
    b. neglected coal and iron technology in favor of the textile industry
    c. benefitted from the discovery of great coal deposits in Germany in the 1820s
    d. would remain far behind Great Britain's until the twentieth century

Answer: a, difficult, page 717

53. The most modern cotton-manufacturing system on the Continent by the 1840s was in:
    a. Russia
    b. France
    c. Italy
    d. Belgium

Answer: d, medium, page 717

54. The Industrial Revolution in the United States:
    a. never matched Great Britain's due to a lack of internal transportation
    b. employed large numbers of women in factories, especially the textile mills
    c. utilized a labor-intensive economy with many skilled workers
    d. occurred predominantly in the southern states

Answer: b, easy, page 718

55. The "American system" benefitted the United States' Industrial Revolution in that it:
    a. utilized America's large pool of artisans
    b. revolutionized industrial production by saving labor
    c. prevented immigrants, women, and children from working in dangerous factories
    d. bridged the gap in wealth between the rich and poor

Answer: b, difficult, page 717

56. Contrary to the growing myth, in America by 1860, _____ percent of the
     population in cities held 70 to 80 percent of the wealth compared to 50 percent
     in 1800.
     a.   10
     b.   30
     c.   60
     d.   75

Answer: a, easy, page 719

57. By 1850, the European population:
     a.   could not be closely approximated as government statistics were not
          yet kept
     b.   was close to figures from 1800
     c.   was over 150 million
     d.   was over 250 million

Answer: d, easy, page 719

58. The European population explosion of the nineteenth century:
     a.   is mainly explained by the increased birthrates across Europe
     b.   was largely attributable to the disappearance of famine from western
          Europe
     c.   was due to the lack of emigration
     d.   occurred despite the preponderance of major epidemic diseases

Answer: b, medium, page 719

59. The only European country with a declining population in the nineteenth
     century was:
     a.   Ireland
     b.   Italy
     c.   Austria
     d.   France

Answer: a, easy, page 720

60. The Great Irish Famine of 1845-1851:
     a.   witnessed the emigration of 300,000 people from Ireland to Britain
          and the United States
     b.   would have been worse had it not been for earlier large-scale

industrialization throughout the countryside
    c.   saw over one million people die of starvation and disease
    d.   was due to peasant dependence on the turnip

Answer: c, easy, page 720

61.   Urbanization in the first half of the fifteenth century:
    a.   was less dramatic for the Continent than Great Britain
    b.   caused over fifty percent of the British population to live in cities by 1850
    c.   was a phenomenon directly tied to industrialization
    d.   all of the above

Answer: d, medium, page 721

62.   Which of the following statements best applies to urban life in the early nineteenth century?
    a.   Government intervention prevented consumer fraud and food adulteration.
    b.   A tremendous decline in death rates accounted for the increased population of most large cities.
    c.   Lower-class family dwellings were on the whole much better than in the countryside.
    d.   Filthy sanitary conditions were exacerbated by the city authorities' denial of public responsibility.

Answer: d, difficult, page 721

63.   Urban living conditions in the early Industrial Revolution were <u>not</u> characterized by:
    a.   wealthy inhabitants living on the outer ring of the city
    b.   overcrowded tenements
    c.   widespread, charitable acts by the wealthy toward the urban poor
    d.   appalling sanitary conditions

Answer: c, easy, page 722

64.   Edwin Chadwick:
    a.   was a leader in expressing the dislike of the middle class for the working poor
    b.   wrote the <u>Treatise on Adulteration of Foods and Culinary Poisons</u>, which immediately solved the problem of food poisoning in Britain
    c.   advocated modern sanitary reforms that resulted in Britain's first

Public Health Act
d.   was representative of the new entrepreneurial, industrial class

Answer: c, medium, page 723

65.   Most prominent among the new industrial entrepreneurial class in the Industrial
Revolution was:
a.   the bourgeoisie
b.   the lower classes
c.   the richest ten percent of society
d.   the traditional aristocracy

Answer: a, easy, page 724

66.   Members of the new industrial entrepreneurial class in the early nineteenth
century:
a.   particularly excluded aristocrats
b.   were responsible for the predominance of giant corporate firms by
1850
c.   were often from dissenting religious minorities
d.   were more often from the lower classes than the bourgeoisie

Answer: c, difficult, page 724

67.   The early industrial entrepreneur in Great Britain:
a.   often had to control singlehandedly the entire factory
b.   had to expand constantly to feel secure
c.   often came from a mercantile background
d.   all of the above

Answer: d, medium, page 724

68.   The largest group of urban workers in the first half of the nineteenth century
was composed of:
a.   artisans and craftsmen
b.   domestic servants
c.   industrial workers
d.   members of guilds

Answer: a, easy, page 725

69.   The new social class of industrial workers in the early Industrial Revolution:
a.   drastically altered traditional female working patterns

b.   worked under appallingly dangerous conditions for incredibly long hours
c.   excluded large numbers of children from factory work
d.   all of the above

Answer: b, medium, page 725

70.   Working conditions in the early decades of the Industrial Revolution:
a.   were poor in all areas except for pottery and craft workshops
b.   were poor despite close government regulation of factories
c.   were satisfactory in the coal mines following the invention of steam power
d.   were probably worst in the cotton mills with their high temperatures and hazardous air

Answer: d, easy, page 726

71.   The harsh treatment of children in the workplace during the early Industrial Revolution:
a.   physically toughened and strengthened the children for their adult lives
b.   matched the contemporary brutal treatment of children in general
c.   did not occur in mining operations, where children were too small to be of any good
d.   was often prevented by parish officials who employed children as pauper apprentices

Answer: b, easy, page 728

72.   Women who worked in the early factories of the Industrial Revolution:
a.   were given the same pay as men
b.   instigated dramatic change in pre-industrial kinship patterns
c.   never represented a large percentage of the workers in textile factories
d.   did not cause a significant transformation in female working patterns

Answer: d, medium, page 728

73.   The Industrial Revolution's effect on the standard of living:
a.   especially benefitted the middle and upper classes
b.   led to increased disparity between the richest and poorest classes
c.   led to an overall increase in real wages for the working classes
d.   all of the above

Answer: d, easy, page 729

74.   The economies of the newly industrialized nations were free from:
    a.   short-term economic depressions
    b.   high unemployment figures
    c.   crises of overpopulation
    d.   none of the above

Answer: d, medium, page 729

75.   The Chartist movement in Britain:
    a.   was the skilled craftsmen's attempt to destroy industrial machinery
    b.   gave millions of men and women a sense of working-class consciousness
    c.   coerced Parliament into instituting universal male suffrage
    d.   none of the above

Answer: b, medium, page 730 + DOC 7

76.   Robert Owen was responsible for:
    a.   leading a series of bitter strikes in Britain in the 1810s
    b.   forming the largest trade union in Europe, the Amalgamated Society of Engineers
    c.   the brilliant success of the Grand National Consolidated Trades Union
    d.   none of the above

Answer: d, medium, page 730

77.   All of the following were political demands of the Chartists except:
    a.   the formation of a national federation of trade unions
    b.   annual sessions of Parliament
    c.   universal male suffrage
    d.   payment of the members of Parliament

Answer: a, medium, page 730

78.   The Luddites:
    a.   received little local support in their areas of activity
    b.   attacked industrial machines that affected their livelihood
    c.   were composed of the lowest unskilled workers in Great Britain
    d.   was the first movement of working-class consciousness of the Continent

Answer: b, easy, page 730

79. Efforts at industrial reform in the 1830s and 1840s in Great Britain achieved all of the following except:
    a. the establishment of a national system of trade unions by 1847
    b. the reduction of working hours for children to no more than 12 hours a day
    c. the outlawing of women and children in coal mines
    d. the requirement of daily education for working children

Answer: a, medium, page 732

80. All of the following acts of the British government aided the industrial working class except:
    a. the Ten Hours Act
    b. the Factory Acts
    c. the Combination Acts
    d. the Coal Mines Act

Answer: c, easy, page 732

SUGGESTED FILMS:

The Industrial Revolution in England. Encyclopedia Britannica, 26 min. (black/white).

Man and the Industrial Revolution. McGraw-Hill Films, 20 min. (color).

The Ascent of Man: The Drive for Power. Time-Life Films, 52 min. (color).

An Age of Revolutions. International Film Bureau, 26 min. (color).

Civilization: Heroic Materialism. Time-Life Films, 52 min. (color).

The Crystal Year. National Educational Television, 30 min. (black/white).

CHAPTER 22: REACTION, REVOLUTION, AND ROMANTICISM, 1815-1850

CHAPTER OUTLINE

Reform in Great Britain
The Growth of the United States
The Revolutions of 1848
Yet Another French Revolution
Central Europe
Italy
THE EMERGENCE OF AN ORDERED SOCIETY
The Development of New Police Forces
The Reform of Prisons

ROMANTICISM
The Characteristics of Romanticism
Romantic Poets and the Love of Nature
Romanticism in Art and Music
The Revival of Religion in the Age of Romanticism

SUGGESTED LECTURE TOPICS

1. "The Forces of Conservatism: Theory and Practice"

2. "The Forces of Change: Theory and Practice"

3. "The Romantic Movement" [a slide lecture]

4. "The Failure of Revolutions"

MAPS AND ARTWORK

1. Natural states vs. fragmented principalities, Map 22.1.

2. Language vs. nation: How well do they fit and what modern conflicts are still evident? Map 22.3.

3. The Rise of Portraiture.

DISCUSSION QUESTIONS FOR THE PRIMARY SOURCES (BOXED DOCUMENTS)

"The Voice of Conservatism: Metternich of Austria": Based on Metternich's discussion, how would you define conservatism? What experience obviously conditioned Metternich's ideas? Based on this selection, discuss the actual policies Metternich would have wanted his government to pursue? (page 738)

"University Students and German Unity": Would you call Heinrich von Gagern a nationalist? Why or why not? As seen in this selection, why were nationalism and liberalism allies during the first half of the nineteenth century? (page 745)

"The Voice of Liberalism: John Stuart Mill on Liberty": How does Mill's ideas fit into the concept of democracy, safety and national security? What is more important: the individual or society? (page 749)

"The Voice of Reform: Macauley on the Reform Bill of 1832": What arguments did Macauley use to support the Reform Bill of 1832? Was he correct? Why or why not? (page 755)

"Revolutionary Excitement: Carl Schurz and the Revolution of 1848 in Germany": Why was Schurz so excited when he heard the news about the revolution in France? Do you think being a university student would help explain his reaction? Why or why not? (page 759)

"The Voice of Italian Nationalism: Giuseppe Mazzini and Young Italy": Based on the principles outlined here, define nationalism. Why have some called nationalism a "secular religion?" (page 762)

"The New British Police: 'We Are Not Treated as Men'": What were the complaints of the British constables? What main issue did the complaints raise? To what extent is this issue still prevalent in our own society? (page 765)

"Gothic Literature: Edgar Allan Poe" and "William Blake and the Romantic Attack on Science": What characteristics of Romanticism are revealed in Poe's tale and Blake's poem? (pages 769 and 770)

EXAMINATION QUESTIONS

Essays

1. Discuss the Congress of Vienna: What did it try to accomplish in Europe? How well did it succeed in achieving its goals?

2. What were the chief ideas associated with the ideology of conservatism in the first half of the nineteenth century? How were these ideas put into practice between 1815 and 1830?

3. What were the chief ideas associated with the ideologies of liberalism, nationalism, and early or utopian socialism? Why were liberalism, nationalism, and early socialism considered revolutionary by many people?

4. There were two revolutionary waves in Europe in the 1820s and 1830s. Compare the revolutions of the 1820s to the revolutions of the 1830s in terms of location, motives, and successes. Be sure to assess the role of liberalism and nationalism in these revolutions.

5. How was Great Britain able to avoid revolution in the 1830s and 1840s?

6. Discuss the revolutions of 1848 in France, central Europe, and Italy: What caused them? What did they achieve initially? Why did the revolutionary forces fail? What did the revolutions actually achieve?

7. How did Europe respond to the need for order in society in the first half of the nineteenth century?

8. Discuss the major ideas of Romanticism and show how they were related to the political and social forces of the age.

Identifications

9. Congress of Vienna
10. Reflections on the Revolution in France
11. Concert of Europe
12. Germanic Confederation
13. Burschenschaften
14. liberalism
15. Thomas Malthus
16. David Ricardo
17. Self-Help
18. Charles Fourier
19. Flora Tristan
20. July Ordinances
21. John Marshall
22. Andrew Jackson

23. <u>Grossdeutsch</u>/<u>Kleindeutsch</u>
24. bobbies
25. Johann Wolfgang von Goethe
26. William Wordsworth
27. Caspar David Friedrich
28. Ludwig van Beethoven
29. Romanticism

Multiple Choice

30. The Treaty of Paris after Napoleon's defeat:
    a. required huge indemnities from France
    b. required France to return all her acquired territories
    c. actually had a French representative, Prince Talleyrand, help make the terms
    d. did not deal with the problems created by Napoleon's occupation of Europe

Answer: d, easy, page 735

31. The Congress of Vienna:
    a. gave Prussia complete control over Polish lands
    b. created policies that would maintain the balance of power among the members of the Quadruple Alliance
    c. failed to achieve long-lasting peace among European nations
    d. treated France leniently following Napoleon's One Hundred Days

Answer: b, medium, page 735

32. The foreign minister and diplomat who dominated the Congress of Vienna was:
    a. Klemens von Metternich
    b. Prince Talleyrand
    c. Tsar Alexander I
    d. Napoleon

Answer: a, easy, page 730

33. Klemens von Metternich:
    a. supported much of the revolutionary ideology after Napoleon's defeat
    b. thought that a free press was necessary to maintain the status quo
    c. believed European monarchs shared the common interest of stability

     d. was anti-religious and supported atheistic causes

Answer: c, medium, page 736

34. Conservatism, the dominant political philosophy following the fall of Napoleon,:
     a. was rejected by Metternich at the Congress of Vienna as inappropriate in the new liberal age
     b. expressed that individual rights remained the best guide for human order
     c. was best expressed in Edmund Burke's <u>Reflections on the Revolution in France</u>
     d. was too radical for Joseph de Maistre, the French spokesman for a cautious, revolutionary conservatism

Answer: c, easy, page 737

35. Conservatism of the nineteenth century supported all of the following <u>except</u>:
     a. obedience to political authority
     b. organized religion to maintain social order
     c. suppression of revolutionary upheavals
     d. the elevation of individual rights

Answer: d, medium, page 739

36. The Concert of Europe was most successful at:
     a. ending the political domination of the Holy Alliance in Greece
     b. thwarting Britain's attempts to intervene and crush revolts in Italy and Spain
     c. crushing the colonial revolts in Latin America
     d. none of the above

Answer: d, medium, page 739

37. The most important factor in preventing the European overthrow of the newly independent nations of Latin America was:
     a. British naval power
     b. the Monroe Doctrine
     c. the size of South America
     d. a pacifist movement in Europe

Answer: a, medium, page 741

38. The Greek revolt was successful largely due to:

a. a well-trained guerrilla army
b. the Turks' lack of fortitude
c. European intervention
d. all of the above

Answer: c, easy, page 741

39. Which of the following statements concerning the conservative European governments of 1815-1830 is <u>false</u>?
    a. British politics were marked by repressive measures and violence against public discontent.
    b. With French intervention, Spain remained despotic after crushing a liberal revolution.
    c. The ultra-conservative French kings, Louis XVIII and Charles X, rescinded all of Napoleon's radical innovations.
    d. Italy remained divided into nine states under Austrian domination throughout the period.

Answer: c, difficult, page 743

40. Which of the following areas was most directly controlled by the Austrians after 1815:
    a. Britain
    b. France
    c. Spain
    d. Italy

Answer: d, easy, page 743

41. The growing forces of liberalism and nationalism in central Europe were best characterized by:
    a. the increased liberal reforms of Frederick William III of Prussia between 1815 and 1840
    b. the national affinity and unity felt by the many Austrian ethnic groups under Frederick II
    c. the liberal constitutions of the states of the German Confederation
    d. the <u>Burschenschaften</u>, the radical student societies of Germany

Answer: d, medium, page 744

42. The purpose of the Germanic Confederation was to:
    a. prevent Austria from becoming too powerful
    b. provide a common defense against France or Russia

   c. form a central authority to govern Germany
   d. prevent Prussia from becoming too powerful

Answer; b, medium, page 744

43. The <u>Burschenschaften</u> or student societies of Germany wanted:
   a. to spread German nationalism and comradeship
   b. to dismantle the armed forces of Germany
   c. a multi-ethnic European super state
   d. regional concerns to dominate political thinking in Germany

Answer: a, difficult, page 744

44. Tsar Alexander I of Russia did all of the following <u>except</u>:
   a. become more reactionary after the defeat of Napoleon
   b. grant a constitution, freeing the serfs
   c. become involved in mysticism
   d. continue a program of arbitrary censorship

Answer: b, medium, page 746

45. Following the death of Alexander I in 1825, Russian society under Nicholas I became:
   a. a police state due to Nicholas's fear of internal and external revolution
   b. the most liberal of the European powers
   c. an industrial power after the abolition of serfdom
   d. increasingly influenced by ultra-conservative societies, such as the Northern and Southern Unions

Answer: a, easy, page 747

46. _____ argued that population must be held in check for any progress to occur.
   a. Adam Smith
   b. Thomas Malthus
   c. Joseph de Maistre
   d. Tsar Alexander I

Answer: b, medium, page 747

47. Which of the following statements best applies to Samuel Smiles?
   a. He was an advocate of a social welfare system.
   b. He believed the poor should be ignored.

c. He believed that individual effort could overcome poverty.
d. He believed poverty existed because of overpopulation.

Answer: c, medium, page 748

48. Liberals in the nineteenth century believed in all of the following except:
    a. an official state religion
    b. freedom of speech
    c. representative government
    d. equality before the law

Answer: a, difficult, page 748

49. The growing movement of nationalism in nineteenth-century Europe:
    a. was resisted by liberal thinkers, who felt that all ethnic groups should live together harmoniously
    b. advocated the formation of one European nation to end economic and military conflicts
    c. was especially inspired in Germany by the philosophical works of Hegel
    d. found its best expression in the writings of John Stuart Mill

Answer: c, difficult, page 750

50. The utopian socialists of the first half of the nineteenth century were best characterized by:
    a. Charles Fourier, who worked out detailed plans for cooperative communities called phalansteries
    b. Flora Tristan, who rejected the programs for female equality proposed by other socialists
    c. Louis Blanc, who wished for the demise of government in favor of individuals providing for their own welfare
    d. Henri de Saint-Simon, who established a cooperative community in the United States that quickly failed

Answer: a, medium, page 751

51. Louis-Philippe's bourgeois policies in France from 1830 to 1848 found support from:
    a. Charles X
    b. the Party of Resistance
    c. the Party of Movement
    d. Adolphe Thiers

Answer: b, medium, page 753

52. King Louis-Philippe in France:
    a. did all he could to help the industrial workers
    b. cooperated with François Guizot and the Party of Resistance
    c. allowed for great reforms in the electoral system
    d. was the son of Charles X

Answer: b, easy, page 753

53. The most successful nationalistic European revolution in 1830 was in:
    a. Poland
    b. Belgium
    c. Italy
    d. Scandinavia

Answer: b, medium, page 753

54. The primary force in the revolutions of Belgium, Poland, and Italy in 1830 was:
    a. nationalism
    b. religion
    c. racism
    d. socialism

Answer: a, easy, page 754

55. Which of the following statements best applies to Thomas Macaulay's thoughts on reform?
    a. He opposed giving any concessions to the middle class.
    b. He supported reforms as a way of preventing a revolution.
    c. He was convinced that reforms were unnecessary due to Britain's democratic heritage.
    d. He was afraid reforms would cause the collapse of the government.

Answer: b, medium, DOC 4

56. The Reform Bill of 1832 in Britain primarily benefitted the:
    a. landed aristocracy
    b. upper-middle class
    c. working class
    d. clergy

Answer: b, easy, page 756

57. All of the following were true of American politics through 1850 <u>except</u>:
    a. the assertion of the Supreme Court's power under John Marshall
    b. the extension of suffrage to almost all adult, white males
    c. the victory of the Federalists over the Republicans in 1812
    d. the growth of mass democratic politics and liberal reforms under Andrew Jackson

Answer: c, medium, page 756

58. The revolution of 1848 in France resulted in:
    a. the continued rule of Louis-Philippe but with radical reforms
    b. new elections to the national Assembly, resulting in the dominance of the radical republicans
    c. Europe's first socialist state under the guidance of the workshops
    d. an authoritarian order under Louis Napoleon

Answer: d, easy, page 758

59. The French revolution of 1848 saw all of the following <u>except</u>:
    a. the abdication of the throne by Louis-Philippe
    b. a severe industrial and agricultural depression leading to it
    c. a coalition formed between the moderate and radical republicans
    d. the bloody suppression of a working-class revolt by government forces

Answer: c, medium, page 758

60. The social and political upheavals in central Europe through 1848-1849 led to:
    a. the failure of the Frankfurt Assembly in Germany
    b. an independent state for Hungary
    c. the victory of the <u>Grossdeutsch</u> solution in a united German-Austrian state
    d. the continued dominance of Metternich in Austrian politics

Answer: a, difficult, page 758

61. The student response in Germany to the French revolution of 1848 was one of:
    a. outrage and a call for war on France
    b. disbelief and despair for the coming destruction
    c. joy, that the French had been weakened greatly
    d. enthusiasm and optimism for republican reforms in Germany

Answer: d, medium, DOC 5

62. Giuseppe Mazzini's nationalist organization Young Italy:
    a. liberated Italy's northern provinces from Austrian control
    b. failed to achieve his goal of <u>risorgimento</u> by 1849
    c. helped inspire successful liberal constitutions throughout Italy
    d. used the liberals in governments to extend suffrage to Italy's working classes

Answer: b, difficult, page 761 + DOC 6

63. The most important lesson learned by Italian revolutionaries in 1848 was:
    a. that if led, the whole of Italy would rise up for freedom
    b. that without foreign intervention, Austria could not be expelled from Italy
    c. that Piedmont would continue to resist Italian unity
    d. that the pope would always be a source of support for the creation of an Italian state

Answer: b, easy, page 762

64. Which of the following statements best applies to European social control agencies in the nineteenth century?
    a. Military units increasingly played a large role in maintaining social order.
    b. Capital punishment was increasingly used as a means of dealing with crime.
    c. German police forces never matched the British police in power and social acceptance.
    d. The British and French adopted the American system of solitary confinement for their prisons.

Answer: d, easy, page 766

65. Professional civilian police forces first appeared in 1828 in:
    a. Germany
    b. Russia
    c. Italy
    d. France

Answer: d, easy, page 764

66. By 1848, the British police forces were:

a. extremely well paid, but under strict discipline
b. not well paid, but highly respected
c. outlawed as being potentially revolutionary
d. complaining of low wages and shoddy leadership

Answer: d, medium, page 765 + DOC 7

67. Police forces and prison reform were geared toward:
    a. the creation of more disciplined societies
    b. appeasing the public outcry against the barbarism of the ordeal
    c. protecting the poor from being exploited
    d. adding an element of fear to society

Answer: a, easy, page 769

68. All of the following were characteristics of Romanticism <u>except</u>:
    a. a strong, pantheistic worship of nature
    b. the rejection of the supernatural and unfamiliar
    c. a preoccupation with sentiment, suffering, and self-sacrifice
    d. a romantic reverence for history that inspired nationalism

Answer: b, difficult, page 768

69. The romantic movement had its roots in:
    a. Turkey
    b. Britain
    c. Germany
    d. France

Answer: c, easy, page 767

70. Identify the correct relationship between the romantic writer and his main work:
    a. Goethe-<u>Sorrows of the Young Werther</u>
    b. Walter Scott-<u>Frankenstein</u>
    c. Thomas Carlyle-<u>Lucinde</u>
    d. William Wordsworth-<u>Prometheus Unbound</u>

Answer: a, easy, page 767

71. The romantic movement can be viewed as a(n):
    a. reaction against the Enlightenment's preoccupation with reason
    b. continuation of Enlightenment ideals and practices
    c. attempt to create a socialist society

d. a movement of lower-class, less literate people

Answer: a, difficult, page 767

72. The American romantic author of <u>The Fall of the House of Usher</u> was:
    a. Mary Shelley
    b. Thomas Carlyle
    c. Edgar Allan Poe
    d. Hans Christian Anderson

Answer: c, easy, DOC 8

73. The most important form of literary expression for the romantics was:
    a. educational texts
    b. poetry
    c. the novel
    d. the play

Answer: b, easy, page 768

74. Romantic painters included:
    a. Delacroix
    b. Turner
    c. Constable
    d. all of the above

Answer: d, medium, page 771

75. William Blake summed up the romantic view of science by:
    a. calling for the creation of a new social order based on rationalism and technology
    b. writing the poem <u>Milton,</u> which called for ethics in science and continued experimentation
    c. acknowledging that it was a necessary evil for the benefit of humanity
    d. denouncing its proclaimed knowledge and accusing it of destroying imagination

Answer: d, easy, DOC 9

76. Romanticism in art and music was well characterized by:
    a. Chateaubriand, whose many paintings anticipated the Impressionist movement
    b. Beethoven, whose dramatic compositions bridged the gap between

classicism and Romanticism
 c. Delacroix, who broke classical conventions by using only blacks and whites in his paintings
 d. Friedrich, whose "program" music played upon the listeners' emotions

Answer: b, easy, page 772

77. Religion in the age of Romanticism experienced:
 a. a Catholic revival, especially in Germany
 b. lost the favor of many artists and intellectuals
 c. a decline in Protestantism in Britain
 d. the mass popularization of eastern religions in Europe

Answer: a, medium, page 773

SUGGESTED FILMS

Revolutions and Reforms: Europe, 1815-1848. Coronet Instructional Films, 16 min. (color).

1848. Radim Films, 22 min. (black/white).

Civilization: Fallacies of Hope. Time-Life Films, 52 min. (color).

Prophets and Promise of Classical Capitalism. Films Inc., 60 min. (color).

Romanticism: Revolt of the Spirit. Learning Corporation of America, 27 min. (color).

The Spirit of Romanticism. Encyclopedia Britannica, 27 min. (color).

English Literature: Romantic Period. Coronet Instructional Films, 14 min. (color).

Blake. BBC/Time-Life Films, 53 min. (color).

Beethoven: Ordeal and Triumph. McGraw-Hill, 53 min. (color).

Beethoven and His Music. Coronet Instructional Films, 12 min. (color).

SUGGESTIONS FOR MUSIC

Ludwig van Beethoven, <u>The Nine Symphonies</u> (Deutsche Grammophon: -2563656-2563663)

Ludwig van Beethoven, <u>Moonlight Sonata</u> (Philips-CD412575-2)

Ludwig van Beethoven, <u>Concerto for Violin and Orchestra in D Major</u> (Deutsche Grammophon-139021)

Ludwig van Beethoven, <u>Missa Solemnis</u> (Angel-3679)

Felix Mendelssohn, <u>A Midsummer Night's Dream</u> (DG-4153532)

Felix Mendelssohn, <u>Violin Concerto in E Minor</u>; <u>Fingal's Cave</u> (Musical Heritage Society-1847K)

Franz Schubert, <u>Piano Quintet in A Major</u> (Trout) (London-417459-2)

Hector Berlioz, <u>Symphonie Fantastique</u> (Philips-411425-2)

CHAPTER 23: AN AGE OF NATIONALISM AND REALISM, 1850-1871

CHAPTER OUTLINE

THE FRANCE OF NAPOLEON III
    Louis Napoleon: Toward the Second Empire
    The Second Napoleonic Empire
    Foreign Policy: The Crimean War

NATIONAL UNIFICATION: ITALY AND GERMANY
    The Unification of Italy
    The Unification of Germany
        The Danish War, 1864
        The Austro-Prussian War, 1866
        The Franco-Prussian War, 1870-1871

NATIONALISM AND REFORM: THE NATIONAL STATE IN MID-CENTURY
    The Austrian Empire
    Imperial Russia
    Great Britain
    The United States: Civil War and Reunion

INDUSTRIALIZATION AND THE MARXIST RESPONSE
    Industrialization on the Continent
    Marx and Marxism

CULTURAL LIFE IN AN AGE OF REALISM

A New Age of Science
Charles Darwin and the Theory of Organic Evolution
Auguste Comte and Positivism
Realism in Literature and Art
            Literature
            Art
Music: The Twilight of Romanticism

A REVOLUTION IN HEALTH CARE

SUGGESTED LECTURE TOPICS

1. "The Unification of Germany: Myths and Realities in the Light of Twentieth-Century German History"

2. "The Growth of the European Nation-State"

3. "The Triumph of Scientific Thought in the Nineteenth Century"

4. "Realism" [a slide lecture]

MAPS AND ARTWORK

1. Unification of Italy and Germany: 1868 vs. 1848. Maps 23.1, 23.2 with 22.5.

2. Multi-national/ethnical state, map 23.3, compared with modern examples of identity problems with the Soviet Union and Yugoslavia.

3. Photographs vs. painting: Which has more impact? Why?

DISCUSSION QUESTIONS FOR THE PRIMARY SOURCES (BOXED DOCUMENTS)

"Louis Napoleon Appeals to the People": What were Louis Napoleon's arguments to the French people? Why did they have such a strong appeal? Can Louis Napoleon be looked upon as a precursor of modern authoritarian politics? Why or why not? (pages 778 and 779)

"Garibaldi and Romantic Nationalism": Why did Garibaldi become such a hero to the Italian people? (page 784)

"Bismarck 'Goads' France into War": What did Bismarck do to the Ems telegraph? What does this affair tell us about Bismarck's motives? (page 788)

"Emancipation: Serfs and Slaves": Compare and contrast the "emancipation proclamations" of Alexander II and President Lincoln. Were both equally effective? (page 792)

"The Classless Society": What steps did Marx believe would lead to a classless society? Although Marx criticized early socialists as utopian and considered his own socialism scientific, why does his own socialism appear equally utopian? (page 801)

"Darwin and the Descent of Man": What is Darwin's basic argument in The Descent of Man? Why did so many people object to it? (page 804)

"Realism: Charles Dickens and an Image of Hell on Earth": What image of Birmingham do you get from this selection by Dickens? Why is it so powerful? What does it reveal about Dickens himself? (page 806)

"Anesthesia and Modern Surgery": In what way does this document demonstrate the impact that modern science made on Western society by the middle decades of the nineteenth century? (page 810)

EXAMINATION QUESTIONS

Essays

1. Assess the accomplishments and failures of Louis Napoleon's regime in terms of the impact his policies had on France.

2. Evaluate the unification of Italy and Germany: What were the roles of Cavour and Bismarck in the unification of their countries? What role did war and diplomacy play in the two unification movements?

3. Despite the defeat of the revolutions of 1848, the forces of liberalism and nationalism triumphed after 1850. To what extent is this true in the Austrian Empire, Russia, and Great Britain?

4. What does the author claim that continental industrialization came of age between 1850 and 1871?

5. What are the chief ideas of Marxism? Despite Marx's claim for its scientific basis, why can Marxism be viewed primarily as a product of its age?

6. How did the expansion of scientific knowledge affect the Western worldview and the everyday lives of Europeans during the mid-nineteenth century?

7. How did Realism differ from Romanticism? How did Realism reflect the economic and social realities of Europe during the middle decades of the nineteenth century?

Identifications

8. Crimean War
9. Red Shirts
10. Zollverein
11. realpolitik
12. The Austro-Prussian War
13. North German Confederation
14. Ausgleich
15. Tsar Alexander II
16. zemstvos
17. Lord Palmerston
18. American Civil War
19. Karl Marx
20. Communist Manifesto
21. On the Origins of Species
22. positivism
23. Realism
24. Franz Liszt
25. Madame Bovary
26. Jean-François Millet
27. Louis Pasteur
28. Elizabeth Blackwell

Multiple Choice

29. In establishing the Second Empire, Napoleon III:
    a. received the overwhelming support of the people
    b. granted the National Assembly stronger legislative powers
    c. rescinded universal male suffrage
    d. cared little about public opinion

Answer: a, medium, page 778

30. All of the following occurred in the early part of the Second Napoleonic Empire except:
    a. the reconstruction of Paris
    b. the granting of the freedom of speech, assembly, and the press
    c. government-subsidized industrial expansion
    d. improved social welfare for the working class

Answer: b, difficult, page 778

31. Under the "liberal empire" of Napoleon III in the 1860s:
    a. tariffs on foreign goods were lowered
    b. the Legislative Corps was permitted more say in affairs of state
    c. trade unions and the right to strike were legalized
    d. all of the above

Answer: d, easy, page 780

32. The immediate origins of the Crimean War involved:
    a. French expansionism in the Black Sea
    b. Austrian expansion in the Balkans
    c. Russia's right to protect Christian shrines in Palestine
    d. the Turks' assassination of a British ambassador

Answer: c, medium, page 780

33. An overall result of the Crimean War was:
    a. the reinforcement of the Concert of Europe until World War I
    b. continued Russian expansionism in Europe for the next two decades
    c. increased involvement for Great Britain in continental affairs
    d. an international situation where Italian and German unification became possible

Answer: d, difficult, page 781

34. In their efforts for unification, Italian nationalists in the 1850s looked for

leadership from:
   a.   the pope
   b.   the kingdom of Piedmont
   c.   the house of Habsburg
   d.   the kingdom of the Two Sicilies

Answer: b, medium, page 781

35.   The prime minister of Piedmont who organized the Italian unification
      movement was:
      a.   Giuseppe Mazzini
      b.   Giuseppe Garibaldi
      c.   Camillo di Cavour
      d.   Nandor Eber

Answer: c, easy, page 782

36.   The leader of the Red Shirts who helped unify Italy through his military
      leadership was:
      a.   Giuseppe Garibaldi
      b.   Prince Napoleon
      c.   Victor Emmanuel II
      d.   Camillo di Cavour

Answer: a, medium, page 783

37.   As leader of the Italian unification movement, Camillo di Cavour:
      a.   had no preconceived policy as to how unification would be achieved
      b.   personally led Italian troops against Austria in 1859-1860
      c.   joined Italy with Prussia in the Austro-Prussian War of 1866
      d.   saw Napoleon III as Italy's most bitter enemy

Answer: a, difficult, page 783

38.   Giuseppe Garibaldi was all of the following except:
      a.   an avid believer in romantic democratic republicanism
      b.   Camillo di Cavour's right-hand man in all military decisions
      c.   the inspirational leader of the Red Shirts
      d.   responsible for the unification of all of Italy after 1860

Answer: b, medium, page 783

39.   The final act of Italian unification occurred in 1870 when:

a. Garibaldi's Red Shirts defeated the kingdom of the Two Sicilies
b. Savoy was defeated with the aid of Prussian troops
c. Rome became the capital city following the withdrawal of French troops
d. the Piedmont received Lombardy as a result of Napoleon III's peace with Austria

Answer: c, easy, page 784

40. Before Otto von Bismarck, Prussia was characterized by:
    a. a deteriorating army under William I
    b. an unfair voting system determined by wealth
    c. a resentful middle class that had little control of the legislature's lower house
    d. a parliament that had no power to reject the king's legislation

Answer: b, medium, page 785

41. Otto von Bismarck, the Prussian-born leader of German unification,:
    a. instituted the Zollverein, the German customs union that inspired rapid industrial growth
    b. followed a rigid plan for unification at all costs
    c. was a liberal from lower-class origins who used the Prussian parliament to achieve his goal
    d. practiced realpolitik in conducting domestic and foreign policy

Answer: d, easy, page 786

42. The Zollverein describes:
    a. the German states' customs union
    b. a German nationalist group that looked to Prussia for unification
    c. the lower house of the Prussian parliament
    d. Bismarck's liberal reforms

Answer: a, easy, page 785

43. Otto von Bismarck was all of the following except:
    a. from the aristocratic Junker class of Prussia
    b. an extreme warmonger
    c. a moderate who favored diplomacy whenever possible
    d. the foremost nineteenth-century practitioner of "realpolitik"

Answer: b, medium, page 785

44. A result of Bismarck's Austro-Prussian War was:
     a. the incorporation of Austria into the North German Confederation
     b. a harsh treaty against Austria that reduced it to a second-rate power
     c. the Prussian liberals' disgust over Bismarck's expansionistic policies
     d. none of the above

Answer: d, easy, page 787

45. The creation of the North German Confederation following the Austro-Prussian War:
     a. did not include the Catholic south German states
     b. proved that nationalism and authoritarian government could be combined
     c. divided parliament into the Bundesrat and Reichstag, both responsible to the Prussian king
     d. all of the above

Answer: d, medium, page 787

46. The immediate origins of the Franco-Prussian War concerned:
     a. the assent of a French prince to the Spanish throne
     b. Bismarck's editing of a telegraph from King William I
     c. the French invasion of Alsace and Lorraine
     d. Napoleon III's annexation of Schleswig and Holstein

Answer: b, difficult, page 788

47. The Franco-Prussian War of 1870-1871 was concluded with:
     a. a harsh treaty imposed on France by Bismarck
     b. the proclamation of the Second German Empire
     c. the complete unification of all Germany
     d. all of the above

Answer: d, easy, page 789

48. The Ausgleich or Compromise of 1867:
     a. created a loose federation of ethnic states within the Austrian Empire
     b. freed the serfs and eliminated compulsory labor services within the Austrian Empire
     c. made Austria part of the North German Confederation
     d. created the dual monarchy of Austria-Hungary

Answer: d, medium, page 790

49. The creation of the dual monarchy of Austria-Hungary:
    a. allowed the Magyars and German-speaking Austrians to dominate the ethnic minorities
    b. enabled Alexander von Bach to become an absolute leader
    c. left Hungary an independent nation in domestic affairs
    d. overturned the Ausgleich (Compromise) of 1867

Answer: a, difficult, page 790

50. The reforms of Tsar Alexander II did not include:
    a. government sponsorship of popular societies like the People's Will
    b. the mir-based land redistribution system
    c. the abolition of serfdom
    d. the formation of local, self-governing assemblies called zemstvos

Answer: a, easy, page 792

51. The Russian zemstvos were:
    a. radical, populist societies that supported revolutionary causes
    b. local assemblies with self-governing powers
    c. agreements between peasants and landowners concerning land distribution
    d. the emancipation proclamation that set groups of serfs free

Answer: b, medium, page 793

52. Tsar Alexander's reforms in the 1860s and 1870s:
    a. appeased both Russian conservatives and liberals
    b. made Russia's peasants the most economically prosperous in all of Europe
    c. led to his assassination in 1881
    d. particularly failed in the area of legal and court reforms

Answer: c, medium, page 793

53. The British liberal who was responsible for an impressive series of reform acts between 1868 and 1874 was:
    a. Henry John Temple
    b. Lord Palmerston
    c. William Gladstone
    d. Benjamin Disraeli

Answer: c, difficult, page 796

54.   As British prime minister from 1855 to 1865, Lord Palmerston was responsible for:
    a.   instituting universal male suffrage for all of Great Britain
    b.   chauvinistically defending British interests worldwide
    c.   rigidly defending the interests of the lower industrial working class
    d.   opening civil service positions to competitive exams

Answer: b, easy, page 795

55.   Slavery in the United States prior to the American Civil War:
    a.   increased despite the decline of the American cotton industry
    b.   was a divisive issue that was solved with the Kansas-Nebraska Act of 1854
    c.   was a divisive issue that was solved with the Compromise of 1850
    d.   became a major issue of debate with the push of Americans past the Mississippi

Answer: d, medium, page 796

56.   The American Civil War of 1861-1865:
    a.   was solved by the Missouri Compromise
    b.   was of a destructive nature due to the equal resources of the North and South
    c.   was a precursor of twentieth-century total warfare
    d.   did not completely eradicate slavery in all the states

Answer: c, difficult, page 797

57.   Industrialization of the Continent from 1850 to 1870 witnessed:
    a.   Germany and France surpass Great Britain in iron production
    b.   railroads become the major aspect of industrial expansion
    c.   the complete replacement of hand looms by power looms in the textile industries
    d.   charcoal iron smelting replace coke-blast smelting in the iron industries

Answer: b, medium, page 798

58.   The continental governments played a crucial role in European industrialization between 1850 and 1870 by:
    a.   eliminating the barriers to international trade

b. allowing the working classes to organize large-scale trade organizations
c. replacing the risky joint-stock investment banks with government subsidies
d. all of the above

Answer: a, easy, page 798

59. The philosophy of Karl Marx and Friedrich Engels was <u>not</u> influenced by:
    a. British classical economics
    b. their lower-class backgrounds
    c. the political and social theories inspired by the French Revolution
    d. the dialectical philosophy of Hegel

Answer: b, easy, page 799

60. <u>The Communist Manifesto</u> of Marx and Engels:
    a. was a guidebook for the European workers in the revolutions of 1848
    b. viewed the bourgeoisie as leading the proletariat in the overthrow of the aristocracy
    c. saw the successful realization of its ideas in the First International
    d. based all historical development on class struggles

Answer: d, medium, page 800

61. Which of the following statements is derived from Karl Marx's philosophy?
    a. "Political power and class antagonisms will disappear with the victory of the proletariat."
    b. "Ideas precede actualities and material conditions in the course of history."
    c. "The ruling ideas of each age have been the ideas of the masses."
    d. "The bourgeoisie is destined to win the struggle with the proletariat once the epidemic of overproduction is solved."

Answer: a, medium, page 800

62. According to Karl Marx, the final product of the struggle between the bourgeoisie and the proletariat would be:
    a. a classless society
    b. the dictatorship of the proletariat
    c. the wielding of political power by the proletariat
    d. a Utopian society

Answer: a, easy, page 800

63.   The First International:
    a.   failed due to Marx's preoccupation with <u>Das Kapital</u>
    b.   became the largest working-class organization in Europe in the nineteenth century
    c.   was rejected by Marx as a "bourgeois-dominated institution"
    d.   none of the above

Answer: d, difficult, page 801

64.   The theoretical discoveries in science in the nineteenth century led to all of the following <u>except</u>:
    a.   a renewal of spiritual beliefs
    b.   a belief in material reality as the only reality
    c.   great advances in mathematics and thermodynamics
    d.   technological improvements that affected all Europeans

Answer: a, medium, page 802

65.   Which of the following statements best applies to Charles Darwin and his evolutionary theory?
    a.   It revolved around the idea of "survival of the fit," in which advantageous variants determine survival.
    b.   His <u>On the Origins of Species</u> described man's evolution from animal origins through natural selection.
    c.   His works were revolutionary as they were the first to propose a theory of evolution.
    d.   His ideas were accepted by religion communities as they once again gave human beings a place in the universe.

Answer: a, difficult, page 803

66.   The evolutionary ideas found in Charles Darwin's <u>On the Origins of Species</u> were based on all of the following except:
    a.   his observations of plant and animal life in the South Pacific
    b.   Thomas Malthus's theory of population
    c.   Jean-Baptiste Lamarck's theory of creationism
    d.   the theory of natural selection

Answer: c, easy, page 803

67.   Charles Darwin's <u>The Descent of Man</u>:

    a. is filled with expressions of doubt and hesitancy over the new evolutionary theory
    b. expressed the first theory of genetic mutations
    c. was originally regarded by many scientists as a "degrading" work
    d. placed humans in the center of a rational universe

Answer: c, medium, page 803 + DOC 6

68. The author of <u>System of Positive Philosophy</u> and founder of the philosophical school of positivism was:
    a. Gustave Flaubert
    b. Charles Darwin
    c. Nicholas Fabian
    d. Auguste Comte

Answer: d, easy, page 804

69. Auguste Comte was responsible for:
    a. posing an evolutionary scheme for all human knowledge
    b. founding the discipline of sociology
    c. helping make science and materialism so popular in the mid-nineteenth century
    d. all of the above

Answer: d, easy, page 804

70. The dominant literary and artistic movement in the 1850s and 1860s was:
    a. Romanticism
    b. Realism
    c. Positivism
    d. Modernism

Answer: b, medium, page 805

71. Identify the <u>false</u> relationship among the realist artists and their works:
    a. William Thackeray--<u>The Old Curiosity Shop</u>
    b. Gustave Courbet--<u>The Stonebreakers</u>
    c. Jean-François Millet--<u>The Sower</u>
    d. Gustave Flaubert--<u>Madame Bovary</u>

Answer: a, difficult, page 805

72. In addition to examining everyday life, the literary realists of the

mid-nineteenth century were interested in:
    a.   completely eschewing romantic imagery, as shown in the works of
         Charles Dickens
    b.   employing emotional and poetic language to cause social reform
    c.   allowing their characters to speak for themselves
    d.   showing the positive values of middle-class life

Answer: c, medium, page 805

73.   Realist art in the mid-nineteenth century:
    a.   was praised by critics for showing the beauty of ordinary people
    b.   was best characterized by the urban depictions of Jean-François Millet
    c.   still contained an element of romantic sentimentality, best shown in
         Gustave Courbet's paintings
    d.   was particularly interested in the natural environment

Answer: d, difficult, page 807

74.   The New German School emphasized:
    a.   abstract form
    b.   emotional content
    c.   spiritual ideas
    d.   all of the above

Answer: b, medium, page 807

74.   _____ has been called the "Greatest Pianist of All Time."
    a.   Wagner
    b.   Beethoven
    c.   Liszt
    d.   Mozart

Answer: c, easy, page 807

76.   Vital to the growth of medical science in the nineteenth century was the germ
    theory of disease discovered by:
    a.   Robert Koch
    b.   Louis Pasteur
    c.   Alfred Lewis
    d.   Harriet Hunt

Answer: b, easy, page 808

77. Which of the following statements concerning nineteenth-century medicine is false?
    a. Women like Elizabeth Blackwell broke through great obstacles to become licensed physicians.
    b. Although private practices improved greatly, public health and hygiene were still ignored.
    c. The development of anesthetic agents made surgery much more bearable for patients.
    d. The Johns Hopkins University School of Medicine helped set a standard for medical training.

Answer: b, easy, page 809

78. Joseph Lister was most noted in medicine for:
    a. founding the science of bacteriology
    b. founding the British Medical Association in 1832
    c. discovering a new disinfectant to eliminate infections during surgery
    d. developing pasteurization

Answer: c, medium, page 809

SUGGESTED FILMS

<u>Nationalism</u>. Encyclopedia Britannica, 20 min. (black/white).

<u>The Unification of Italy</u>. Coronet Instructional Films, 13 min. (black/white).

<u>Bismarck: Germany from Blood and Iron</u>. Learning Corp. of America, 30 min. (color).

<u>Karl Marx: The Massive Dissent</u>. BBC Films, 60 min. (color).

<u>Marxism: The Theory That Split a World</u>. Learning Corporation of America, 25 min. (color).

<u>Charles Darwin</u>. University of California Extension Media Center, 24 min. (color).

<u>Darwin and Evolution</u>. McGraw-Hill, 28 min. (color).

<u>Early Victorian England and Charles Dickens</u>. Encyclopedia Britannica, 34 min.

(black/white).

The Charles Dickens Show. International Film Bureau, 52 min. (color).

The Changing World of Charles Dickens. Learnex Corp. of Florida, 27 min. (color).

Louis Pasteur. University of California Extension Media Center, 24 min. (color).

CHAPTER 24: SOCIETY AND POLITICS IN THE "AGE OF PROGRESS," 1871-1914

CHAPTER OUTLINE

THE SECOND INDUSTRIAL REVOLUTION
Technological Innovations and New Products
TheDevelopment of Markets
Economic Patterns
    European Trends
    The Union of Science and Technology
    Agricultural Crisis
    Toward a World Economy

CITIES AND SOCIAL STRUCTURE IN AN AGE OF MASS SOCIETY
Transformation of the Urban Environment
    Public Health and Housing
    Urban Reconstruction
The Social Structure of Mass Society
    The Elite
    The Middle Classes
    The Working Classes

THE "WOMAN QUESTION": FEMALE EXPERIENCES
Women and Work
    New Job Opportunities
    Prostitution
Marriage, Family, and Children
    The Middle-Class Family

The Working-Class Family
The Rise of the Feminist Movement

THE SOCIALIST MOVEMENT
    The Socialist Parties
    Trade Unions
    Anarchism

THE NATIONAL STATE: DOMESTIC POLITICS
    Great Britain
    France
    The Mediterranean Powers: Spain and Italy
        Spain
        The New Italian State
    The New Germany
        The German Empire Under William II
    Austria-Hungary
    Imperial Russia
        The Drive to Industrialization
        The Revolution of 1905
    The Balkans and the Ottoman Empire
    The United States

SUGGESTED LECTURE TOPICS

1. "The Impact of the Second Industrial Revolution on the Transformation of Europe"

2. "The Middle Classes and Nineteenth-Century European Society"

3. "Nationalism in the Age of Mass Society: The Role of Mass Politics"

4. "The Socialist Movement"

MAPS AND ARTWORK

1. Development of industrialization, map 24.1, compared with map 21.2.

2. The view of the city: The ideal vs. reality.

DISCUSSION QUESTIONS FOR THE PRIMARY SOURCES (BOXED
DOCUMENTS)

"The Department Store and the Beginnings of Mass Consumerism": What does this
document tell us about the growth of a new mass consumerism? Who were these
new consumers? (page 818)

"The Housing Venture of Octavia Hill": Discuss the housing venture of Octavia
Hill. What did she hope to achieve? Was she successful? What are the obvious
limitations to her efforts? (page 823)

"Advice to Women: Be Dependent" and "Advice to Women: Be Independent": How
do you explain the differences between these two approaches to the role of women?
Which position did the feminist movement favor? Why? (pages 830 and 831)

"The Voice of Evolutionary Socialism: Eduard Bernstein": Based on this document,
define the phrase "evolutionary socialism." (page 835)

"A Parliamentary Debate on Old Age Pensions": Discuss these two different
approaches to old age pensions. How do you explain the differences? (page 840)

"Parisian Violence": What does this document reveal about French politics following
France's defeat by Prussia? Is it an unbiased account? Why or why not? (page 842)

"Russian Workers Appeal to the Tsar": What did the Russian workers want? What
does the reaction of imperial officials reveal about the Russian political system in
1905? (page 848)

EXAMINATION QUESTIONS

Essays

1. Explain what is meant by the Second Industrial Revolution and discuss its impact
on European society.

2. What do we mean by the phrase "mass society" and how was the growth of this
mass society related to changes in the urban environment?

3. Discuss the structure of European society between 1870 and 1914. Why do historians focus so much attention on the middle class during this period?

4. What was the position of women during the second half of the nineteenth century? What did women hope to achieve in the feminist movement? To what extent were they successful by 1914?

5. Compare and contrast middle-class and working-class families. How do you explain the similarities and the differences?

6. To what extent did the emergence and development of socialist parties and trade unions meet the needs of the working classes between 1871 and 1914?

7. Between 1871 and 1914, two major domestic political issues involved the achievement of liberal practices and the growth of political democracy. To what extent were these realized in Great Britain, France, Germany, Austria-Hungary, and Russia?

8. Between 1871 and 1914, two major social and political issues revolved around the rise of socialist parties and enactment of social welfare measures to meet the demands of the working classes. How successful were these developments in Great Britain, France, Germany, Austria-Hungary, and Russia?

Identifications

9. Second Industrial Revolution
10. cartels
11. mass society
12. Octavia Hill
13. English Boy Scouts
14. Emmeline Pankhurst
15. German Social Democrats
16. Second International
17. Evolutionary Socialism
18. trade union movement
19. anarchism
20. "the Irish question"
21. Fabians
22. Paris Commune
23. Third Republic
24. Kulturkampf

25. Count Edward von Taaffe
26. Sergei Witte
27. Tsar Nicholas II
28. "Bloody Sunday"

Multiple Choice

29. Which of the following was <u>not</u> a development of the Second Industrial Revolution:
    a. Great Britain rapidly developed its steel and chemical industries to surpass Germany by 1910.
    b. The development of electricity provided a common source of power for homes, shops, and industrial enterprises.
    c. The development of the internal combustion engine gave rise to the automobile and airplane.
    d. Steel replaced iron as a cheaper and lighter alternative in building industrial goods.

Answer: a, medium, page 815

30. Choose the correct relationship between the inventor and his invention:
    a. Henry Bessemer--converter furnace for steel
    b. Guglielmo Marconi--incandescent-filament lamp
    c. Alexander Graham Bell--internal combustion engine
    d. Thomas Edison--mass production line

Answer: a, easy, page 815

31. The development of markets after 1870 was best characterized by:
    a. decreased competition through free trade agreements
    b. the dismantling of the cartels that hindered free trade
    c. wealthy urban consumers in Europe who desired consumer products
    d. an abandonment of overseas markets, especially by Britain, due to their small profit potential

Answer: c, medium, page 817

32. Germany began to replace Britain as Europe's industrial leader by the early twentieth century largely due to:
    a. Britain's careless and radical changes made to its industries
    b. its cautious approach and doctrine of "sticking to what works" in

industry
c. Britain's reliance on cartels to invest large sums of money in new industries
d. its encouragement of formal scientific and technical education

Answer: d, medium, page 820

33. By 1900, which of the following nations was <u>not</u> advanced industrially:
    a. Britain
    b. Germany
    c. France
    d. Spain

Answer: d, easy, page 819

34. The growth of urban centers in the nineteenth century:
    a. occurred primarily in eastern Europe
    b. was due to birth rates that dramatically exceeded death rates
    c. saw London grow from a population of 960,000 to over 6 million by 1900
    d. varied little with growth rates in rural areas

Answer: c, medium, page 821

35. The driving force behind immigration to the cities was:
    a. economic necessity
    b. a desire for culture
    c. curiosity
    d. masochism

Answer: a, easy, page 821

36. Reforms in urban living included all of the following <u>except</u>:
    a. the development of pure water and sewerage systems
    b. model homes built for the poor by wealthy philanthropists
    c. the demolition of old, unneeded defensive walls, replaced by wide avenues
    d. a concerted effort to clean up polluted rivers and lakes

Answer: d, difficult, page 821

37. Octavia Hill's housing venture was designed to:
    a. give the poor an environment they could use to improve themselves

    b. give the poor charity since they could never help themselves

    c. let the wealthy know what it was like to be poor

    d. break down class barriers in London

Answer: a, medium, DOC 2

38. The wealthy elite of late nineteenth-century Europe:
    a. came to be dominated by wealthy, upper-middle-class families with fortunes in industry
    b. consisted mostly of the landed aristocracy in industrialized nations
    c. controlled only slightly more of the wealth in proportion to the working classes
    d. was most open to change in Germany where 50 percent of the diplomatic corps came from the wealthy middle class

Answer: a, difficult, page 825

39. Real wages for industrialized nations between 1871 and 1910:
    a. declined dramatically
    b. increased only for the wealthy elite
    c. increased for the average person
    d. declined by 50 percent in Britain

Answer: c, medium, page 825

40. The middle classes of nineteenth-century Europe:
    a. were composed mostly of shopkeepers and manufacturers who barely lived above the poverty line
    b. offered little opportunity for women in improving their lot
    c. were very concerned with propriety and shared values of hard work and Christian morality
    d. viewed progress with distrust as they did not wish to lose their economic gains

Answer: c, medium, page 826

41. The largest segment of European society in the nineteenth century was composed of:
    a. skilled artisans such as winemakers and cabinet makers
    b. unskilled day laborers and domestic servants who worked for very low wages
    c. semi-skilled laborers such as carpenters and bricklayers
    d. urban workers in eastern Europe and peasants in western Europe

Answer: b, medium, page 826

42. Employment opportunities for women during the Second Industrial Revolution:
    a. changed mostly in quality, not quantity, with the expansion of the service sector
    b. declined dramatically as prostitution became illegal
    c. increased greatly with working-class men pushing their wives to work outside the home
    d. declined when pieceworking was abandoned as inefficient and "sweatshops" were outlawed

Answer: a, difficult, page 828

43. For Elizabeth Poole Sanford, women should:
    a. avoid being self-sufficient
    b. strive to become equal to men
    c. accept their roles at home until a new government was elected
    d. make it known to their husbands that they were dissatisfied

Answer: a, easy, DOC 3

44. European middle-class families during the late nineteenth century:
    a. were more concerned with displaying the work ethic than in displaying wealth and following proper decorum
    b. stressed functional knowledge for their children to prepare them for their future roles
    c. could usually hire servants to keep the women of the house from having to do house work
    d. increasingly became less cohesive as togetherness was no longer an important value

Answer: b, medium, page 829

45. The domestic ideal of the nineteenth-century middle-class family was:
    a. everyone working outside the home for the common good
    b. togetherness with leisure time being very important
    c. an almost military environment with the husband as commander
    d. for girls and boys to grow up to be merchants and bankers

Answer: b, difficult, page 829

46. Changes in the standard of living from 1890 to 1914 in Europe affected the working-class family:

a. as more children were produced, which provided more family income
b. negligibly, since most families could not afford any consumer goods beyond necessities
c. due to the severe reduction in real wages
d. by allowing working-class parents to devote more attention to their children

Answer: d, medium, page 832

47. Between 1890 and 1914, working-class families witnessed:
a. an increasing reliance on the incomes of the husband and children
b. an increasing reliance on the income of the wife
c. an increasing reliance on social welfare
d. an increasing reliance on wealthy philanthropists

Answer: a, easy, page 832

48. The feminist movement of the late nineteenth century was well known for:
a. the identical concerns it shared with the socialist movement
b. achievements in nursing by Florence Nightingale and Amalie Sieveking
c. its most vocal and radical followers in Germany like Millicent Fawcett
d. achieving women's suffrage throughout Europe before World War I

Answer: b, medium, page 833

49. In Henrik Ibsen's A Doll's House:
a. women are depicted as necessarily subservient to men
b. the female character, Nora, loves her life of dependence
c. there is a violent uprising by women against society
d. the main character, Nora, leaves her husband to experience life

Answer: d, medium, DOC 4

50. The leader of socialist revisionism who wrote Evolutionary Socialism was:
a. Eduard Bernstein
b. August Bebel
c. Jean Jaurès
d. Friedrich Engels

Answer: a, easy, page 835 + DOC 5

51. The most successful socialist party in the nineteenth century was in:
a. Germany

b. Poland
c. Russia
d. Spain

Answer: a, easy, page 834

52. Eduard Bernstein stressed the need for:
    a. violent overthrow of capitalist governments
    b. the extermination of all individualists
    c. working in politics to create socialism
    d. totally disregarding The Communist Manifesto

Answer: c, difficult, page 835

53. An issue that brought socialists together in the nineteenth century was:
    a. nationalism
    b. revisionism
    c. the need for military action
    d. class differences

Answer: d, difficult, page 836

54. The trade union movement prior to World War I:
    a. was strongest in France after the dissolution of the Second International in 1890
    b. occurred despite trade unions being banned by most state governments
    c. varied from state to state, but was generally most productive when allied with socialist parties
    d. was primarily for unskilled laborers, especially the New Model unions

Answer: c, medium, page 837

55. Trade unions in the nineteenth century reflected all of the following except:
    a. an expression of nationalistically oriented socialism
    b. the extreme liberalism of Russia
    c. the decline of the labor movement in Britain
    d. an evolutionary expression of socialism

Answer: b, medium, page 836

56. Anarchist movements were most successful in:
    a. industrialized countries like Great Britain and Germany
    b. toppling national governments through assassination

c. restoring legitimacy to radical movements through peaceful dialogue

d. none of the above

Answer: d, easy, page 837

57. All of the following were major developments in British politics before 1914 <u>except</u>:
    a. the continual growth of political democracy
    b. the peaceful and successful settlement of the "Irish question"
    c. the transformation of the Fabians into the Labor Party
    d. the reduction of the House of Lords' power

Answer: b, easy, page 839

58. Which of the following national groups had realized nationhood by 1871?
    a. Irish
    b. Hungarians
    c. Czechs
    d. Germans

Answer: d, difficult, page 838

59. The Liberals who controlled the House of Commons from 1906 to 1914 made reforms that:
    a. provided unemployment and sickness benefits and pensions for workers
    b. were stubbornly resisted by Conservative leader David Lloyd George
    c. had a revolutionary impact felt almost immediately in Britain
    d. lowered the wealthy classes' tax burden, causing wide social unrest

Answer: a, medium, page 839

60. The political group that sought to further the cause of the working class in nineteenth-century Britain was:
    a. the Liberal party
    b. the Conservative party
    c. the Labour party
    d. the Social Democrats

Answer: c, easy, page 839

61. The debate over old age pensions in Britain in 1908:
    a. ended with Parliament deciding to use tribute from conquered nations to support pensions

    b. could not be resolved and led to a civil war
    c. brought about an increased tax burden on the wealthy to pay for it
    d. was hardly a debate as everyone support pensions

Answer: c, medium, page 839

62. Splits between the French working and middle classes:
    a. were largely solved by the liberal reforms of the Third Republic
    b. enabled the Third Republic to elect a new monarch in 1875
    c. led to a strong parliamentary system of government
    d. were further widened by the brutal suppression of the Paris Commune in 1871

Answer: d, medium, page 840

63. Which statement best characterizes the Third Republic of France?
    a. Politically, it was very stable.
    b. It had at least fifty cabinet changes from 1875 to 1914.
    c. Monarchists, clergy, and the army were its chief supporters.
    d. It was more violent than the Great Fear of the French Revolution.

Answer: b, easy, page 841

64. The relevance of Alfred Dreyfus to the history of the Third Republic was in:
    a. demonstrating the anti-Semitism and democratic fragility of the Republic
    b. crushing the attempted coup d'etat of General Boulanger
    c. making France the world leader in instituting labor legislation
    d. none of the above

Answer: a, medium, page 842

65. The newly formed Italian nation (1870) was best characterized by:
    a. a parliamentary government established by King Alfonso XII and dominated by the Liberals and Conservatives
    b. a strong sense of solidarity and community that united its varied areas
    c. heavy industrialization and literacy, especially in the south
    d. a weak, national government under the system of <u>trasformismo</u>

Answer: d, difficult, page 844

66. Which of the following statements best applies to Spain and Italy in the late nineteenth century?
    a. Spain was once again becoming a powerful state.

b. Italian unity was vigorously supported by the papacy
c. Italy was becoming a preeminent colonial power.
d. Both countries remained second-rate European powers

Answer: d, easy, page 843

67. Under the chancellorship of Bismarck, Germany:
    a. realized the growth of a real political democracy through universal male suffrage
    b. passed social welfare legislation to woo workers away from the Social Democrats
    c. engaged in the <u>Kulturkampf</u> or crusade to make Catholicism Germany's national religion
    d. maintained a military second only to that of France on the Continent

Answer: b, medium, page 845

68. Which statement best applies to the Germany under chancellor Otto von Bismarck?
    a. Prussia lost much of its influence on state politics
    b. coalitions were used by Bismarck to get what he wanted and then dropped
    c. socialism was almost completely stamped out by the Prussian army
    d. almost all regional differences disappeared under the charismatic leadership of Bismarck

Answer: b, easy, page 844

69. The growth of Germany under William II included all of the following <u>except</u>:
    a. the expansion of the Social Democratic party
    b. a growing conflict between modernization and traditionalism
    c. the discrediting of radical rightwing parties
    d. continued industrial expansion

Answer: c, easy, page 845

70. Which of the following statements best applies to the Dual Monarchy of Austria-Hungary before World War I?
    a. Both Austria and Hungary had working parliamentary systems.
    b. The Magyars dominated politics in Austria under Emperor William II.
    c. The nationality problem remained unresolved and led to strong German nationalist movements.
    d. Prime minister Count Edward von Taafe was ousted in 1893 by the

Slavic minorities for his failure to make concessions to them.

Answer: c, difficult, page 845

71. Imperial Russia under Tsar Nicholas II
    a. defeated Japan in the Russo-Japanese War in 1905
    b. became an industrial power under Sergei Witte, Nicholas's minister of finance
    c. was a bastion of liberal reforms in Europe after the successful 1905 revolution
    d. had little difficulty with socialist parties, unlike other European nations

Answer: b, easy, page 847

72. Sergei Witte, the Russian minister for finance from 1892 to 1903, did all of the following except:
    a. push a policy of railroad construction
    b. attempt to limit protective tariffs
    c. try to get foreign investment and capital
    d. make possible the growth of a modern steel industry

Answer: b, medium, page 847

73. The result of Father George Gapon's petition to the tsar in 1905 was the:
    a. Workers' Fair Wages Act
    b. the overthrow of the tsar
    c. the "Bloody Sunday Massacre" in St. Petersburg
    d. complete industrial freeze during a six-month long strike

Answer: c, medium, DOC 8

74. Choose the correct relationship between the country and its political status prior to World War I:
    a. Greece--Russian protectorate
    b. Switzerland--Austrian protectorate
    c. Romania--independent state
    d. Belgium--duchy of France

Answer: c, easy, page 850

75. The Ottoman Empire regained the Balkans before 1914.
    a. True
    b. False

Answer: b, easy, page 850

76. Which of the following statements was <u>not</u> true of the United States in 1900:
    a. Americans on average shared in the nation's wealth rather equally.
    b. It was the world's richest nation and greatest industrial power.
    c. Over 40 percent of the population lived in cities.
    d. National amendments failed to maintain equal rights between blacks and whites.

Answer: a, medium, page 850

77. Radical Reconstruction following the American Civil War:
    a. accomplished little as a system of sharecropping replaced slavery
    b. was never honestly attempted and was only a "paper" solution
    c. was so successful that half of the southern states had black governors by 1900
    d. saw the dissolution of such groups as the KKK

Answer: a, easy, page 850

SUGGESTED FILMS

<u>Paris, 1900</u>. Brandon, MacMillan Films, 81 min. (black/white).

<u>The City at the End of the Century</u>. A. Mokin Productions, 19 min. (color).

<u>Women on the March: The Struggle for Equal Rights</u>. National Film Board of Canada, 30 min. (black/white).

<u>Turn of the Century</u>. McGraw-Hill Films, 30 min. (black/white).

<u>Europe, the Mighty Continent: Social Classes 1900</u>. Time-Life Films, 52 min. (color).

<u>Europe, the Mighty Continent: The Glory of Europe 1900</u>. Time-Life Films, 52 min. (color).

<u>Europe, the Mighty Continent: A World to Win</u>. Time-Life Films, 52 min. (color).

<u>English History: Nineteenth Century Reforms</u>. Coronet Instructional Films, 13 min.

(black/white).

The Dreyfus Affair. Texture, 15 min. (black/white).

The Engines of War. Open University Films, 24 min. (color). [Austrian society]

Last Years of the Tsars. Films, Inc., 19 min. (black/white).

Nicholas and Alexandra: Prelude to Revolution, 1904-1905. Learning Corporation of
America, 30 min. (color).

CHAPTER 25: IMPERIALISM, INTERNATIONAL RIVALRY, AND CULTURE IN THE "AGE OF PROGRESS," 1871-1914

CHAPTER OUTLINE

THE EXPANSION OF EUROPE
Population Increase and Demographic Transformation
Migrations

THE NEW IMPERIALISM
Causes of the New Imperialism
The Creation of Empires
    Africa
    Asia
Native Responses to Imperialism
    China
    Japan
    India

INTERNATIONAL RIVALRY AND THE COMING OF WAR
The Bismarckian System
New Directions and New Crises
    Crises in the Balkans, 1908-1913

INTELLECTUAL AND CULTURAL DEVELOPMENTS: TOWARD THE MODERN CONSCIOUSNESS
Developments in the Sciences: The Emergence of a New Physics
Flight to the Irrational

Sigmund Freud and the Emergence of Psychoanalysis
The Impact of Darwin: Social Darwinism and Racism
    Anti-Semitism
The Attack on Christianity and the Response of the Churches
Literature and the Arts: Toward Modernism
        Literature: Naturalism and Symbolism
    The Arts
    Music

EDUCATION AND LEISURE IN AN AGE OF MASS SOCIETY
    Mass Education
    Mass Leisure
        Background to Mass Leisure: Rational Recreation
        Forms of the New Mass Leisure

SUGGESTED LECTURE TOPICS

1. "The New Imperialism: Causes and Consequences"

2. "The Diplomatic Background to World War I: Was War Inevitable?"

3. "Nationalism and Mass Education: What is the Relationship Between Them?"

4. "The Emergence of Modernism in the Arts" [a slide lecture]

MAPS AND ARTWORK

1. Population growth: What impact did it have in 1900 and throughout the twentieth century? Map 25.1.

2. The scramble for empire: Africa, Map 25.2, and Asia, Map 25.3, showing the similarities and differences.

3. Instability in the Balkans: the Road to world war, Maps 25.4a and 25.4b.

4. Impressionism's impact on the art world.

DISCUSSION QUESTIONS FOR THE PRIMARY SOURCES (BOXED DOCUMENTS)

"The White Man's Burden" and "The Black Man's Burden": What arguments did Kipling present to justify European expansion in Africa and Asia? How does the selection by Edward Morel undermine those arguments? (pages 860 and 861)

"The Emperor's 'Big Mouth'": What did Emperor William II mean to say? What did he actually say? What does this interview with William II reveal about the emperor's attitudes and character? (page 871)

"Freud and the Concept of Repression": What did Freud mean by the concept of repression? (page 878)

"The Voice of Zionism: Theodor Herzl and the Jewish State": What is Zionism and how does this selection from Herzl reflect it? (page 881)

"Symbolist Poetry: Art for Art's Sake": In what way does Rimbaud's poem reveal the essence of Symbolism? (page 884)

"The Fight Song: Sports in the English Public School": As seen in this selection, what was the purpose of the "fight song" in the English public school? (page 895)

EXAMINATION QUESTIONS

Essays

1. Discuss the various explanations for late nineteenth-century imperialism. Which do you believe is the best explanation? Why?

2. One historian has written that the history of colonial expansion was "one of long-range schemes than one of individual acts and decisions that appear almost accidental when viewed singly." Does the practice of imperialism in Africa and Asia substantiate this statement? Why or why not?

3. What was the Bismarckian system of alliances? Discuss the breakdown of this system and show how a new system of alliances emerged between 1880 and 1914. Did this new system of alliances lead to war or did Bismarck's?

4. What might European diplomats have done between 1880 and 1914 to avoid war?

5. What do we mean by the phrase "modern consciousness" and how did it begin to emerge between 1871 and 1914 in the sciences, philosophical thought, and psychology?

6. How did Social Darwinism affect the development of a new wave of racism (especially anti-Semitism), in the last half of the nineteenth century? How did Jewish people respond to this anti-Semitism?

7. Why and how did Christianity experience "threats" between 1871 and 1914? How did the churches respond to these threats?

8. How is Modernism evident in literature and the arts between 1871 and 1914? How do these literary and artistic products reflect the political and social developments of the age?

9. How were the promises and problems of the new mass society reflected in education and leisure?

Identifications

10. "new imperialism"
11. "the White Man's Burden"
12. Cecil Rhodes
13. Boxer Rebellion
14. Meiji Restoration
15. Triple Alliance/Triple Entente
16. First Moroccan Crisis
17. Balkan Wars
18. Max Planck
19. Albert Einstein
20. Friedrich Nietzsche
21. Sigmund Freud
22. Social Darwinism
23. the Volk
24. The Jewish State
25. Syllabus of Errors
26. Emile Zola
27. the Symbolists
28. Igor Stravinsky
29. Primativism
30. Impressionism/Post-Impressionism

31. "rational recreation"

Multiple Choice

32. From 1880 to 1910, the European population:
    a. increased most dramatically in France
    b. declined in general
    c. declined only in the economically backward areas of southern Europe
    d. grew dramatically in eastern Europe

Answer: d, easy, page 856

33. The greatest recipient of the mass migrations from Europe at the turn of the twentieth century was:
    a. Canada
    b. the United States
    c. Brazil and Portugal
    d. Latin America

Answer: b, easy, page 858

34. The "new imperialism" of the late nineteenth century was similar to earlier forms of European imperialism in that:
    a. it concentrated on North and South America
    b. it remained on the fringes of the contacted cultures in the form of trading posts
    c. it showed the Europeans' willingness to dominate less technologically oriented peoples
    d. its motives were overwhelmingly linked to economic necessity

Answer: c, medium, page 859

35. Imperialism in the late nineteenth century was justified by Europeans as:
    a. necessary for maintaining international prestige
    b. a moral responsibility to bring religion and civilization to other peoples
    c. part of the natural order of Social Darwinism
    d. all of the above

Answer: d, medium, page 859

36. "The White Man's Burden" describes:

a. Rudyard Kipling's justification for European imperialism
b. the Social Darwinists' plea to stop Western imperialism
c. the Marxists' argument whereby capitalism would be destroyed through imperialism
d. none of the above

Answer: a, medium, DOC 1

37. European imperialism in Africa was best characterized by:
    a. grossly mismatched battles against natives won easily by Europeans
    b. the domination of German colonies in north Africa by 1900
    c. rivalries between European powers leading to full-scale conflicts
    d. cooperative agreements reached between native Africans and Europeans

Answer: a, difficult, page 864

38. The only European nation that was unsuccessful at African colonization before 1900 was:
    a. Germany
    b. Belgium
    c. France
    d. Italy

Answer: d, difficult, page 863

39. British imperialism in Africa was associated with all of the following except:
    a. the slaughter of 11,000 Muslims in the Sudan
    b. the creation of the International Association for the Exploration and Civilization of Central Africa
    c. the occupation of Egypt to protect Suez Canal interests
    d. Cecil Rhodes' involvement in south African affairs

Answer: b, difficult, page 863

40. Which of the following statements best applies to Western imperialism in Asia?
    a. Russia showed little interest in Asia until after 1918.
    b. The British acquired the Philippines from France and Japan from Russia by 1914.
    c. China was divided by the great powers into spheres of influence under the "open door" policy.
    d. The United States played the largest role in Southeast Asia after 1895.

Answer: c, easy, page 865

41. The "open door" policy in China:
    a. gave Great Britain direct control of nearly the entire mainland
    b. allowed the Manchu rulers to select the Western power with which it would trade
    c. led to widespread confusion and warfare among the Western powers
    d. none of the above

Answer: d, medium, page 865

42. The Asian country that avoided direct colonization by Western powers was:
    a. China
    b. Japan
    c. the Philippines
    d. Indochina

Answer: b, easy, page 865

43. The Boxer Rebellion occurred in:
    a. Japan
    b. Korea
    c. Siam
    d. none of the above

Answer: d, medium, page 866

44. Choose the correct relationship between the Asian nation and its response to Western imperialism:
    a. China--educated classes entered the British civil service, but underlying tones of resentment remained
    b. India--anti-foreign violence broke out in the Boxer Rebellion, but only resulted in harsher colonial rule
    c. Japan--rapidly adopted Western military and industrial techniques to become an imperial power
    d. all of the above are correct

Answer: c, difficult, page 866

45. The Meiji Restoration in Japan did not involve:
    a. the close adoption of Western industrial methods
    b. the leadership of the shogun
    c. Western forms of government

d. the creation of a powerful military state

Answer: b, medium, page 866

46. The British allowed the practice of <u>Sati</u> to continue in India.
    a. True
    b. False

Answer: b, easy, page 868

47. British rule in India in the late nineteenth century witnessed:
    a. educated Indians achieve high positions in the civil service
    b. an organized independence movement threaten British rule
    c. a series of internal wars among Indians destroy the countryside
    d. the bulk of the native population remain malnourished and illiterate

Answer: d, medium, page 868

48. The Bismarckian system of alliances:
    a. successfully preserved the status quo in Europe until Bismarck's
        dismissal
    b. was refuted by the Congress of Berlin in 1878
    c. gave Germany control of the Balkans until World War I
    d. was opposed by the Triple Alliance of Italy, Russia, and France

Answer: a, easy, page 868

49. The Triple Alliance from 1882 to World War I united in a defensive alliance:
    a. Germany, Austria, and Italy
    b. Russia, Austria, and Germany
    c. France, Russia, and Austria
    d. Great Britain, France, and Russia

Answer: a, difficult, page 869

50. Following William II's dismissal of Bismarck in 1890, Germany:
    a. became increasingly active in foreign policy and pursuing its "place in
        the sun"
    b. became closely allied with Great Britain
    c. abandoned plans for building a navy while concentrating on its army
    d. succeeded in splitting the Entente Cordiale between France and Britain

Answer: a, difficult, page 870

51. The division of the European powers into two major blocs was precipitated by:
    a. the tactless posturing of William II
    b. diplomats who listened to nationalistic cries rather than rationalistic calculation
    c. Germany's construction of a large navy
    d. all of the above

Answer: d, medium, page 871

52. The First Moroccan Crisis of 1905-1906 succeeded in:
    a. driving Great Britain back into its policy of "splendid isolation"
    b. pushing the European powers into two rigid confederations
    c. driving a wedge between France and Great Britain as William II had planned
    d. awarding control of most of Morocco to Germany

Answer: b, difficult, page 872

53. The crises in the Balkans between 1908 and 1913 did <u>not</u> include:
    a. Russia backing down to Germany over Austro-Serbian conflicts
    b. Austria granting Serbia its Adriatic port in Albania
    c. the Balkan League's victory over the Turks in 1912
    d. the defeat of Bulgaria in the second Balkan War in 1913

Answer: b, easy, page 874

54. Max Planck's discovery of "quanta" energy:
    a. brought Newtonian physics into serious question
    b. proved that atoms radiate energy in a steady stream
    c. reaffirmed the belief in contemporary science as an accurate picture of reality
    d. all of the above

Answer: a, medium, page 875

55. Albert Einstein:
    a. developed the quantum theory with the aid of Max Planck
    b. was readily accepted into the European scientific community
    c. developed a theory in which neither time nor space exists independent of human experience
    d. maintained the Newtonian scheme of the universe as one created by God

Answer: c, difficult, page 875

56. Friedrich Nietzsche, Henri Bergson, and Georges Sorel were all united in their:
    a. fervent belief in political democracy
    b. praising of their "age of progress"
    c. devotion to rational thought and reason
    d. glorifying of the irrational

Answer: d, medium, page 876

57. The nineteenth-century intellectual who reacted against Christianity and reason while advocating the rise of the "Superman" was:
    a. Todd Fabian
    b. Georges Sorel
    c. Henri Bergson
    d. Friedrich Nietzsche

Answer: d, easy, page 876

58. To Sigmund Freud, the key to solving psychologically disturbed patients' conflicts was through:
    a. tracing repression back to its childhood origins
    b. the use of electrotherapy
    c. the overriding of the pleasure principle
    d. the intentional destruction of the superego

Answer: a, medium, DOC 4

59. Not a central part of Sigmund Freud's psychoanalytic theory was:
    a. the ongoing battle between the id, ego, and superego
    b. the belief in the superiority of rational, conscious ideas in determining human behavior
    c. entering the unconscious through dreams and free thought association
    d. uncovering and unblocking early sexual repressions

Answer: b, difficult, page 878

60. Exponents of Social Darwinism in the late nineteenth century called for:
    a. international struggle to prove the survival of the fittest
    b. communist expansion as the only method of dealing with social pressures
    c. an end to warfare to ensure human survival
    d. improved medical care for the weak and diseased

Answer: a, difficult, page 879

61. The most popular exponent of Social Darwinism in the late nineteenth century was:
    a. Houston Chamberlain
    b. Theodor Herzl
    c. Herbert Spencer
    d. Henri Bergson

Answer: c, easy, page 879

62. The German concept of the <u>Volk</u>:
    a. proclaimed a belief in the superiority of German culture
    b. led to a belief in the Jews as the destroyers of the Aryan race
    c. is representative of the misguided directions of Social Darwinism in the nineteenth century
    d. all of the above

Answer: d, medium, page 879

63. Which of the following statements best characterizes the rising anti-Semitism in Europe before World War I?
    a. a growing sentiment to segregate Jews and limit their immigration arose, especially in Germany
    b. a series of systematic massacres, or pogroms, against Jews occurred in Germany and France
    c. journalists like Theodor Herzl called for an international movement to crush Zionism
    d. anti-Semitic parties, such as Benjamin Disraeli's in Britain, gained support until 1914

Answer: a, medium, page 880

64. The worst treatment of Jews in the late nineteenth century and early twentieth century came in the form of pogroms in:
    a. Germany
    b. Russia
    c. France
    d. Austria

Answer: b, easy, page 880

65. The conclusion of Theodor Herzl's <u>The Jewish State</u> was:

    a. Jews should remain in their European states and wait for the tide of anti-Semitism to turn.
    b. the Zionist movement was a Utopian dream that should be abandoned
    c. the creation of a Jewish nation in Palestine was both feasible and advisable
    d. a separate Jewish homeland would never be tolerated by the European nations

Answer: d, medium, page 880 + DOC 5

66. The growing challenges to the Christian churches from science and modern thought resulted in: .
    a. a harsh criticism of socialism and modernization in De Rerum Novarum by Pope Leo XIII
    b. Pope Pius IX's Syllabus of Errors, which admitted the shortcomings of the Catholic church
    c. a picture of a non-divine Jesus in Ernst Renan's Life of Jesus
    d. the Catholic church's adoption of the religious movement known as Modernism

Answer: c, medium, page 882

67. All of the following had an adverse effect on Christianity in the late nineteenth century except:
    a. Darwin's theory of evolution
    b. the Paris Commune of 1871
    c. new findings in anthropology and sociology
    d. urbanization and industrialization

Answer: b, difficult, page 882

68. One of the more liberal, compromising popes of the nineteenth century was Leo XIII who was responsible for:
    a. the creation of the Salvation Army in 1865
    b. issuing De Rerum Novarum, which upheld aspects of socialism and capitalism
    c. adopting the Modernism movement as part of Catholic doctrine
    d. issuing the Syllabus of Errors, which praised the nationalist and socialist movements in Europe

Answer: b, medium, page 883

69. The Syllabus of Errors:

a. reversed the growing tide of anti-clericalism in Europe in the 1880s
b. stated that the papacy should never reconcile itself with progress and liberalism
c. was Pope Leo XIII's most liberal encyclical
d. overturned the doctrine of papal infallibility, first claimed at the First Vatican Council

Answer: b, difficult, page 883

70. Choose the correct relationship between author and his modernistic work:
a. Emile Zola--<u>War and Peace</u>
b. W. B. Yeats--<u>Rougon-Macquart</u>
c. Fyodor Dostoevsky--<u>Crime and Punishment</u>
d. Leo Tolstoy--<u>The Brothers Karamazov</u>

Answer: c, easy, page 885

71. The nineteenth-century literary movement of Naturalism, which pessimistically accepted the material world as real, was best exemplified by:
a. Emile Zola
b. Stéphane Mallarmé
c. Leo Tolstoy
d. Arthur Rimbaud

Answer: a, medium, page 883

72. The Symbolist movement in late nineteenth-century Europe was concerned with:
a. creating art simply for its own sake
b. highly personalized forms of poetry
c. reacting against Realism, as objective reality was impossible
d. all of the above

Answer: d, easy, page 885 + DOC 6

73. An important trend in art before 1914 was:
a. the focus on individual consciousness as the source of true meaning
b. lushly adorned architectural designs, shown in the buildings of Frank Lloyd Wright
c. the movement of Post-Impressionism, based on objective reality and imitation
d. a return to religious motifs, as shown in the paintings of Walter Gropius

Answer: a, difficult, page 885

74. The Post-Impressionist movement was characterized by:
    a. an obsession with the realistic portrayal of nature
    b. the capture of primitive and unconscious life, as in Henri Matisse's paintings
    c. an attention to structure and form, as in the geometric paintings of Paul Gauguin
    d. the spiritual paintings of Pablo Picasso

Answer: c, difficult, page 886

75. All of the following artists were associated with the Post-Impressionist movement except:
    a. Paul Cezanne
    b. Vincent van Gogh
    c. Paul Gauguin
    d. Vasily Kandinsky

Answer: d, easy, page 886

76. The most readily accepted modernistic artistic endeavor before World War I was:
    a. the atonal and expressionistic music of Stravinsky and Schönberg
    b. the Fauvist movement in painting, led by Henri Matisse
    c. the functionalist movement of Vasily Kandinsky
    d. the architectural designs of Louis Sullivan in the "new city" of Chicago

Answer: d, medium, page 888

77. The Romantic movement in music has a fascination with:
    a. rock music
    b. exotic and primitive cultures
    c. the Ottoman Empire
    d. none of the above

Answer: b, medium, page 889

78. A chief exponent of musical primitivism was:
    a. Edward Grieg
    b. Henrik Ibsen
    c. Claude Debussy

d. Igor Stravinsky

Answer: d, difficult, page 890

79. The first state-run system of elementary education arose in:
    a. Russia
    b. Great Britain
    c. Germany
    d. the United States

Answer: c, difficult, page 890

80. The primary motive for government-sponsored mass education in the late
    nineteenth century was:
    a. for the personal and social improvement of the masses
    b. to instill patriotism and nationalism into the masses
    c. to break down long-established gender stereotypes among the sexes
    d. to inculcate the masses with religious and moral values

Answer: b, medium, page 891

81. The state-run systems of education among the Western nations in the late
    nineteenth century:
    a. generally applied only to male children
    b. remained optional up until after World War I
    c. saw women make up the minority of trained teachers
    d. virtually eliminated adult illiteracy in France and Great Britain

Answer: d, easy, page 892

82. The new patterns of mass leisure in the late nineteenth century were determined
    by:
    a. the increase in the lower classes' real wages
    b. the new mechanized urban transportation systems
    c. the rhythms of machine and clocks in the factories
    d. all of the above

Answer: d, easy, page 892

83. The movement of "rational recreation" was designed to:
    a. instill the values of self-control and respectability in the lower classes
    b. provide intellectual stimulation for the middle and upper classes
    c. reinstitute earlier rural forms of mass entertainment

    d. keep the upper and lower classes in a strictly stratified social order

Answer: a, medium, page 893

84. New forms of mass leisure in the late nineteenth century included all of the following except:
    a. professional sporting events
    b. mass tourism, as established by Thomas Cook in Great Britain
    c. the serious editorial and political newspapers known as the "yellow press"
    d. amusement parks and dance halls

Answer: c, easy, page 893

85. The new team sports of the late nineteenth century:
    a. were unorganized, spontaneous activities arranged just for fun
    b. helped distract people from the realities of their work lives
    c. allowed for a continuation of older leisure patterns of active community participation
    d. would remain small-scale, exclusive activities until the mid-twentieth century

Answer: b, medium, page 895

SUGGESTED FILMS

Europe, the Mighty Continent: Hey-Day Fever. Time-Life Films, 52 min. (color).

Europe, the Mighty Continent: Day of Empire Has Arrived. Time-Life Films, 52 min. (color).

Europe, the Mighty Continent: The Drums Begin to Roll. Time-Life Films, 52 min. (color).

Doomed Dynasties of Europe. Radim Films, 16 min. (black/white).

Imperialism and European Expansion. Coronet Instructional Films, 13 min. (black/white).

Stanley Finds Livingstone. CBS-TV, 28 min. (black/white).

Zulu. CCM Films, 13 min. (color).

The Boxer Rebellion. Teaching Film Custodians, 21 min. (color).

China: Agonies of Nationalism 1800-1927. Films Inc., 29 min. (black/white).

India's History: British Rule to Independence. Coronet Instructional Films, 11 min. (color).

The Christians: The Roots of Disbelief. McGraw-Hill Films, 39 min. (color).

The Scientific Challenge to Religion. University Films, 29 min. (black/white).

The Life of Emile Zola. Warner, 32 min. (black/white).

A Third Testament: Tolstoy. BBC/Time-Life Films, 53 min. (color).

The Impressionists. University Education and Visual Arts, 20 min. (black/white).

Van Gogh. Pictura Films Coronation, 17 min. (black/white).

From Renoir to Picasso. Audio Brandon Films Inc., 32 min. (black/white).

Picasso: Artist of the Century. Films Inc., 60 min. (color).

SUGGESTIONS FOR MUSIC

Richard Wagner, Parsifal

Richard Wagner, Der Ring des Nibelungen-Das Rheingold, Die Walküre, Siegfried, Götterdämmerung (London-414100-2LM15)

Igor Stravinsky, The Rite of Spring (Columbia-ML5277)

Igor Stravinsky, Firebird Suite (Columbia-ML5182)

Igor Stravinsky, Petrushka (London-4177758-2)

Jean Sibelius, Finlandia (Philips-420490-2)

Piotr Tchaikovsky 1812 Overture (CBS-MLK 39433)

Antonín Dvorák, <u>Symphony No. 9</u> ("From the New World") (Angel-CDM-69005)

Claude Debussy, <u>La Mer</u>, (CBS-MYK-37261)

CHAPTER 26: THE BEGINNING OF THE TWENTIETH-CENTURY CRISIS: WAR AND REVOLUTION

CHAPTER OUTLINE

THE ROAD TO WORLD WAR I
Nationalism and Internal Dissent
Militarism
The Outbreak of War: The Summer of 1914

THE WAR
1914-1915: Illusions and Stalemate
1916-1917: The Great Slaughter
    Daily Life in the Trenches
The Widening of the War
    Entry of the United States
The Home Front: The Impact of Total War
    Total War: Political Centralization and Economic
        Regimentation
    Public Order and Public Opinion
    The Social Impact of Total War

WAR AND REVOLUTION
The Russian Revolution
    The March Revolution
    The Bolshevik Revolution
    Civil War
The Last Year of the War

213

Revolutionary Upheavals in Germany and Austria-Hungary

THE PEACE SETTLEMENT

SUGGESTED LECTURE TOPICS

1. "The Causes of World War I: The Unending Controversy"

2. "The Military Strategy of World War I: The Problem of Yesterday's War Plans and Today's Reality"

3. "The Impact of Total War on the Home Front in World War I"

4. "Why Did the Bolshevik Revolution Succeed?"

5. "Versailles: Prelude to Another War?"

MAPS AND ARTWORK

1. The breakup of the old system. Compare Map 26.1 with 26.5. What impact did this have on the interwar period?

2. The war in the West (Map 26.2) compared with the forgotten war in the east (Map 26.3.)

3. Propaganda in the arts (page 914), and photographs.

DISCUSSION QUESTIONS FOR THE PRIMARY SOURCES (BOXED DOCUMENTS)

"You Have to Bear the Responsibility for War or Peace": How do the telegrams exchanged between William II and Nicholas II reveal why Europeans went to war in 1914? What does it reveal about the relationship of Germany's and Russia's monarchs? (page 903)

"The Excitement of War": What does the excerpt from Stefan Zweig reveal about the motivations of many people for war? What does it reveal about the power of nationalism in 1914? (page 905)

"The Reality of War: Trench Warfare" and "The Reality of War: War and the Family": How do Remarque's novel and the letters of John Mott capture the "reality" of World War I? (page 909)

"The Songs of World War I": Based on their war songs, what ideas or themes maintained the will of German, American, and British soldiers to continue fighting? (page 911)

"Ten Days That Shook the World: Lenin and the Bolshevik Seizure of Power": What impressions did John Reed give of Lenin? How do you know his account is biased? (page 921)

"The Voice of Peacemaking: Woodrow Wilson" and "The Voice of Peacemaking: Georges Clemenceau": How did the peacemaking aims of Wilson and Clemenceau differ? How did their different views affect the deliberations of the Paris Peace Conference and the nature of the final peace settlement? (pages 926 and 928)

EXAMINATION QUESTIONS

Essays

1. Discuss the causes of World War I: What were the major long-range causes of the war? How important were the decisions made by European statesmen during the summer of 1914 in causing the war? What nation, if any, was the most responsible for causing the war?

2. Discuss the course of the first two years of World War I: Why did many people expect a short war? Why was it not a short war? Why did World War I become a "war of attrition"? Why did the warring nations, worn out by the end of 1916, not make peace?

3. Why can 1917 be viewed as the year that witnessed the decisive turning point of World War I?

4. How did wartime governments maintain public order and mobilize public opinion during the course of the war?

5. Discuss the effects of World War I on political life, economic affairs, the social classes, and women.

6. Write a brief history of the Russian Revolution by discussing the following questions: What caused the Russian Revolution? How did Lenin and the Bolsheviks manage to seize and hold power despite their small numbers? How did the Bolsheviks secure their power during the civil war?

7. What were the chief aims of the Paris Peace Conference? To what extent were these aims incorporated into the actual peace treaties?

8. Why can Versailles be seen only as a truce between the world wars?

Identifications

8. Schlieffen Plan
9. First Battle of the Marne
10. trench warfare
11. Central Powers
12. "unlimited submarine warfare"
13. DORA
14. Erich Ludendorff
15. Georges Clemenceau
16. Rasputin
17. soviets
18. Bolsheviks
19. Leon Trotsky
20. Communists
21. Menseviks
22. Red Army
23. Cheka
24. Free Corps
25. Rosa Luxemburg
26. Paris Peace Conference
27. Woodrow Wilson
28. League of Nations
29. Treaty of Versailles

Multiple Choice

30. Which of the following trends helped lead to the outbreak of the Great War?
    a. conservative leaders hoped to crush internal socialist movements through war
    b. European generals were inflexible in their military policies
    c. European states felt they had to uphold the power of their allies for their own internal security
    d. all of the above

Answer: d, medium, page 900

31. Before the outbreak of World War I in 1914, the general outlook for the future by most Europeans was:
    a. highly optimistic with material progress expected to create an "earthly paradise"
    b. one of extreme indifference and reckless abandon
    c. extremely negative, with most people believing that Armageddon was near
    d. largely determined by state agencies

Answer: a, medium, page 900

32. The immediate cause of World War I was:
    a. an uprising of Catholic peasants in Bavaria
    b. the assasination of Archduke Francis Ferdinand
    c. the German invasion of Poland
    d. the German naval blockade of Britain

Answer: b, easy, page 900

33. The outbreak of the Great War was greatly accelerated by the Schlieffen Plan, which was:
    a. Germany's promise of full-fledged support for Austrian military actions against Serbia
    b. the Black Hand's plan for the assassination of Archduke Ferdinand of Austria
    c. Germany's military plan to invade France through Belgium before attacking Russia
    d. Russia's mobilization plan against both Germany and Austria-Hungary

Answer: c, medium, page 902

34. The rivalry between which two states for domination of southeastern Europe helped create serious tensions before World War I?

a. Germany and Italy
b. Russia and Italy
c. Austria-Hungary and Russia
d. Britain and France

Answer: c, easy, page 901

35. The newly created state of _____ was a thorn in Austria-Hungary's side and a primary cause of World War I:
    a. Serbia
    b. Bulgaria
    c. Greece
    d. Italy

Answer: a, medium, page 901

36. The Great Powers were not dissapointed in the war in 1914.
    a. True
    b. False

Answer: a, easy, page 904

37. On the eve of the outbreak of general war in Europe in 1914, William II of Germany was:
    a. plotting the downfall of Nicholas II of Russia
    b. intentionally provoking Russia to extend German influence on Europe
    c. engaged in conversation with Nicholas II to avoid war if possible
    d. encouraging Russia to intercede on behalf of Serbia

Answer: c, easy, DOC 1

38. In August 1914, the perception of the upcoming war among Europeans was that:
    a. it would be the dawn of a new socialist Europe
    b. it would redeem Europe by ending selfishness while reviving social commitment
    c. it would mark the end of European civilization
    d. its long-term nature would revive Europe's economy

Answer: b, difficult, page 905

39. Most Europeans believed that the Great War would:
    a. be much like the American Civil War in terms of length
    b. be over in just a few weeks

    c. last forever creating a state of perpetual heroics
    d. make Europe a unified society under one leader

Answer: b, easy, page 904

40. The most important consequence of the first year of World War I was:
    a. a stalemate on the Western front as a result of the First Battle of the Marne
    b. Italy's decision to switch to the German-Austrian alliance
    c. the collapse of German armies on the Russian front
    d. Serbia's rapid advancement into Austria-Hungary

Answer: a, medium, page 906

41. Germany and its allies were most successful in the early stages of the war in:
    a. France, where they quickly eliminated the Allied forces
    b. Serbia, which was knocked out of the war in 1915
    c. Italy, which was quickly overrun by the Austrians
    d. all of the above

Answer: b, easy, page 906

42. The development of trench warfare in France was characterized by:
    a. quick advances and seizures of enemy trenches
    b. fewer casualties due to elaborate fortifications
    c. dreary boredom and static daily routines
    d. high morale and assurance of victory among the troops

Answer: c, medium, DOC 3

43. The war in the east was best characterized by:
    a. more mobility than the trench warfare on the Western Front
    b. relatively little loss of life and tiny skirmishes
    c. trench warfare as in France
    d. the overwhelming superiority of the Russian military forces

Answer: a, medium, page 906

44. The usual tactic of trench warfare was to:
    a. surround the enemy and starve it into submission
    b. use a heavy bombardment and then launch a massive frontal assault
    c. attempt to outflank the enemy and attack the relatively undefended

positions
    d. meet the opposing force on the "field of honor" between the trenches in hand to hand combat

Answer: b, easy, page 907

45. As soldiers on both sides realized that no one could gain an advantage in trench warfare:
    a. savage treatment of prisoners became commonplace
    b. new weapons were developed to kill rather overrun the enemy
    c. a "live and let live" attitude emerged with its own rules of etiquette
    d. they were encouraged by their superiors to not fight and wait for a peaceful resolution

Answer: c, easy, page 910

46. A favorite song of the _____, "The Watch on the Rhine" expressed patriotism and heroism of the fighting men:
    a. British
    b. Americans
    c. French
    d. Germans

Answer: d, easy, DOC 4

47. The entry of the United States into World War I in April 1917:
    a. gave the nearly-defeated Allies a psychological boost
    b. was greatly feared by the German Naval Staff
    c. was a response to Turkey's entrance into the war among the Central Powers
    d. put an end to Germany's use of unlimited submarine warfare

Answer: a, difficult, page 912

48. As the war expanded from Europe:
    a. British forces in Africa destroyed the Ottoman Turks
    b. Germany successfully used its colonies to wage war on a world scale
    c. Italy played a leading role in fighting off the new allies of the Central Powers
    d. China played a key role

Answer: a, medium, page 910

49. The United States entered the war as a result of:
    a. a surprise German attack on the Philippines
    b. Germany's unrestricted submarine warfare
    c. the strong expansionist desires of Woodrow Wilson
    d. the assassination of the American ambassador to Austria-Hungary

Answer: b, easy, page 912

50. Which of the following statements concerning the economies of the wartime powers is <u>false</u>?
    a. Russia, Italy, and Austria-Hungary failed to develop the necessary wartime industrial economies.
    b. Britain's Liberal government doomed the Ministry of Munitions' centralization attempts to failure.
    c. Germany, under Walter Rathenau, was most successful in developing a planned economy.
    d. A strong war economy in France was hampered by disputes between civil and military authorities.

Answer: b, difficult, page 913

51. Which of the following was <u>not</u> a result of the need for a prolonged war effort in Europe?
    a. the use of conscription
    b. the use of government planned economies
    c. the use of propaganda
    d. the end of compulsory labor on the home front

Answer: d, difficult, page 912

52. As public morale weakened in the later stages of the war,
    a. workers' strikes became less frequent as they were brutally suppressed
    b. the liberal French government under Georges Clemenceau found it impossible to stifle internal dissent
    c. propaganda posters and weapons became less important
    d. police powers were expanded to include the arrest of dissenters as traitors

Answer: d, medium, page 914

53. Internal opposition to the war in the European nations came largely from:
    a. the factory owners and businessmen
    b. the liberals and the socialists

c. the government ministries
d. ethnic minorities and women

Answer: b, easy, page 914

54. The women workers of World War I played an important role in:
    a. winning women the right to vote immediately following the war
    b. gaining equal industrial wages with men by the end of the war
    c. achieving permanent job security in the once male-dominated workplace
    d. all work areas except the textile industry

Answer: a, medium, page 916

55. The total war of World War I had the most visible effect on European society in:
    a. bringing an end to unemployment
    b. ending crime
    c. causing church attendance to soar
    d. creating a positive outlook for young people

Answer: a, easy, page 915

56. Expectations for women during the war were:
    a. that they would occupy a permanent place in the work force
    b. that they would return to their "normal" lives when the war ended
    c. very bleak as they still could not gain employment
    d. had little to do with any social changes that subsequently appeared

Answer: b, medium, page 916

57. Which group experienced the heaviest casualties during the war?
    a. the common infantrymen
    b. the leaders who were assassinated behind the lines
    c. medical personnel who were favorite sniper targets
    d. junior officers who led the advances

Answer: d, difficult, page 916

58. Which of the following benefitted from the Great War?
    a. small industrial firms
    b. middle-class professional people
    c. trade unions
    d. unskilled workers and peasants

Answer: c, difficult, page 916

59. One group that benefitted from World War I was:
    a. civil servants who received job security
    b. large industrial munitions factory owners
    c. chldren who were treated with special care during the war
    d. criminals who had to be released during wartime

Answer: b, easy, page 918

60. The collapse of Russia's tsarist regime in March 1917 was aided by all of the following except:
    a. the leadership of the Mensheviks in forming the new Provisional Government
    b. a general strike in Petrograd
    c. the tremendous wartime losses of Russian soldiers due to incompetent leadership
    d. strife in the ruling dynasty, as evidenced by the influence of Rasputin

Answer: a, easy, page 919

61. The Russian army's woes during World War I included all of the following except:
    a. not enough manpower
    b. poor leadership
    c. lack of armaments
    d. great losses in battle

Answer: a, medium, page 918

62. Which of the following statements best applies to Nicholas II's tsarist regime?
    a. Rasputin, an alleged holy man, ran a very efficient government.
    b. Alexandra, Nicholas's wife, kept him insulated from domestic disturbances.
    c. It was patriotically supported throughout the war.
    d. Many reforms were made to keep the peasants content.

Answer: b, easy, page 918

63. Which of the following statements best applies to Lenin?
    a. He was a central figure in the establishment of the Provisional Government.
    b. He denounced the use of revolutionary violence in his "April Theses."

    c. His middle-class representation led to his desire to form a new, broad, democratically oriented labor party.

    d. As leader of the Bolsheviks, he promised redistribution of all land to the peasants.

Answer: d, medium, page 920

64. Lenin was aided by all of the following <u>except</u>:
    a. being smuggled by the Germans into Russia to cause dissent in April of 1917
    b. simple slogans that promised more to the peasants and workers
    c. the weakness of the Provisional Government
    d. the support of the Russian aristocracy

Answer: d, easy, page 920

65. The Bolsheviks' ascendency to power was made possible by:
    a. their gaining a majority in the new Constituent Assembly
    b. the Military Revolutionary Committee of Lenin and Trotsky
    c. Lenin's renewed military successes along the Eastern Front
    d. the collapse of Alexander Kerensky's Congress of Soviets

Answer: b, medium, page 920

66. Following the Bolshevik seizure of power in November of 1917, Lenin:
    a. accelerated the war effort against Germany
    b. gave control over factories to a few individuals
    c. ratified the redistribution of land to the peasants
    d. successfully campaigned for a Bolshevik victory in the Constituent Assembly

Answer: c, easy, page 922

67. Upon seizing power, Lenin let it be known to the world that he wished for:
    a. everlasting peace among all nations
    b. Communist revolutions to break out worldwide
    c. Western technology and learning to be imported into Russia
    d. a Russian government based on that of the United States

Answer: b, difficult, page 923

68. The success of the Red Army in allowing the Bolsheviks to maintain power was <u>not</u> aided by:

a. the disunity and political differences

b. Allied intervention on behalf of the Red Army

c. the Red Terror carried out by the Red secret police, the Cheka

d. the revolutionary fervor of Trotsky's well-disciplined soldiers

Answer: b, difficult, page 923

69. All of the following groups were opposed to the Bolsheviks <u>except</u>:

a. the Mensheviks

b. the Socialist Revolutionaries

c. the Communists

d. the Allies

Answer: c, medium, page 923

70. The Cheka was a:

a. Serbian terrorist group

b. Slovak national organization

c. Tsarist secret police

d. none of the above

Answer: d, easy, page 923

71. The Second Battle of the Marne was:

a. Germany's final effort to win the war

b. the decisive victory Germany had hoped for

c. a disaster for the Allies

d. decided by the entry of Australia into the war

Answer: a, easy, page 924

72. The series of revolutionary upheavals in central Europe following Germany's defeat led to:

a. the creation of a new socialist state in Germany, led by Karl Liebknecht

b. a military dictatorship in Austria headed by the Free Corps

c. the creation of independent republics within the old Austro-Hungarian Empire

d. a strong Communist influence among most of the German populace

Answer: c, medium, page 925

73. The German November revolution of 1918 resulted in:

a. a parliamentary democracy dominated by the Republicans

  b. the division of Germany among the victorious Allies
  c. the creation of a Communist state similar to the Soviet Union
  d. the creation of a German republic with the Social Democrats in power

Answer: d, difficult, page 925

74. All of the following states were created out of the Austro-Hungarian Empire following World War I <u>except</u>:
  a. Austria
  b. Hungary
  c. Poland
  d. Czechoslovakia

Answer: c, easy, page 925

75. For Woodrow Wilson, the most important thing after the war was to:
  a. punish Germany severely
  b. assure self-determination for all peoples
  c. improve upon America's influence in Europe
  d. bring about the disintegration of the Soviet Union

Answer: b, difficult, page 926 + DOC 9

76. The chief motivation of Georges Clemenceau's terms of armistice was:
  a. to punish Germany and gain some measure of security
  b. to help Germany become a democracy
  c. maintain a peaceful and cooperative atmosphere in Europe
  d. to limit British influence on the Continent

Answer: a, easy, page 927 + DOC 8

77. The Treaty of Versailles:
  a. absolved the Central Powers of full guilt in instigating the war
  b. created Woodrow Wilson's League of Nations
  c. forced Germany to pay reparations for its wartime aggression
  d. created a systemn of mandates for the newly indpendent nations of the old Ottoman Empire

Answer: c, easy, page 928

78. An overall result of the Paris peace settlements of 1919 was that:
  a. Clemenceau's and Lloyd George's revengeful policies toward Germany would lead to future conflicts

b. America would play a central, active role in European affairs

c. the new ethnic-based states in eastern Europe would no longer remain a source of conflict

d. Woodrow Wilson successfully achieved his goals for a lasting European peace

Answer: a, difficult, page 927

79. Which of the following nations was <u>not</u> a member of the Big Three of the Paris Peace Conference?

    a. Russia

    b. Great Britain

    c. United States

    d. France

Answer: a, easy, page 927

80. The feature the Germans were particularly unhappy about in the Treaty of Versailles was:

    a. the loss of land that reduced the nation by half

    b. the reduction of the armed forces

    c. the "War Guilt Clause," which called for reparations

    d. the loss of political sovereignty for the next twenty years

Answer: c, medium, page 928

81. As a result of World War I, eastern Europe:

    a. experienced little or no change

    b. fell subject to the new Russian Communist state

    c. witnessed the emergence of new nation-states

    d. none of the above

Answer: c, easy, page 928

SUGGESTED FILMS

<u>The Great War: 1914-1917</u>. McGraw-Hill Films, 52 min. (black/white).

<u>The Great War--Fifty Years After</u>. NBC, 25 min. (color).

The First Casualty. Heritage Visual Sales, 55 min. (color).

Europe, the Mighty Continent: The Great War. Time-Life Films, 52 min. (color).

Europe, the Mighty Continent: This Generation Has No Future. Time-Life Films, 52 min. (color).

The End of the Old Order. Learning Corp. of America, 24 min. (color).

World War I: A Documentary on the Role of the USA. Encyclopedia Britannica, 27 min. (black/white).

Verdun: End of a Nightmare. Indiana University, 29 min. (black/white).

Russia in World War I. Films Inc., 20 min. (black/white).

Russia: Czar to Lenin. McGraw-Hill Films, 29 min. (black/white).

Lenin. Learning Corp. of America, 39 min. (black/white).

Lenin and Trotsky. CBS, 27 min. (black/white).

Lenin's Revolution. Time-Life Films, 20 min. (black/white).

Nightmare in Red. Contemporary Films, 55 min. (black/white).

Bolshevik Victory. Granada TV, 20 min. (black/white).

Versailles: The Lost Peace. Films Inc., 26 min. (color).

Europe, the Mighty Continent: Are We Making a Good Peace? Time-Life Films, 52 min. (color).

CHAPTER 27: THE FUTILE SEARCH FOR A NEW STABILITY: EUROPE BETWEEN THE WARS, 1919-1939

CHAPTER OUTLINE

AN UNCERTAIN PEACE: THE SEARCH FOR SECURITY
The French Policy of Coercion, 1919-1924
The Hopeful Years, 1924-1929
The Great Depression

THE DEMOCRATIC STATES
Great Britain
France
The Scandinavian Example
The United States

THE RETREAT FROM DEMOCRACY: THE AUTHORITARIAN AND TOTALITARIAN STATES
Fascist Italy
    The Birth of Fascism
    Mussolini and the Italian Fascist State
Hitler and Nazi Germany
    Weimar Germany and the Rise of the Nazis
    The Nazi Seizure of Power
    The Nazi State, 1933-1939
Authoritarianism in Eastern Europe
The Iberian Peninsula
Soviet Russia

> The New Economic Policy
> The Stalin Era, 1929-1939

MASS CULTURE AND MASS LEISURE BETWEEN THE WARS
>   Radio and Movies
>   Mass Leisure

CULTURAL AND INTELLECTUAL TRENDS IN THE INTERWAR YEARS
>   Art and Music
>   Literature
>   Intellectual Trends: Physics and Psychology

SUGGESTED LECTURE TOPICS

1. "The Birth of Fascism: Mussolini and the Italian Model"

2. "Ideology and Opportunism: The Dualistic Nature of Adolf Hitler's Policies"

3. "Propaganda in the Totalitarian State: The Example of Nazi Germany"

4. "Soviet Russia under Stalin: Betrayal of the Communist Dream?"

5. "The Arts in an Era of Uncertainty" [a slide lecture]

MAPS AND ARTWORK

1. Hitler's use of propaganda and rituals.

DISCUSSION QUESTIONS FOR THE PRIMARY SOURCES (BOXED DOCUMENTS)

"The Great Depression: Unemployed and Homeless in Germany": Discuss the plight of the homeless in Germany in 1932. Compare and contrast their situation to that of the homeless in the United States today. (page 939)

"The Struggles of a Democracy: Unemployment and Slums in Great Britain": What economic and social problems are described in these two selections? (page 941)

"The Voice of Italian Fascism": Based on his speech of January 3, 1925, what did fascism mean to Mussolini? (page 946)

"Adolf Hitler's Hatred of the Jews": What was Hitler's attitude toward the Jews? Why did he hate them? (page 950)

"Propaganda and Mass Meetings in Nazi Germany": How did Hitler envision the role of propaganda and mass meetings in the totalitarian state? (page 954)

"The Formation of Collective Farms": What is a collective farm and how was it created? (page 961)

"Mass Leisure: Strength Through Joy": Based on these reports, what were the attitudes of German workers to the regime's "Strength through Joy" programs? Do you think these reports are unbiased and accurate? Why or why not? (page 964)

"The Voice of Dadaism": How does this excerpt from Tristan Tzara reflect the ideas of Dadaism? (page 966)

EXAMINATION QUESTIONS

Essays

1. The decade of the 1920s has been characterized as both an "age of anxiety" and a "period of hope." Why?

2. What are the causes of the Great Depression? How did the European states respond to the Great Depression? How did America cope with the Depression?

3. What are the chief characteristics of totalitarianism? To what extent was Fascist Italy a totalitarian state?

4. What were Hitler's ideas and how did he implement them once he and the Nazis had established the Nazi state in Germany?

5. Why does the author state that the Stalinist era inaugurated an "economic, social, and political revolution that was more sweeping in its results than the revolutions of 1917"?

6. What impact did the growth of mass culture and mass leisure have upon European society in the 1920s and 1930s?

7. How do the cultural and intellectual trends of the 1920s and 1930s reflect a crisis of confidence in Western civilization?

Identifications

8. Treaty of Locarno
9. the Great Depression
10. John Maynard Keynes
11. French Popular Front
12. the New Deal
13. Il Duce
14. squadristi
15. "the Matteotti crisis"
16. National Socialist German Workers' Party
17. Mein Kampf
18. Hindenberg
19. Enabling Act
20. Heinrich Himmler
21. Kristallnacht
22. Joseph Stalin
23. Spanish Civil War
24. New Economic Policy
25. kulaks
26. Dopolavoro
27. Dadaism
28. Salvador Dali
29. Carl Jung

Multiple Choice

30. Efforts to maintain European peace following World War I included:
    a. a three-way alliance between Great Britain, France, and Germany
    b. the addition of an international security force to the League of Nations
    c. a weak system of alliances between France and the Little Entente
    d. increased intervention of Woodrow Wilson and the United States in European diplomacy

Answer: c, medium, page 936

31. French policy toward a defeated Germany following World War I was guided by all of the following except:
    a. a strict enforcement of the Treaty of Versailles
    b. occupation of German industries in the Ruhr Valley
    c. a strict collection of Germany's war reparations
    d. a policy of passive resistance under Raymond Poincaré

Answer: d, medium, page 936

32. Following Germany's failure to pay its war reparations, France occupied Germany's Ruhr Valley, resulting in:
    a. a policy of passive resistance by the German government
    b. economic and political upheavals in Germany
    c. the fall of Raymond Poincaré's French government in 1924
    d. all of the above

Answer: d, easy, page 937

33. The period of 1924-1929 in Europe witnessed:
    a. a growing feeling of optimism for a peaceful future under liberal-socialist governments
    b. the Great Depression destroy Europe's economy
    c. direction occupation of Germany by World War I's victorious powers
    d. the Western powers cut off all ties with Communist Russia

Answer: a, medium, page 937

34. Not among the hopeful signs of permanent European peace in the period 1924 to 1929 was:
    a. the World Disarmament Conference
    b. the Treaty of Locarno
    c. the Kellogg-Briand pact
    d. the Dawes Plan

Answer: a, easy, page 937

35. A major cause of the Great Depression was:
    a. European governments were too involved in their own economies
    b. the recall of American loans from European markets
    c. the underproduction and high prices of agricultural goods in eastern and central Europe

d. all of the above

Answer: b, difficult, page 938

36. An overall effect of the Great Depression in Europe was:
    a. the complete destruction of Communist parties
    b. huge unemployment rates in all nations but Great Britain
    c. the strengthening of liberal, democratic movements in the 1930s
    d. the rise of authoritarian movements in most areas of Europe

Answer: d, difficult, page 943

37. British political life between the wars was primarily dominated by:
    a. the Conservative party
    b. the Labour party
    c. the Liberal party
    d. none of the above

Answer: d, difficult, page 940

38. Great Britain came out of the worst stages of the post-World War I depression under:
    a. John Maynard Keynes
    b. the National Government
    c. David Lloyd George
    d. the Labour-Liberal coalition led by Ramsay MacDonald

Answer: b, medium, page 941

39. The French coalition government formed by the Radical and Socialist parties in the 1920s was:
    a. the Cartel of the Left
    b. the Fascist League
    c. the National Bloc
    d. the Popular Front

Answer: a, medium, page 942

40. The first Popular Front government of France:
    a. solved the depression by eliminating workers' benefits
    b. had as its prime minister the Socialist leader Leon Blum
    c. was responsible for solving the problems of the depression
    d. collapsed in 1926, allowing Raymond Poincaré's Cartel of the Left to

take power

Answer: b, difficult, page 942

41. Under a Social Democratic government and an expanded program of social services, one of the only European nations to prosper during the depression of the 1930s was:
    a. Spain
    b. Belgium
    c. France
    d. Sweden

Answer: d, easy, page 943

42. Franklin Roosevelt's New Deal policies in the United States:
    a. were successful by 1933
    b. virtually eliminated unemployment
    c. brought about government ownership of most industries
    d. none of the above

Answer: d, medium, page 943

43. The totalitarian states of the 1930s and 1940s were <u>not</u> concerned with:
    a. rule by a single party or leader
    b. controlling the intellectual and cultural aspects of life
    c. subordinating individual freedoms to the collective will of the masses
    d. securing the passive obedience of the people toward the goals of the regime

Answer: d, medium, page 944

44. The first fascist state in Europe was:
    a. Italy
    b. Germany
    c. Russia
    d. France

Answer: a, easy, page 944

45. The growth of Mussolini's Fascist movement was aided by:
    a. the inability of the parliamentary parties to form a coalition government
    b. popular, nationalistic resentment toward Italy's treatment following World War I

    c. the violence of the industrial and agricultural strikes of 1919 and 1920
    d. all of the above

Answer: d, easy, page 944

46. Which of the following statements is true of Mussolini's Italian Fascist state:
    a. The government's control over the mass media allowed for successful integration of the masses into the state's plans.
    b. Fascist laws and propaganda attempted to force women to remain at home and out of the factories.
    c. Giuseppe Bottai's radical education policies enabled the state to create thousands of "new Fascist men."
    d. As a totalitarian state, all religion, including Catholicism, was seen as detrimental to creating obedience to the state.

Answer: b, difficult, page 948

47. The assassination of Giacomo Matteotti by Fascists in 1924:
    a. caused Mussolini to become hesitant in his quest for power
    b. won the Fascists unprecedented support in the 1924 elections
    c. forced Mussolini to make a push for full dictatorship
    d. resulted in the passage of the Acerbo Law

Answer: c, difficult, page 946

48. The institutional framework of Mussolini's Fascist dictatorship:
    a. lacked a secret police force
    b. included highly popular and well attended Fascist youth organizations
    c. was primarily aimed at aiding the workers and peasants
    d. never created the degree of totalitarian control found in Russia and Germany in the 1930s

Answer: d, medium, page 948

49. Women in Mussolini's Fascist Italy:
    a. were coerced into factory work to aid industrial production
    b. were regarded as equal to men in social status
    c. were largely forced through government legislation to become homemakers
    d. were aided by the government's emphasis on birth control

Answer: c, easy, page 948

50. The Lateran Accords of 1929:
    a. nationalized all church property
    b. recognized Catholicism as the sole religion of Italy
    c. marked the Catholic church's official condemnation of the Fascist state
    d. eliminated government support for the Catholic church

Answer: b, medium, page 948

51. The city in which Hitler spent his formative years and developed his fundamental ideas was:
    a. Berlin
    b. Munich
    c. Vienna
    d. Hamburg

Answer: c, easy, page 949

52. All of the following were major influences on Hitler's ideology except:
    a. the operas of Richard Wagner
    b. the demagogic and mass party methods of Karl Lueger
    c. the anti-Semitic literature of Gustav Stresemann
    d. the racial and nationalistic ideas of Lanz von Liebenfels

Answer: c, medium, page 949

53. The successful early growth of Hitler's Nazi party can be attributed to all of the following except:
    a. Hitler's oratorical skills
    b. the SA's policies of force and terror
    c. the development of the party into a mass political movement
    d. the success of the Beer Hall Putsch

Answer: d, easy, page 950

54. Mein Kampf:
    a. depicted Hitler's plan to take power through a massive rebellion
    b. displayed a set of ideas that would guide Hitler throughout his entire political life
    c. excluded any trace of Hitler's anti-Semitism
    d. was immediately seen by German politicians as the dangerous work of a madman

Answer: b, medium, page 951

55. The German president at the time of Hitler's maneuvers to gain sole political power over Germany was:
    a. Heinrich Bröning
    b. Paul von Hindenberg
    c. Franz von Papen
    d. Herman Göring

Answer: b, easy, page 952

56. Hitler's "legal seizure" of power was aided by all of the following <u>except</u>:
    a. the political maneuverings of Franz von Papen
    b. the Enabling Act
    c. continual Nazi electoral success in 1932-1933
    d. the support of the rightwing elites of Germany

Answer: c, medium, page 952

57. The <u>Gleichschaltung</u> describes:
    a. the coordination of all institutions under Nazi control
    b. the purge of the SA leadership in June 1934
    c. the subordination of the German army under Hitler
    d. Hitler's plan for securing "living space" from the other nations

Answer: a, easy, page 953

58. The Nazis pursued the creation of a totalitarian state by only one means, terror.
    a. True
    b. False

Answer: b, medium, page 954

59. Which of the following statements concerning Hitler's "total state" is <u>false</u>"
    a. Hitler's mass demonstrations and rallies usually succeeded in evoking mass enthusiasm and excitement for Hitler's ideas.
    b. Governmental administration was marked by constant personal and institutional chaos.
    c. It was intended to be a purified racial state based on Aryan supremacy and Jewish subordination.
    d. In opposition to Fascist Italy, women were coerced into performing industrial labor to build up the state's military power.

Answer: d, easy, page 955

60. Economic and labor conditions in Nazi Germany were characterized by:
   a. nationalization of all industry
   b. a confusing, chaotic system of labor unions
   c. continuous high unemployment rates until World War II
   d. strict control of the workers under the German Labor Front

Answer: d, difficult, page 955

61. The Nazi leader Heinrich Himmler was responsible for:
   a. forming Nazi professional organizations for civil servants, doctors, and teachers
   b. carrying out the racial and terroristic policies of the SS
   c. guiding the German Labor Front
   d. the indoctrination of Nazi ideals into Hitler Youth organizations

Answer: b, medium, page 955

62. Hitler's anti-Semitic policies in the 1930s:
   a. included the Nuremberg laws, which centered on the forced emigration of most Jews from Germany
   b. reached their most violent phase during the events of <u>Kristallnacht</u>
   c. did not exclude Jews from legal, medical, and teaching positions
   d. would remain minimal and unorganized until World War II

Answer: b, easy, page 956

63. The Nazi policies toward women:
   a. differed fundamentally from those of Fascist Italy
   b. eliminated females from all professional occupations
   c. were aimed at bridging the differences between the sexes
   d. were geared toward bringing about the triumph of the Aryan race

Answer: d, easy, page 956

64. The only eastern European country to maintain political democracy throughout the 1930s was:
   a. Czechoslovakia
   b. Romania
   c. Poland
   d. Greece

Answer: a, medium, page 957

65. The dominant form of government in eastern Europe in the 1920s and 1930s was:
    a. authoritarianism
    b. Soviet Russia-style Communism
    c. parliamentary democracy
    d. Christian Socialism

Answer: a, medium, page 957

66. The Spanish Civil War ended with the victory of:
    a. King Alfonso XIII and General Miguel Primo de Rivera
    b. an antifascist coalition, aided by Soviet troops and supplies
    c. the National Front, aided by Italian and German arms and money
    d. General Francisco Franco, who established a conservative, authoritarian regime

Answer: d, easy, page 958

67. Lenin's New Economic Policy in the early 1920s:
    a. put Russia on the path of rapid industrialization at the expense of the peasantry
    b. was a modified form of the capitalist system
    c. forced communism to move forward as both industry and agriculture were nationalized
    d. failed to reverse the patterns of famine and industrial collapse that began in 1921

Answer: b, difficult, page 958

68. Joseph Stalin's emergence as leader of the Communist party was aided by:
    a. Lenin's recommendation that he become sole leader
    b. his alliance with Trotsky and the Right in the Politburo
    c. his position as general secretary
    d. strong support of the left in the Politburo, which favored the spread of Communism abroad

Answer: c, medium, page 959

69. The Stalinist era in the 1930s witnessed:
    a. the decline of industrialization in favor of the collectivization of agriculture
    b. real wages and social conditions for the industrial labor force improve dramatically

     c. millions of ordinary citizens arrested and sent into forced labor camps
     d. an abundance of permissive social legislation

Answer: c, difficult, page 960

70. The collectivization of agriculture under Stalin was characterized by:
     a. widespread famine due to peasant hoarding and slaughter of livestock
     b. the cooperation of the kulaks
     c. the destruction of the collective farms
     d. immediate financial benefits for most of the peasants

Answer: a, difficult, page 960

71. The new forms of mass communication and leisure created between the wars:
     a. saw cinema become an increasingly popular form of entertainment
     b. were used by fascist nations for propaganda purposes
     c. witnessed radio production and broadcasting companies increase dramatically
     d. all of the above

Answer: d, easy, page 962

72. The Dopolavaro was instituted in:
     a. England
     b. France
     c. Spain
     d. Italy

Answer: d, easy, page 963

73. Strength through Joy:
     a. was Joseph Goebbels's most effective Nazi propaganda film
     b. was Fascist Italy's most popular national recreation agency
     c. attempted to monitor and homogenize the leisure time of the German workers
     d. failed miserably in its attempts to draw German workers to vacation package tours

Answer: c, difficult, page 963

74. Artistic and intellectual trends in the interwar years were concerned with:
     a. a rejection of the avant-garde
     b. a sense of disillusionment with Western civilization

    c. realistic forms of art, as with the Dadaists
    d. an acceptance of modern art forms, especially in Germany and Russia

Answer: b, medium, page 964

75. Identify the <u>false</u> relationship between the artist and his artistic movement:
    a. Arnold Schönberg--socialist realism
    b. Salvador Dali--Surrealism
    c. Walter Gropius--Bauhaus
    d. Kurt Schwitters--Dadaism

Answer: a, difficult, page 965

76. The Dadaist movement in art was known for all of the following <u>except</u>:
    a. an expressed contempt for the Western tradition
    b. an effort to put a sense of purpose back into life
    c. anti-art
    d. the junk-based collages of Kurt Schwitters

Answer: b, difficult, page 965

77. Arnold Schönberg was best known for his:
    a. "socialist realism" paintings
    b. atonal, experimental music
    c. revolutionary directions in theater
    d. surrealistic, nightmarish paintings

Answer: b, easy, page 966

78. Art in Nazi Germany centered around:
    a. the use of modern, abstract forms to reflect Germany's "new order"
    b. the functionalistic methods of the Bauhaus school
    c. realistic scenes that glorified the strong and the heroic
    d. all of the above

Answer: c, medium, page 966

79. <u>Not</u> associated with the new literary techniques of the 1920s was:
    a. the "stream of consciousness"
    b. James Joyce
    c. Herman Hesse
    d. Ernest Rutherford

Answer: d, easy, page 967

80. The physicist Walter Heisenberg was most noted for:
    a. proposing that uncertainty was at the bottom of all physical laws
    b. being among the first team to split the atom
    c. resurrecting the scientific predictability of classical physics
    d. the development of the atomic bomb

Answer: a, medium, page 968

81. All of the following concepts were central to the psychological theories of Carl Jung except:
    a. the collective unconscious
    b. the process of individuation
    c. the uncertainty principle
    d. universal archetypes

Answer: c, difficult, page 968

SUGGESTED FILMS

Aftermath of World War I. McGraw-Hill Films, 26 min. (black/white).

League of Nations: The Hope of Mankind. Time-Life Films, 52 min. (color).

The Great Depression: A Human Diary. Mass Media Associates, 52 min. (black/white).

Franklin D. Roosevelt: The New Deal. ACI Productions, Inc., 22 min. (black/white).

Europe, the Mighty Continent: Form, Riflemen, Form! Time-Life Films, 52 min. (color).

The Rise of the Dictators. Time-Life Films, 52 min. (color).

Mussolini. McGraw-Hill Films, 26 min. (black/white).

Benito Mussolini. Contemporary Films, 26 min. (black/white).

<u>Duce</u>. Hearst Metronome News, 14 min. (black/white).

<u>The Rise of Adolf Hitler</u>. McGraw-Hill Films, 27 min. (black/white).

<u>Rise of Hitler</u>. Time-Life, 29 min. (black/white).

<u>From Kaiser to Fuhrer</u>. McGraw-Hill Films, 30 min. (black/white).

<u>Minister of Hate: Goebbels</u>. McGraw-Hill Films, 27 min. (black/white).

<u>The Twisted Cross</u>. McGraw-Hill Films, 54 min. (black/white).

<u>Triumph of the Will</u>. Phoenix Films, 110 min. (black/white). [Nazi propaganda film]

<u>Stalin and Russian History, 1879-1927</u>. Centron Films, 29 min. (black/white).

<u>Stalin and Russian History, 1928-1953</u>. Centron Films, 31 min. (black/white).

<u>Stalin vs. Trotsky</u>. Films Inc., 25 min. (black/white).

<u>Stalin's Revolution</u>. Time-Life Films, 20 min. (black/white).

<u>The Rise of Soviet Power</u>. McGraw-Hill Films, 30 min. (black/white).

<u>The Spanish Turmoil</u>. Time-Life Films, 64 min. (black/white).

<u>The Spanish Civil War</u>. Films Inc., 26 min. (black/white).

<u>Germany-Dada</u>. University Education and Visual Arts, 55 min. (color).

<u>Surrealism</u>. International Film Bureau, 24 min. (color).

<u>Vienna: Stripping the Facade</u>. Media Guild Films, 25 min. (color).   [Schönberg]

SUGGESTIONS FOR MUSIC

Arnold Schönberg, <u>Pierrot Lunaire</u> (CBS-MT-42072)

Arnold Schönberg, <u>Verklärte Nacht</u> (DG-415326-2)

Kurt Weill, <u>The Threepenny Opera</u> (Columbia-02L257)

Béla Bartók, <u>Concerto for Orchestra</u> (Philips-411132-2)

Béla Bartók, <u>The Miraculous Mandarin</u> (Mercury-MG50038)

Alban Berg, <u>Wozzeck</u> (DG-423587-2)

CHAPTER 28: THE DEEPENING OF
THE EUROPEAN CRISIS: WORLD WAR II

CHAPTER OUTLINE

THE AFTERMATH OF THE WAR: THE EMERGENCE OF THE COLD WAR
The Conferences at Teheran, Yalta, and Potsdam

SUGGESTED LECTURE TOPICS

1. "The Role of Hitler in World War II"

2. "The Nazi New Order: What Did It Mean for Europe?"

3. "The Destructiveness of Two World Wars and The Crisis of Twentieth-Century Western Civilization"

4. "Hitler's Other War: The Holocaust"

5. "The Defeat of the Axis: An Unholy Alliance"

MAPS AND ARTWORK

1. German lands vs. non-German acquisitions (language, culture, history) Map 28.1.

2. German and Japanese advances: What were their strategic plans? Maps 28.2 and 28.3.

3. Creation of the modern state, Map 28.4.

4. Holocausts and the totality of war.

DISCUSSION QUESTIONS FOR THE PRIMARY SOURCES (BOXED DOCUMENTS)

"Hitler's Foreign Policy Goals": According to Hitler, what were Germany's possible foreign policy goals? Which one did he prefer? Why? What were its consequences? (page 975)

"The Munich Conference": Compare the responses of Churchill and Chamberlain to the Munich agreement? Why did they disagree so much? (page 978)

"A German Soldier at Stalingrad": What does this excerpt tell you about German soldiers in World War II? (page 986)

"Hitler's Plans for a New Order in the East": What new order did Hitler envision in the east? what would its achievement have meant for the peoples of eastern Europe? (page 989)

"The Holocaust: The Camp Commandant and the Camp Victims": What death camp procedures did the Nazis create for the extermination of the Jews? Why were the Germans so meticulous in these procedures? (page 993)

"The Bombing of Civilians": What common elements do you find in these three different descriptions of bombing raids? What effect did aerial bombing have on the nature of warfare? (page 997)

"Emergence of the Cold War: Churchill and Stalin": What do the statements of Churchill and Stalin tell us about the origins of the Cold War? (page 1002)

EXAMINATION QUESTIONS

Essays

1. Discuss the major steps taken by Hitler from 1933 to 1939 that ultimately led to war. Could Hitler have been prevented from plunging Europe into war? How?

2. How do you account for the early successes of the Germans from 1939 to 1941?

3. When and why did the initiative in World War II pass out of Germany's hands?

4. Compare maps of the fighting fronts in World War I (pages 903 and 904) and World War II (pages 979 and 980) and discuss what this comparison reveals about the nature of land fighting in the two wars. How do you explain the differences you find?

5. Why did Germany lose the war? Was it a forgone conclusion?

6. How did the Nazis attempt to establish a New Order in Europe after their military victories? What were the results of their efforts?

7. Discuss the Final Solution: What was it? Who was responsible for it? How did it work?

8. Compare the home fronts of Great Britain, the Soviet Union, the United States, and Germany. What differences and similarities do you find? How did the organization of each home front affect the outcome of the war?

9. How did the attempt to arrive at a peace settlement after World War II lead to the beginnings of the new conflict known as the Cold War?

Identifications

10. Lebensraum
11. appeasement
12. "diplomatic revolution"
13. Neville Chamberlain
14. Munich Conference
15. Blitzkrieg
16. Battle of Britain
17. Pearl Harbor
18. Luftwaffe
19. New Order
20. Auschwitz
21. Great Patriotic War
22. Arthur Harris
23. "food-rationing"
24. Albert Speer
25. Hiroshima and Nagasaki
26. Cold War
27. Teheran Conference
28. Potsdam Conference
29. Iron Curtain

Multiple Choice

30. World War II was largely made possible by:
    a. Great Britain's aggressive plans on Europe
    b. a power vacuum in central Europe that only Germany could fill
    c. Soviet expansionism and interference in western Europe's affairs

    d. the League of Nations

Answer: b, medium, page 973

31. The idea of <u>Lebensraum</u> maintained that:
    a. a nation's power depended on the amount and kind of land it occupied
    b. only large populations could maintain a powerful country
    c. authority must be dictated from a powerful leader
    d. air power was the key to a successful military

Answer: a, medium, page 974

32. For Hitler, it was most important that Germany:
    a. develop its navy
    b. maintain satisfactory trade arrangements with the rest of Europe
    c. seek to expand its territory
    d. develop its air force

Answer: c, difficult, page 974

33. Germany and Hitler were most interested in expanding to the:
    a. north
    b. south
    c. east
    d. west

Answer: c, easy, page 974

34. For Hitler to achieve his goals, he thought:
    a. he must follow a strict time schedule and order of events
    b. he must gain the confidence of the United States
    c. careful consideration must be given to the desires of the Nationalists
    d. his basic plan of racial supremacy and empire was most crucial

Answer: d, difficult, page 974

35. When Hitler came to power on January 30, 1933, Germany was:
    a. the most powerful state in Europe
    b. limited to an army of 100,000 by the Treaty of Versailles
    c. threatened by Poland and Czechoslovakia
    d. already massing its troops in the Rhineland

Answer: b, easy, page 974

36. German advantages before the war included all of the following <u>except</u>:
    a. a large navy that could dominate the Atlantic
    b. the second largest population in Europe
    c. a great industrial capacity
    d. a desire on the part of France and Britain for peace

Answer: a, easy, page 974

37. The British policy of appeasement was based on:
    a. Britain's cowardly nature in world politics
    b. a general admiration of the Germans and their accomplishments
    c. a hatred and distrust of France
    d. a belief that it would maintain stability

Answer: d, medium, page 975

38. By the eve of his invasion of Poland, Hitler had concluded an alliance with:
    a. Japan
    b. Italy
    c. Soviet Union
    d. all of the above

Answer: d, easy, page 979

39. In 1937, Neville Chamberlain, the British prime minister, was:
    a. a strong advocate of appeasement
    b. calling for Britain to declare war on Germany
    c. working with Hitler to divide Europe into spheres of influence
    d. busy denouncing all changes in the status of central Europe

Answer: a, medium, page 977

40. The Munich Conference was:
    a. applauded by Winston Churchill as a "wise and noble agreement"
    b. formulated with the idea that if Germany wanted the Sudentenland it would have to fight for it
    c. criticized by Winston Churchill as setting a bad precedent in Europe
    d. a severe setback for Hitler

Answer: c, easy, DOC 2

41. Following the Munich Conference, Hitler:
    a. had Germany relinquish its claims to Czechoslovakia

    b. systematically took Czechoslovakia

    c. attacked France

    d. launched an attack on the Soviet Union

Answer: b, easy, page 978

42. Hitler took Poland in 1939:
    a. despite interference by the Soviet Union
    b. in a long protracted struggle that cost Germany dearly
    c. upon Poland's request for a restructured government
    d. using the new <u>Blitzkrieg</u> or "lightning war" tactics

Answer: d, easy, page 980

43. Immediately following the fall of Poland:
    a. France and Britain declared war and started an offensive against Germany
    b. France and Britain decided to continue to appease Hitler
    c. France and Britain declared war, but remained relatively inactive militarily
    d. Germany turned on its Russian allies

Answer: c, medium, page 980

44. The Maginot was in:
    a. Russia
    b. Poland
    c. Czechslovakia
    d. France

Answer: d, easy, page 980

45. Following the Allied evacuation at Dunkirk, France:
    a. soon surrendered and the Vichy government was set up as a puppet state
    b. went on the offensive and bogged Germany down in Normandy
    c. Italian forces moved to shore up Allied defenses and give them time to regroup
    d. the United States declared war on Germany

Answer: a, difficult, page 981

46. Hitler's plan for defeating Britain relied on:
    a. the support of Soviet troops in a massive amphibious invasion

     b. Germany's <u>Luftwaffe</u> gaining control of the skies
     c. V-2 rockets to destroy British industrial power
     d. a giant tunnel under the English Channel

Answer: b, medium, page 981

47. The war in North Africa was best characterized by:
     a. the overwhelming superiority of the Italian troops
     b. Hitler's lack of the commitment needed to secure the Suez Canal
     c. Hitler's easy lines of supply that allowed the war to drag on
     d. the intense fighting due to the strategic importance of its rubber supplies

Answer: b, medium, page 981

48. Japan's imperialist tendencies were motivated by all of the following <u>except</u>:
     a. the economic crisis of the 1930s
     b. the desire to be self-sufficient in raw materials
     c. a rapidly expanding population
     d. a Marxist ideology that governed state policies

Answer: d, medium, page 983

49. The Grand Alliance included all of the following countries <u>except</u>:
     a. Britain
     b. the Soviet Union
     c. France
     d. the United States

Answer: c, difficult, page 984

50. After the attack on Pearl Harbor, the main priority for the United States was:
     a. defeating Japan as quickly as possible
     b. recovering the Hawaiian Islands
     c. defeating Germany and then turning its resources on Japan
     d. to remain neutral, while buying time to build up industrial and military supplies

Answer: c, difficult, page 984

51. The turning point of the North African campaign came:
     a. at El Alamein where the British stopped Rommel in the summer of 1942
     b. when South African troops crossed the Sahara and overwhelmed Rommel
     c. with the revolt of the Vichy French in North Africa

      d. when the Italians joined the Allied cause in 1942

Answer: a, medium, page 984

52. The decisive Battle of Stalingrad was best characterized by:
    a. the Russians fighting to the last man until an exhausted German army took the city
    b. a gradual breakdown in German morale until the Germans were surrounded and forced to surrender
    c. the lack of conviction on the part of the Russians to defend their city
    d. the decisive role that the Soviet air force played in halting the German advance

Answer: b, easy, DOC 3

53. American naval superiority in the Pacific was:
    a. never in question, even after Pearl Harbor due to the great size of the United States navy
    b. precarious right up until the end of the war, with the United States generally relying on British support
    c. achieved after the decisive defeat of a Japanese carrier group at Midway
    d. really not necessary since the United States had no intention of trying to take back all the Pacific Islands

Answer: c, medium, page 985

54. The Allied advance in Italy was:
    a. extremely slow due to staunch resistance from the Italians
    b. extremely rapid with the whole of Italy conquered by November of 1943
    c. greatly aided by the influx of Soviet troops in the north
    d. very slow due to the extremely effective defensive lines of the Germans

Answer: d, medium, page 985

55. In order to open up a "second front" in western Europe, the Allies:
    a. quickly advanced through Italy into France in 1943
    b. invaded Normandy in history's greatest naval invasion
    c. landed in the Iberian peninsula and advanced through southern France
    d. lured Germany south to Italy and invaded the north German coast

Answer: b, easy, page 985

56. The final human toll of World War II may have numbered as many as:

    a. 500,000
    b. 5 million
    c. 100,000
    d. 50 million

Answer: d, medium, page 987

57. The Nazi Empire was:
    a. strictly organized into efficient states that paid tribute to Germany
    b. never much larger than the size of present-day Germany and Austria
    c. never organized systematically or governed efficiently
    d. for the most part composed of independent states that collaborated with Hitler

Answer: c, difficult, page 988

58. The Nazi rule of Europe was most ruthless in:
    a. eastern Europe because the Slavs were considered racially inferior
    b. France due to the long rivalry between France and Germany
    c. Norway, Denmark, and the Netherlands due to their close proximity to Germany
    d. Italy because the Italians were generally disloyal

Answer: a, medium, page 988

59. Hitler's intentions for his eastern conquests included:
    a. making the area into a giant strip-mine for natural resources
    b. setting up a puppet Slavic state to serve as a buffer zone
    c. massive Germanic colonization of these lands
    d. the creation of a giant, wildlife preserve in which no humans could live

Answer: c, difficult, page 988

60. Germany's policy of forced labor of conquered peoples:
    a. helped cause more resistance to the Nazis
    b. crushed the morale of peoples so they could not revolt
    c. gave Germany a critical advantage in industrial production
    d. was really quite exaggerated and was no more brutal than Allied practices

Answer: a, medium, page 990

61. A major source of resistance to the Nazis came from:

    a. the German people who were very effective in disrupting Hitler's plans

    b. Communists, especially after the invasion of the Soviet Union

    c. the Vichy French who would fight to the last person

    d. the Austrians who felt Austria should be the leader of Aryan Europe

Answer: b, easy, page 990

62. The SS's Security Service under _____ was given administrative responsibility for the final solution.
    a. Himmler
    b. Göering
    c. Bormann
    d. Heydrich

Answer: d, difficult, page 991

63. Hitler's "Final Solution" to the Jewish problem called for:
    a. the extermination of all European Jews
    b. the forced deportation of the Jews to Madagascar
    c. the resettlement of Jews in ghettos, isolated from other Europeans
    d. breeding "Jewish genes" out of the Jewish population itself

Answer: a, easy, page 992

64. The most efficient means developed for the extermination camps was:
    a. the use of specially trained SS units to round up "undesirables" and execute them by machine gun fire
    b. simply to intern prisoners and starve them to death
    c. to gas the victims and then cremate the remains
    d. the introduction of the plague

Answer: c, medium, page 992

65. Nazi atrocities at Auschwitz:
    a. were largely exaggerated by war propagandists
    b. were willingly carried out by most SS men who had few qualms about killing
    c. were reserved for just the Jews, with gypsies and other groups being sent to labor camps
    d. included cruel and painful "medical" experiments on inmates

Answer: d, medium, page 992

66. By far the nation that lost the most people in World War II was:
    a. France
    b. Germany
    c. Soviet Union
    d. United States

Answer: c, medium, page 994

67. The most thorough mobilization of people and resources in World War II occurred in:
    a. Britain
    b. United States
    c. Germany
    d. France

Answer: a, difficult, page 993

68. The only country to use women as combatants in World War II was:
    a. Germany
    b. Soviet Union
    c. Japan
    d. Britain

Answer: b,medium, page 995

69. The brunt of the Soviet war effort was borne by:
    a. small factory owners and craftsmen
    b. heavy industry
    c. the peasantry
    d. members of the Communist party

Answer: c, difficult, page 995

70. The mobilization of the United States included all of the following except:
    a. full employment by 1943
    b. substantial internal migration
    c. the internment of Japanese-Americans in guarded camps
    d. the shutdown of some small factories

Answer: a, medium, page 995

71. When Germany was preparing for war in 1939:
    a. the populace was euphoric as in 1914

    b. the populace feared that it would spell disaster for Germany
    c. consumer goods were cut in favor of war materials
    d. none of the above

Answer: b, difficult, page 996

72. Civilian bombing was done mainly:
    a. to reduce the number of people available to participate in war
    b. to exact revenge on the enemy
    c. to break the will of a people to resist
    d. by the Germans and was never an Allied strategy

Answer: c, medium, page 996

73. Black Americans in World War II:
    a. comprised a large percentage of the military forces
    b. were segregated into their own military units
    c. moved into many high paying positions in industry
    d. remained relatively sedentary compared to the internal migration of other Americans

Answer: b, medium, page 995

74. In the Allied bombing strategy, Americans participated:
    a. primarily in the nighttime saturation bombing of civilian populations
    b. only when British bomber wings needed reinforcements
    c. primarily in daytime, precision bombing of German strategic targets
    d. primarily as fighter pilots assigned to guard British bomber wings

Answer: c, difficult, page 997

75. Allied bombing raids on German civilians:
    a. produced stubborn resistance from the German people
    b. destroyed the average German's will to fight
    c. was only done to retaliate for German bombing
    d. occurred mostly by accident when bombing strategic targets

Answer: a, medium, page 998

76. The official reason for dropping atomic bombs on Japan was:
    a. to punish Japan for Pearl Harbor
    b. to test out the new weapon to see how powerful it was
    c. the shortage of explosive materials in the United States

d. to save the lives an invasion of Japan would entail

Answer: d, difficult, page 999

77. The leaders of the Big Three who met at Teheran in November of 1943 were:
    a. Stalin, Roosevelt, and Churchill
    b. Stalin, Roosevelt, and Chamberlain
    c. Lenin, Roosevelt, and Churchill
    d. Stalin, Truman, and Churchill

Answer: a, easy, page 999

78. The chief concern of the Allied conferences at Teheran, Yalta, and Potsdam was:
    a. how to end the war on favorable terms in the event of defeat
    b. determining spheres of influence of the individual Allies in postwar Europe
    c. how to rebuild the economy of Germany after the war
    d. whether or not to let China in on the spoils of the war

Answer: b, difficult, page 999

79. Following the war, Germany was divided into:
    a. two zones of occupation, west and east
    b. twenty small security districts
    c. four occupation zones under the United States, Soviet Union, Britain, and France
    d. three countries based on ethnicity

Answer: c, medium, page 1001

80. The chief argument between Truman and Stalin at Potsdam in July of 1945 was over:
    a. free elections in eastern Europe
    b. numbers of tanks on each side
    c. what to do with German prisoners of war
    d. whether or not the Soviet Union would be in the United Nations

Answer: a, difficult, page 1002

81. Churchill and Stalin were:
    a. basically in agreement, unlike Truman and Stalin
    b. quite willing to divide Europe into spheres of influence

c. largely agreed on creating a buffer zone between the east and the west
d. bitterly opposed after the war in a new Cold War

Answer: d, medium, page 1003

SUGGESTED FILMS

Munich Tragedy. Educational Film Enterprises, 27 min. (black/white).

Chamberlain versus Hitler. Films, Inc., 25 min. (black/white).

Under the Clouds of War. Time-Life Films, 20 min. (black/white).

Europe, the Mighty Continent: With Hardship in Their Garment. Time-Life Films, 52 min. (color).

The World at War Series. Thames Television, 26 parts, each 51 min. (color).

Battle of Britain. Wolper Films, 50 min. (black/white).

De Gaulle vs. Pétain: Struggle for France. United Artists, 30 min. (black/white).

D-Day. Metromedia Films, 50 min. (black/white).

Nazi Concentration Camps. National Audio-Visual Center, 59 min. (black/white).

Genocide. Thames Television, 52 min. (color). [Hitler's Final Solution]

Legacy of Anne Frank. McGraw-Hill Films, 29 min. (color)

The Warsaw Ghetto. Time-Life Films, 51 min. (black/white).

The Music of Auschwitz. CBS, Inc., 16 min. (color).

Night and Fog. McGraw-Hill, 31 min. (black/white).

Total War. Learning Corporation of America, 26 min. (black/white).

The A-Bomb Dropped on Japan. Fleetwood, 4 min. (black/white).

The Decision to Drop the Bomb. Films, Inc., 32 min. (black/white).

Tale of Two Cities: Hiroshima and Nagasaki. National Audio-Visual   Center, 12 min. (black/white).

1945. Contemporary Films, 28 min. (color).

Trial at Nuremberg. Films, Inc., 55 min. (black/white).

Aftermath of World War II. McGraw-Hill, 25 min. (color).

CHAPTER 29: COLD WAR AND A NEW EUROPE, 1945-1970

CHAPTER OUTLINE

THE DEVELOPMENT OF THE COLD WAR
The Confrontation of the Superpowers
The Cuban Missle Crisis and the Move Toward Détente

RECOVERY AND RENEWAL IN EUROPE
Decolonization
The Soviet Union: From Stalin to Khrushchev
Eastern Europe: The Soviet Satellite States
Western Europe: Domestic Politics
   France: The Domination by De Gaulle
   West Germany
   Great Britain
   Italy
Western Europe: The Move Toward Unity

THE EMERGENCE OF A NEW SOCIETY
Social Structure
The Emergence of the Welfare State
The Permissive Society
Education and Student Revolt

SUGGESTED LECTURE TOPICS

1. "The Cold War, 1945-1970"

2. "The Resurgance of Western Europe: the Stagnation of Eastern Europe"

3. "De-Colonization and the New Global Community"

MAPS AND ARTWORK

1. A world armed to its teeth. Maps 29.1 and 29.2.

2. The independence movement. Maps 29.3, 29.4 and 29.5.

3. New European Economic Power (?), Map 29.6.

DISCUSSION QUESTIONS FOR THE PRIMARY SOURCES (BOXED DOCUMENTS)

"Truman Doctrine": What motifs does Truman evoke in this section, both American and Russian? What future impact will this speech have for American Foreign Policy? How did Truman justify his request for aid? Does he bear some responsibility for beginning the Cold War? (page 1008)

"The Cuban Missle Crisis: Khrushchev's Perspective": How does Khrushchev's account differ from America's version? Do you think that Khrushchev could know it was a highpoint in his career? (page 1014)

"Frantz Fanon and the Wretched of the Earth": Compare the Algerians' response with other groups fighting for independence. What does this account tell us about the worth of human life? (page 1017)

"Khrushchev Denounces Stalin": According to Khrushchev, what were Stalin's crimes? What do you think was the purpose of Khrushchev's denunciation of Stalin? (page 1021)

"Soviet Repression in Eastern Europe: Hungary, 1956": Based on this selection, what was Soviet policy in the 1950s toward its Eastern European satellite states? Compare this policy to Soviet policy in Eastern Europe in the late 1980s? What impact did this change of policy have on Eastern Europe? (page 1025)

"De Gaulle Calls for French Autonomy": What does this speech reveal about De Gaulle's wishes for France? Was he realistic? Why or why not? (page 1026)

"The Times They Are A-Changin'. The music of youthful protest.": Who are the opponents in the song? Have they changed today? How releveant is this song in today's world? (page 1033)

"1968: The Year of Student Revolts": Based on these selections, what were the issues that generated the student unrest of the 1960's? Do you find similar issues today? (page 1034)

EXAMINATION QUESTIONS

Essays

1. What was the Cold War? What were the major turning points in its development (through 1970)?

2. What are the major developments in the history of the Soviet Union since 1945? How have Soviet policies affected the history of Eastern Europe?

3. What were the major developments in domestic politics in Western Europe and how were they expressed in France, West Germany, Great Britain, and Italy? What efforts toward unity were made by Western European states? How did the policies of the United States affect those efforts?

4. Discuss the major social changes that have occurred in Western society since 1945.

5. What role has popular culture played in the Western world since 1945?

6. Discuss how the balance of power has moved from Europe to the United States and the Soviet Union.

7. How has the world developed into two armed camps?

8. Trace the development and history of "containment" of the United States from Truman to Vietnam.

9. Compare and contrast Stalin's policies with Khrushchev's.

10. Compare and contrast the political, social and economic histories of Eastern and Western Europe.

Identifications

11. Truman Doctrine
12. Marshall Plan
13. NATO
14. COMECON
15. Nikita Khrushchev
16. Cuban Missle Crisis
17. Vietcong
18. Joseph Tito
19. János Kádár
20. Charles de Gaulle
21. Konrad Adenauer
22. the Common Market
23. social welfare
24. permissive society
25. Herbert Marcuse

Multiple Choice

26. Which of the following statements concerning the Cold War is <u>false</u>?
    a. The Soviet Union's blocade of West Berlin failed to stop the creation of a separate West German state.
    b. American involvement in the Korean War reinforced America's determination to stop Communist expansion.
    c. The Marshall Plan was the Soviet Union's attempt to offer economic support to war-torn European nations.
    d. Soviet involvement in Greece's civil war led to the proclamation of the Truman Doctrine.

Answer: c, medium, page 1008

27. The Cold War resulted from:
    a. the Soviet Union's need to secure its western border
    b. the United States' desire to maintain its wartime power and prestige
    c. the European tradition of power politics
    d. all of the above

Answer: d, easy, page 1008

28. The Truman Doctrine did all of the following <u>except</u>:
      a. condemn the victory of the Communists in the Chinese civil war
      b. call for $400 million in aid for the defense of Greece and Turkey
      c. express America's fear of Communist expansion in Europe
      d. announce the United States' intention to support "free peoples" throughout the world

Answer: a, medium, page 1008

29. The Marshall Plan:
      a. intended to rebuild European prosperity and stability
      b. was viewed by the Soviet Union as Capitalist imperialism
      c. did not intend to shut out the Soviet Union or Eastern Europe
      d. all of the above

Answer: d, easy, page 1009

30. The battle between East and West over Germany in the Cold War resulted in:
      a. the creation of an independent West German state under Walter Ulbricht
      b. a successful plan of industrial and economic revitalization by the Soviet Union in East Germany
      c. a successful blockade of West Berlin by the Soviet Union
      d. the creation of two separate German states by 1949

Answer: d, difficult, page 1010

31. An overall effect of the Korean War on the Cold War was:
      a. the domination of the Soviet Union over all of Southeast Asia
      b. the end to American and Soviet involvement in Asian affairs
      c. the reinforcement of American determination to contain Soviet power
      d. none of the above

Answer: c, easy, page 1012

32. The United States played a dominant role in all of the following alliances <u>except</u>:
      a. NATO
      b. COMECON
      c. CENTO
      d. SEATO

Answer: b, medium, page 1011

33. The policy used by the Americans against Communism was called:
     a. aggressive retaliation
     b. containment
     c. appeasement
     d. none of the above

Answer: b, easy, page 1012

34. The Cuban Missile Crisis of 1962 concluded with:
     a. improved communications between the United States and the Soviet Union
     b. the installation of Soviet missiles in Cuba
     c. the United States overthrowing Cuba's Soviet-supported government
     d. John Kennedy backing down to the threats of Nikita Khrushchev

Answer: a, easy, page 1013

35. The Vietnam War:
     a. was resolved in 1975 with the Helsinki Agreements
     b. ended in 1973 with the defeat of North Korea
     c. showed the limitations of American power, leading to improved Soviet-American relations
     d. marked the beginning of the total domination of Southeast Asia by the Soviet Union

Answer: c, medium, page 1015

36. The process of decolonization was accelerated by:
     a. the Japanese humiliating the western states by overruning their empire
     b. colonial soldiers fighting for the Allies in World War II
     c. the ideas of self-determination
     d. all of the above

Answer: d, medium, page 1016

37. The process of decolonization throughout the non-Western world following World War II resulted in:
     a. a peaceful resolution of the Arab-Israeli conflict in Palestine
     b. the immediate, peaceful realization of independence among the French colonies
     c. the creation of the "Third World," which has lacked the technological advancements of the "First" and "Second" Worlds
     d. bloody struggles for independence in all of southern Africa

Answer: c, medium, page 1019

38. Post-World War II life in the Soviet Union under Stalin witnessed:
    a. continued poor standards of living for the working classes
    b. an emphasis on the production of consumer goods
    c. a relaxation of restrictions on literary and artistic expressions
    d. the adoption of Western influences into Communist ideology

Answer: a, easy, page 1020

39. The policies of Nikita Khrushchev in the 1950s and early 1960s:
    a. were basically a continuation of Stalinist policies
    b. were bolstered by his continued successes in foreign policy
    c. failed to benefit the Soviet economy and industry
    d. focused on repressing individualistic and intellectual trends

Answer: c, difficult, page 1022

40. Which of the following descriptions among these Eastern European nations is correct?
    a. Poland--The country became anti-Communist.
    b. Yugoslavia--Under the leadership of Tito, it remained dedicated to Stalinist forms of Communism until the 1980s.
    c. Czechoslovakia--The "Prague Spring" of 1968 led to the collapse of its Communist party and the new presidency of Vaclav Havel.
    d. Hungary--The failure of Imry Nagy's independence movement led to the rule of János Kádár for the next thirty years.

Answer: d, medium, page 1023

41. Yugoslavia from World War II through the 1970s was characterized by:
    a. its close alliance with the West in the Cold War
    b. a strict adherence to Stalinist-style Communism
    c. the dominant leadership of Tito, who asserted Yugoslavia's independence from the Soviet Union
    d. all of the above

Answer: c, medium, page 1023

42. The independence movement in Hungary in 1956 resulted in:
    a. the end of Communist rule in Hungary
    b. the leadership of Imry Nagy for the next thirty years

      c. armed Soviet intervention and reassertion of Communist leadership
      d. none of the above

Answer: c, medium, page 1023

43. The "Prague Spring" in Czechoslovakia in 1968:
      a. was triggered by the reforms of Alexander Dubcek
      b. led to the presidency of Vaclav Havel in 1970
      c. witnessed Czechoslovakia's successful withdrawal from the Soviet bloc
      d. brought about the resignation of President Gustav Husák

Answer: a, difficult, page 1024

44. In general, the Western European states in the postwar world have witnessed:
      a. the continual success of Communist parties
      b. the continual success of Socialist parties
      c. a continual decline in industrial production
      d. successful mixed economies and technological growth

Answer: d, easy, page 1025

45. As president of France, Charles de Gaulle's position in the Cold War was to:
      a. closely align France with the Warsaw Pact nations
      b. remain independent from the superpowers
      c. let American policy guide France and the European nations
      d. make France the leading European power in NATO

Answer: b, difficult, page 1026

46. de Gaulle achieved his goal of making France a world power.
      a. True
      b. False

Answer: b, medium, page 1026

47. The first chancellor and "founding hero" of the West German Federal Republic is:
      a. Helmut Kohl
      b. Helmut Schmidt
      c. Willy Brandt
      d. Konrad Adenauer

Answer: d, difficult, page 1027

48. Which of the following statements concerning postwar Great Britain is <u>false</u>?
    a. The National Insurance Act and National Health Service Act made Britain a welfare state in the 1940s.
    b. The Conservative party in the 1950s and 1960s revoked nearly all of the liberal legislation passed by the Labour party in the 1940s.
    c. Britain suffered from losing its pre-war reserves.
    d. By the Suez Canal debaucle, Britain was no longer a superpower.

Answer: b, difficult, page 1028

49. Postwar Italian politics have been characterized by:
    a. the dominance of the Communist party
    b. the weakness and demise of the Christian Democrats
    c. control of Christian Democrats
    d. all of the above

Answer: c, medium, page 1028

50. The free trade union known as the Common Market includes all of the following nations <u>except</u>:
    a. France
    b. Great Britain
    c. the United States
    d. Spain

Answer: c, easy, page 1030

51. The social structure of postwar European society has been greatly affected by a dramatic increase in the number of:
    a. white-collar management and administrative personnel
    b. the number of industrial workers
    c. rural, agricultural workers
    d. all of the above

Answer: a, difficult page 1030

52. The postwar Western world has witnessed a steady decline in:
    a. the number of women in the work force
    b. birthrate and fertility rates
    c. the trend toward early marriages
    d. the use of contraceptive devices

Answer: b, page 1031

53. The Welfare State represented:
     a. an attempt by the state to control the lives of its citizens
     b. a new move in European society
     c. an attempt to make life better and more meaningful
     d. "a" and "c"

Answer: d, medium, page 1031

54. The "permissive society" is characterized by all of the following except:
     a. sexual freedom
     b. experimentation in drugs
     c. the increase of family values
     d. decriminalization of homosexuality

Answer: c, medium, page 1032

55. The outburst of student revolts in the late 1960s was instigated by:
     a. the Vietnam War
     b. overcrowded classrooms and lack of attention from professors
     c. discontent with the materialistic and impersonal nature of the modern
         world
     d. all of the above

Answer: d, medium, page 1031

56. The student revolts of the 1960's in Germany and France successfully brought
     down the government.
     a. True
     b. False

Answer: b, easy, page 1034

SUGGESTED FILMS

Europe: Two Decades. U. S. National Audiovisual Center, 45 min. (black/white).
    [1945- 1965]

Europe, the Mighty Continent: The New Europe--A Certain Amount of Violence.
    Time-Life Films, 52 min. (color).

Europe, the Mighty Continent: A Search for Unity. Time-Life Films, 52 min. (color).

Europe, the Mighty Continent: A European Idea. Time-Life Films, 52 min. (color).

Europe, the Mighty Continent: How are the Mighty Fallen. Time-Life Films, 52 min. (color).

Cold War: Confrontation. Films Inc., 20 min. (color).

The Cold War: The Early Period. McGraw-Hill, 20 min. (black/white).

Vietnam--A Historical Document. Carousel Films, 56 min. (color).

Germany: The Road of Return. Filmfair International, 30 min. (color).

Death of Stalin. McGraw-Hill Films, 54 min. (black/white).

Nikita Khrushchev. Mc-Graw Hill Films, 26 min. (black/white).

Revolution's Orphans. Films Inc., 20 min. (color). [Hungary in 1956]

Hungary and Communism--Eastern Europe in Change. Encyclopedia Britannica, 17 min. (color).

Rise of British Socialism. McGraw-Hill Films, 55 min. (black/white).

The Second Battle of Britain. Carousel Films, 49 min. (color).

Britain: A Changing Culture. McGraw-Hill, 25 min. (color).

The Chancellor: A Portrait of Konrad Adenauer. Hearst, 11 min. (black/white).

Charles De Gaulle. McGraw-Hill Films, 26 min. (black/white).

Revolution in Europe's Role in the World. National Educational Television, 30 min. (color).

Man and the "Second" Industrial Revolution. McGraw-Hill Films, 19 min. (color).

Life at the Top. Sterling Educational Films, 24 min. (color). [social structure]

Since 1945. Films Inc., 30 min. (color). [popular culture]

Albert Camus: A Self-Portrait. Learning Corporation of America, 20 min. (color).

R. Buckminster Fuller: Prospects for Humanity. Indiana University Audio-Visual Center, 30 min. (color).

SUGGESTIONS FOR MUSIC

Olivier Messiaen, Turangalila-symphonie (CBS-M2K-42271)

Olivier Messiaen, Quartet for the End of Time (Angel-CDCB-47463)

Aaron Copland, Appalachian Spring (London-414457-2LH)

Edgard Varése, Poéme electronique (CBS-MG6146)

Karlheinz Stockhausen, Ceylon (Chrysalis-CHR1110)

Philip Glass, Glassworks (CBS-MK37265)

CHAPTER 30: THE CONTEMPORARY WESTERN WORLD (SINCE 1970)

CHAPTER OUTLINE

FROM A COLDWAR TO POST-COLD WAR: TOWARD A NEW WORLD ORDER?
The End of the Cold War

TOWARD A NEW EUROPEAN ORDER
The Revolutionary Era in the Soviet Union
    The Gorbachev Era
    The End of the Soviet Union
Eastern Europe: From Soviet Satellites to Sovereign Nations
    Poland
    Hungary
    Czechoslovakia
    Romania
    Bulgaria and Albania
    East Germany
    Yugoslavia
    After the Fall
Western Europe
    From Western Germany to Germany
    Great Britain
    France
    Italy

NEW DIRECTIONS AND NEW PROBLEMS IN WESTERN SOCIETY
New (and Old) Patterns: Women Since the 1960s
The Feminist Movement: The Search for Liberation
Terrorism
Guest Workers and Immigrants
The Environment and the Green Movements

THE WORLD OF WESTERN CULTURE
Recent Trends in Art, Music, and Literature
Science and Technology
The Philosophical Dilemma: Existentialism
The Revival of Religion
Popular Culture
Popular Culture and the Americanization of the World
Sports
Popular Culture: Toward a New Globalism

TOWARD A GLOBAL CIVILIZATION?

SUGGESTED LECTURE TOPICS

1. "Big Science and Big Environmental Problems: Is There a Relationship?"

2. "The Women's Movement: Promises and Problems"

3. "The Fall and Breakup of the Soviet Union: How Stable is World Peace?"

4. "The Problems of Nationalities and Self-Determination"

5. "Modernism and Post-Modernism in the Arts" [a slide lecture]

MAPS AND ARTWORK

1. The breakup of the Soviet Union; ramifications for the future. Map 30.1.

2. The war in the former Yugoslavia. Map 30.2 compared with 23.3.

DISCUSSION QUESTIONS FOR THE PRIMARY SOURCES (BOXED DOCUMENTS)

"Gorbachev and Perestroika": How revolutionary is Gorbachev's rejection of nuclear war? What impact did his idea of restructuring have on Communism? (page 1044)

"Vaclav Havel: The Call for a New Politics": How different is Havel's view of politics than the mainstream politicians? Do you think his ideas could succeed? (page 1048)

"Bosnia: Two Faces of War": Given the contradictory statements, is it possible to find the truth? (page 1053)

"The Voice of the Women's Liberation Movement": What is Simone de Beauvoir's basic argument? Do you agree with it? Why or why not? (page 1059)

"Violence against Foreigners in Germany": How different are these attacks than those in the 1930s in Germany? (page 1062)

"Small is Beautiful: The Limits of Modern Technology": What was Schumacher's critique of modern technology? To what extent has this critique been substantiated by developments since 1975? (page 1066)

"The Voice of Existentialism" and "Pope John Paul II: An Appeal for Peace": Can these two ideas be reconciled? How far apart are the two views? What hinders peace according to John Paul II? (pages 1068 and 1071)

EXAMINATION QUESTIONS

Essays

1. What are Modernism and Postmodernism and how were they expressed in art, music, and literature since 1945? How do they reflect the political and social developments of the age?

2. What was the role of science and technology in the postwar Western world? What fundamental critiques have been made of science?

3. In what ways were the movement of existentialism and the revival of religion responses to the "despair generated by the apparent collapse of civilized values in the

twentieth century?"

4. In what ways does the postwar feminist movement resemble the feminist movement of the nineteenth century? In what ways is it different?

5. How successful have the former Soviet satellites been in handling post-Communism?

6. What problems have plagued the West during the 1970s and 1980s?

Identifications

7. Mikhail Gorbachev
8. New World Order
9. Leonid Brezhnev
10. <u>perestroika</u>
11. <u>sajudis</u>
12. solidarity
13. Vaclav Havel
14. Nicolae Ceausescu
15. Erich Honecker
16. Slobodan Milosevic
17. Helmut Kohl
18. François Mitterand
19. Margaret Thatcher
20. Simone de Beauvoir
21. Theater of the Absurd
22. <u>Small if Beautiful</u>
23. Existentialism
24. Pope John Paul II

Multiple Choice

25. The term "détente" describes:
    a. the United States' failed intervention in the Vietnam War
    b. the independence movements of the Eastern European nations in the late 1980s
    c. the period of increased hostility between the two superpowers in the 1960s

    d. the reduction of tensions between the superpowers following the Vietnam War

Answer: d, medium, page 1039

26. The success of détente was dampened by:
    a. the United States invasion of Grenada
    b. the Soviet invasion of Hungary
    c. the Soviet invasion of Afghanistan
    d. the United States invasion of Panama

Answer: c, difficult, page 1040

27. The first opportunity for testing the new relationship between the United States and the Soviet Union in the post-Cold War era was:
    a. the Chinese-Vietnamese War
    b. the Arab-Israeli War
    c. the war in Angola
    d. the Gulf War

Answer: d, easy, page 1041

28. The Soviet Union under Leonid Brezhnev:
    a. was completely shut off to Western influences
    b. stressed worker incentives and increased efficiency in industrial production
    c. saw heavy industry decline with improvements in agriculture
    d. none of the above

Answer: d, easy, page 1041

29. The problem of the Soviet Union in the 1970s and 1980s was the lack of vigorous leadership under:
    a. Brezhnev
    b. Yeltsin
    c. Gorbachev
    d. Khrushchev

Answer: a, medium, page 1042

30. Mikhail Gorbachev's radical reforms under "perestroika" have included all of the following except:
    a. the demise of the office of president

b. the creation of a new Soviet parliament

c. the creation of a market economy with limited free enterprise and private property

d. the open discussion of Soviet weaknesses in public

Answer: a, difficult, page 1043

31. One of the most successful independence movements among the Soviet republics during Gorbachev's rule has been led by the <u>Sajudis</u> in:
    a. Afghanistan
    b. Azerbaijan
    c. Lithuania
    d. Georgia

Answer: c, medium, page 1045

32. The breakup of the Soviet republics and the demolition of the Soviet Union allowed Gorbachev to become president of Russia in 1991.
    a. True
    b. False

Answer: b, medium, page 1046

33. The Solidarity movement in Poland:
    a. was temporarily crushed by General Lech Walesa in 1981
    b. failed to gain massive support due to the non-support of the Catholic church
    c. ended the Communist monopoly of power in 1988
    d. was formed by Wladyslaw Gomulka in 1956

Answer: c, easy, page 1046

34. In 1990 the Communist Party in Hungary changed its name to the _____ to appeal to the voters.
    a. Round Table
    b. Hungarian Socialist
    c. Democratic Forum
    d. Kádár Party

Answer: c, medium, page 1047

35. The leader of Czechoslovakia in 1990 who replaced the Communist government was:

    a. Kádár
    b. Husák
    c. Dubcek
    d. Havel

Answer: d, medium, page 1047

36. The brutal, dictatorial Communist government of Nicolae Ceausescu occurred from 1965 to 1989 in:
    a. Czechoslovakia
    b. Bulgaria
    c. East Germany
    d. Romania

Answer: d, easy, page 1047

37. The East German leader Erich Honecker was most noted for:
    a. building the Berlin Wall in 1961
    b. establishing a virtual dictatorship in the 1970s and 1980s
    c. urging the political unification of West and East Germany in the late 1980s
    d. leading an unsuccessful independence movement from the Soviet Union in 1953

Answer: b, medium, page 1050

38. Yugoslavia was divided into warring factions because of:
    a. ethnic diversity
    b. "ethnic cleansing"
    c. Europe's failure to take a stand
    d. all of the above

Answer: d, medium, page 1051

39. The European Community has witnessed:
    a. an increase in stature of Communism in the 1990s
    b. full political unity in 1991
    c. Europe being accustomed to democracy
    d. none of the above

Answer: c, medium, page 1054

40. The unification of Germany has brought about a strong Germany.

a. True
b. False

Answer: b, easy, page 1054

41. All of the following occurred in Great Britain under Margaret Thatcher except:
    a. a popular victory against Argentina in the Falklands War
    b. improved industrial production in all of Britain
    c. serious cutbacks in education
    d. a large military buildup and hard-line approach against Communism

Answer: b, medium, page 1055

42. Identify the false relationship among the European ruler and her or his political party:
    a. Alcide de Gasperi--Christian Democrats
    b. Margaret Thatcher--Labour party
    c. François Mitterand--Socialist party
    d. Helmut Kohl--Christian Democratic Union

Answer: b, difficult, page 1056

43. The Western nation with the highest percentage of married women in the work force since World War II has been:
    a. the United States
    b. the Soviet Union
    c. Sweden
    d. West Germany

Answer: b, medium, page 1057

44. Simone de Beauvoir was responsible for all of the following except:
    a. having a major influence on the women's movements in Europe and the United States
    b. gaining the right to vote for French women following World War I
    c. showing how women have come to be regarded at the Other
    d. the book The Second Sex, which claimed that women have been forced into a position subordinate to men

Answer: b, difficult, page 1058

45. Some believe that international terrorism declined in the 1980s because of:
    a. the breakup of the Soviet Union

b. the Iran-Iraq War

c. American retaliation/action

d. Israeli retaliation/action

Answer: c, medium, page 1060

46. The Green Parties have won impressive in European political races.
    a. True
    b. False

Answer: b, easy, page 1061

47. The postwar art world has been mostly dominated by:
    a. the United States
    b. France
    c. West Germany
    d. Great Britain

Answer: a, easy, page 1065

48. The American artist Jackson Pollock was most noted for:
    a. a return to extreme realism in his paintings
    b. Postmodernist sculptures
    c. Pop Art, which celebrated the whims of popular culture
    d. Abstract Expressionistic paintings

Answer: d, medium, page 1063

49. The major trend in classical music since World War II, as best expressed by Olivier Messiaen, has been:
    a. neoclassicism
    b. serialism
    c. Postmodernism
    d. minimalism

Answer: b, medium, page 1064

50. The "Theater of the Absurd":
    a. is well exemplified in Samuel Beckett's Waiting for Godot
    b. reflected the postwar disillusionment with fixed religious and political ideologies
    c. questioned the ability of language to reflect reality accurately
    d. all of the above

Answer: d, easy, page 1065

51. Identify the <u>false</u> relationship among the modern artists and their artistic fields:
    a. Andy Warhol--Pop Art
    b. Samuel Beckett--Theater of the Absurd
    c. Jackson Pollock--Abstract Expressionism
    d. Vaclav Havel--serialist music

Answer: d, medium, page 1065

52. "Big Science" in the postwar world has witnessed all of the following <u>except</u>:
    a. the bulk of scientific funding goes toward military related projects
    b. the dominance of government sponsorship in scientific research
    c. a return to Newtonian conceptions of the universe in physics
    d. the merging of theoretical science with technology

Answer: c, difficult, page 1066

53. A fundamental critique of the destructive nature of Big Science and modern technology was offered in <u>Small is Beautiful</u>, written by:
    a. Robert Oppenheimer
    b. E. F. Schumacher
    c. Ludwig Wittgenstein
    d. Michael Goric

Answer: b, medium, page 1066

54. The philosophical doctrine of existentialism:
    a. was dominant in the universities of Great Britain and the United States
    b. concentrated on logic and a theory of knowledge
    c. prospered in the optimistic values of the postwar world
    d. was best expressed by Albert Camus and Jean-Paul Sartre

Answer: d, medium, page 1067

55. The philosophical doctrine of existentialism stressed:
    a. the need for people to create their own values and give their lives meaning
    b. a return of God to the universe
    c. the human need to find the sole and true meaning and purpose of the world
    d. a complete withdrawal from an active, involved life

Answer: a, difficult, page 1068

56. American motion pictures in the postwar years have:
    a. been the primary vehicle for the diffusion of American popular culture
    b. destroyed the avant-garde expressions of Europe's "national cinemas"
    c. proven to be unpopular among European audiences
    d. done little to reflect the changing sentiments of contemporary society

Answer: a, medium, page 1070

57. The British punk movement of the late 1970s:
    a. was influenced by an earlier punk movement in the United States
    b. was supported by leftwing art school graduates
    c. was fueled by an economic and unemployment crisis, leading to rebellious and anarchical sentiments
    d. all of the above

Answer: d, easy, page 1072

58. Which of the following statements regarding popular culture since World War II is <u>false</u>?
    a. The politicization of sports and nationalistic sentiments were virtually eliminated by global telecasting.
    b. The United States has exerted the most dominant influence on worldwide cultural expressions.
    c. Advancements in mass communications technology have led to the emergence of global cultures in the 1960s and 1980s.
    d. Rock music and the punk movement have been influenced by migrations of musical forms between the United States and Great Britain.

Answer: a, medium, page 1072

59. Sports in the postwar years have:
    a. become a welcomed refuge from politics
    b. often been marred by nationalistic violence
    c. been economically damaged by the popularity of television
    d. none of the above

Answer: b, easy, page 1073

SUGGESTED FILMS

The Seventies: The Great Powers. Journal Films, 27 min. (color).

The Soviet Union: A New Look. International Film Foundation, 26 min. (color).

Trends. Journal Films, Inc., 27 min. (color). [science and society in 1970s]

A Woman's Place. Xerox Films, 52 min. (color).

Women at Work: Change, Choice, and Challenge. Encyclopedia Britannica, 19 min. (color).

MAP EXERCISES

Chapter XIII

Map Exercise 1: <u>The Iberian Peninsula</u>

Using various shades of pencil, color and label the following:

1.   Aragon
2.   Balearic Islands
3.   Castile
4.   Corsica
5.   France
6.   Granada
7.   Navarre
8.   North Africa
9.   Portugal
10. Sardinia

Pinpoint and label the following:

1.   Barcelona
2.   Lisbon
3.   Madrid
4.   Toledo
5.   Valencia

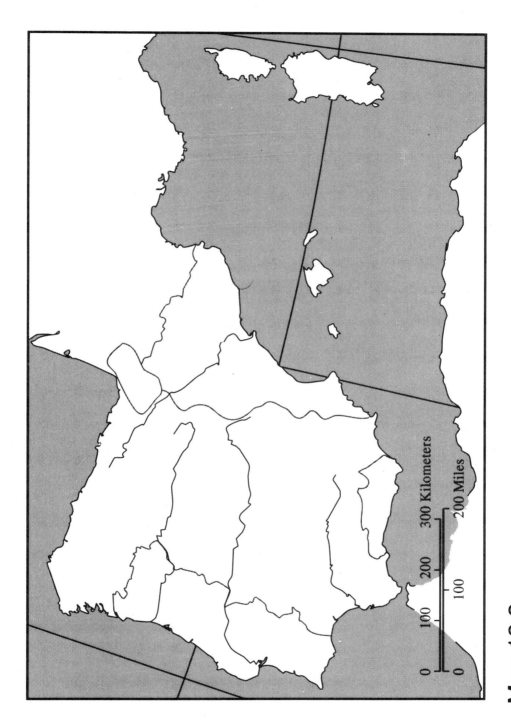

Map 13.3

300 Kilometers

200 Miles

Chapter XIV

Map Exercise 2:   <u>The Empire of Charles V</u>

Using one shade of pencil, color and label the possessions of Charles V and with various other shades show the territories of other princes:

1.   Aragon
2.   Austria
3.   Bavaria
4.   Bohemia
5.   Brandenburg
6.   Castile
7.   France
8.   Holy Roman Empire
9.   Hungary
10.   Netherlands
11.   Ottoman Empire
12.   Papal States
13.   Poland
14.   Portugal
15.   Russia
16.   Saxony
17.   Switzerland
18.   Tuscany

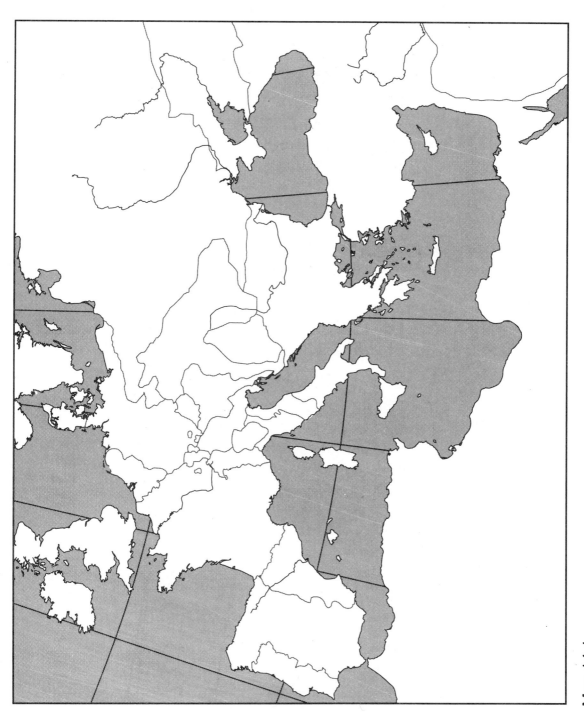

Map 14.1

Chapter XV

Map Exercise 3:   <u>Discoveries and Possessions in the Fifteenth through Early
                    Seventeenth Centuries</u>

Using various shades of pencil, color and label the following:

1.   Brazil
2.   Canton
3.   Caribbean Sea
4.   India
5.   Indian Ocean
6.   Indonesia
7.   Mozambique
8.   New Spain
9.   Peru
10. Philippines

Pinpoint and label the following:

1.   Calicut
2.   Cape of Good Hope
3.   Ceylon
4.   Goa
5.   Hispaniola
6.   Macao
7.   Tenochtitlan
8.   Zanzibar

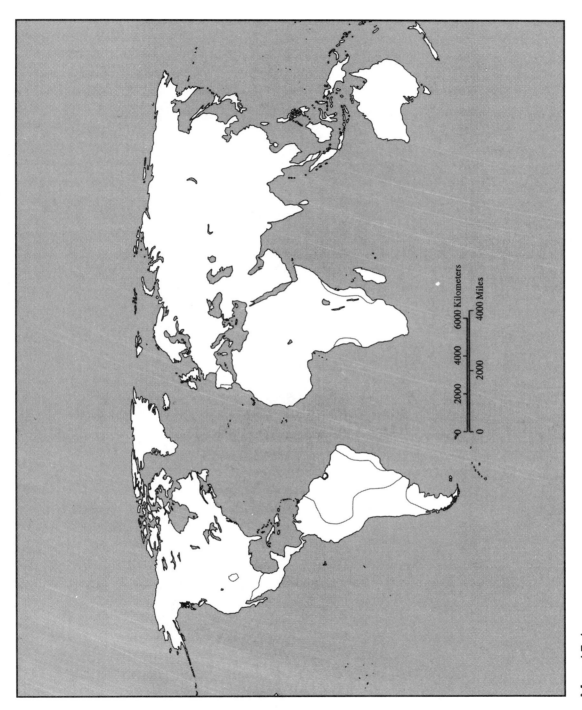

Map 15.1

Chapter XVI

Map Exercise 4: <u>The Thirty Years War</u>

Using various shades of pencil, color and label the following:

1. Baltic Sea
2. Bavaria
3. Bohemia
4. Brandenburg
5. British Isles
6. Denmark
7. Estonia
8. Finland
9. Hungary
10. Kingdom of the Two Sicilies
11. Norway
12. Ottoman Empire
13. Poland
14. Portugal
15. Prussia
16. Russia
17. Sweden
18. Swiss Confederation
19. Tuscany
20. United Provinces

Pinpoint and label the following:

1. Amsterdam
2. Berlin
3. Budapest
4. Danzig
5. Naples
6. Paris
7. Venice
8. Vienna
9. Warsaw

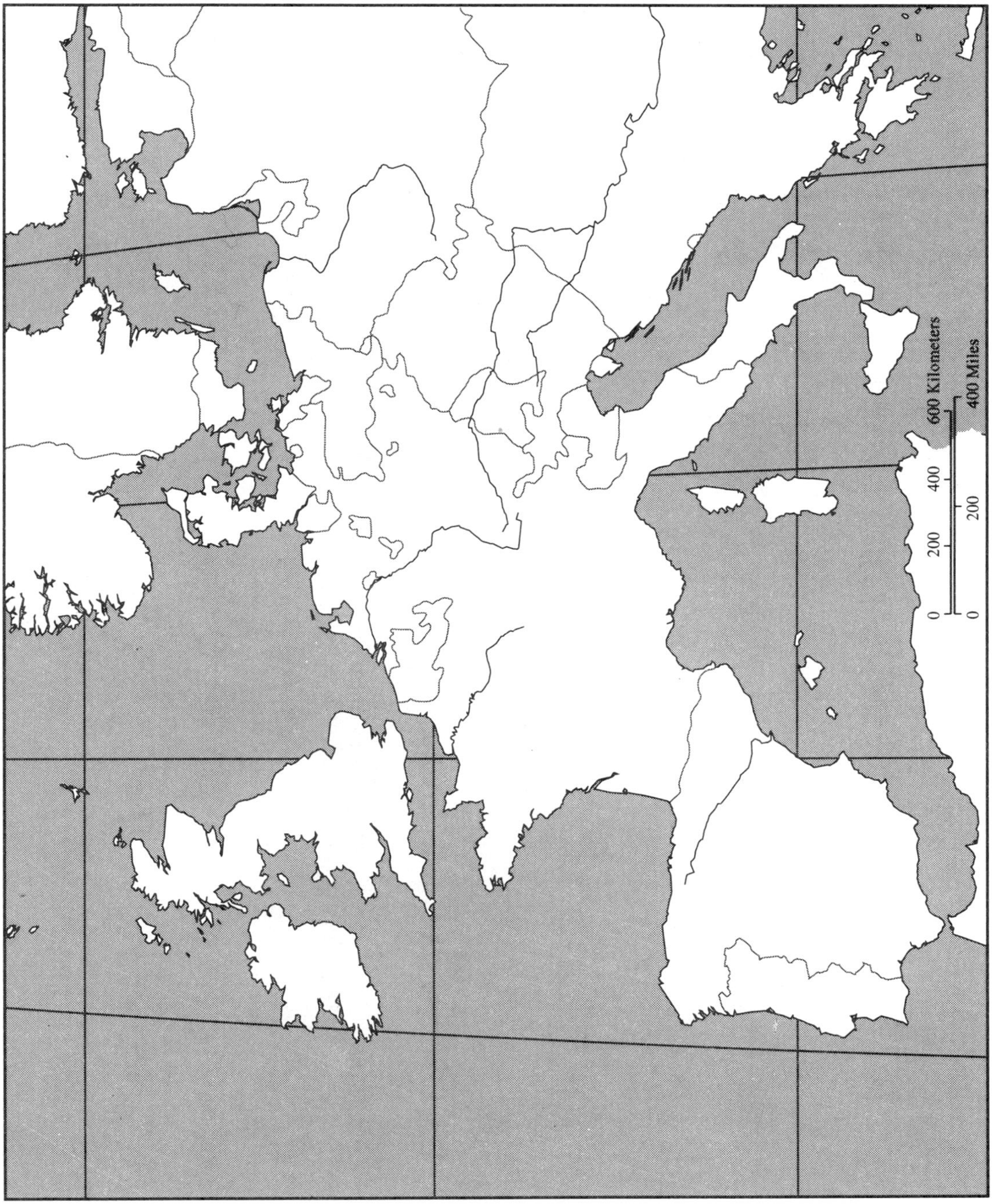

600 Kilometers

400 Miles

400

200

200

0

0

Map 15.3

Chapter XX

Map Exercise 5: <u>Napoleon's Grand Empire</u>

Using various shades of pencil, color and label the following:

1.	Austrian Empire	9.	France
2.	Baltic Sea	10.	Grand Duchy of Warsaw
3.	Bavaria	11.	Kingdom of Naples
4.	Britain	12.	Kingdom of Sicily
5.	Confederation of the Rhine	13.	Prissia
6.	Corsica	14.	Spain
7.	Denmark	15.	Sweden
8.	Elba	16.	Switzerland

Pinpoint and label the following:

1.	Auerstadt	10.	Madrid
2.	Austerlitz	11.	Marseilles
3.	Berlin	12.	Milan
4.	Borodino	13.	Moscow
5.	Brussels	14.	Paris
6.	Copenhagen	15.	Trafalgar
7.	Danzig	16.	Ulm
8.	Jena	17.	Vienna
9.	Kiev	18.	Waterloo

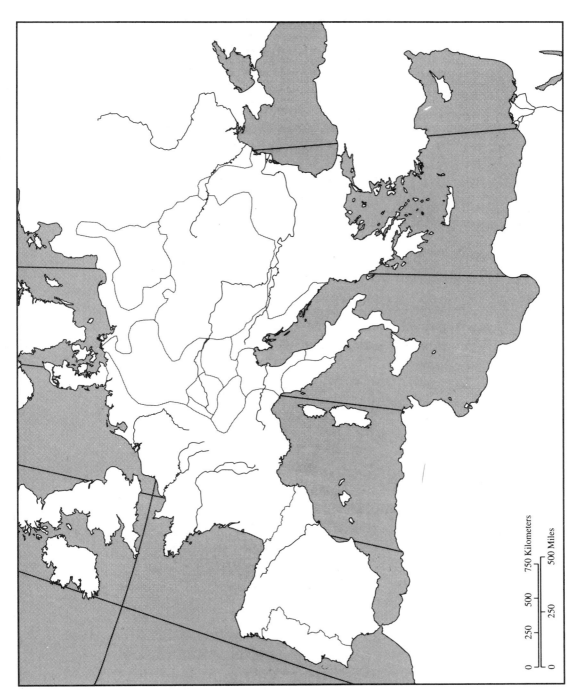

Map 20.3

Chapter XXIII

Map Exercise 6:   <u>The Unification of Germany and Italy</u>

Using various shades of pencil, color and label the following:

<u>Germany</u>	<u>Italy</u>
1. Alsace	1. Lombardy
2. Baden	2. Modena
3. Bavaria	3. Papal States
4. East Prussia	4. Parma
5. Hanover	5. Piedmont
6. Hesse	6. Romagna
7. Lorraine	7. Sardinia
8. Oldenburg	8. Savoy
9. Prussia	9. Tuscany
10. Schleswig-Holstein	10. Two Sicilies
11. West Prussia	11. Umbria
12. Württemburg	12. Venezia

Pinpoint and label the following:

1. Berlin	1. Florence
2. Breslau	2. Genoa
3. Frankfurt	3. Milan
4. Hamburg	4. Naples
5. Leipzeig	5. Palermo
6. Munich	6. Rome
7. Strassburg	7. Cwnixw
8. Trier	
9. Weimar	

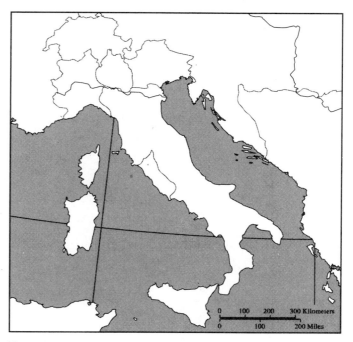

Map 23.1

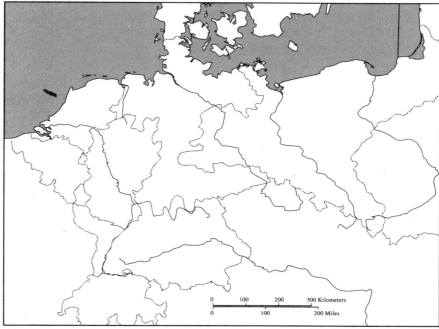

Map 23.2

Chapter XXIV

Map Exercise 7: <u>Europe in 1871</u>

Using various shades of pencil, color and label the following:

1. Algeria
2. Austria-Hungary
3. Austria
4. Belgium
5. Bessarabia
6. Black Sea
7. Bosnia
8. Crimea
9. Croatia-Slovenia
10. Cyprus
11. Denmark
12. Finland
13. France
14. German Empire
15. Great Britain
16. Greece
17. Hungary
18. Italy
19. Luxemburg
20. Montenegro
21. Morocco
22. Netherlands
23. Norway and Sweden
24. Ottoman Empire
25. Poland
26. Portugal
27. Romania
28. Russian Empire
29. Serbia
30. Spain
31. Switzerland
32. Tunisia

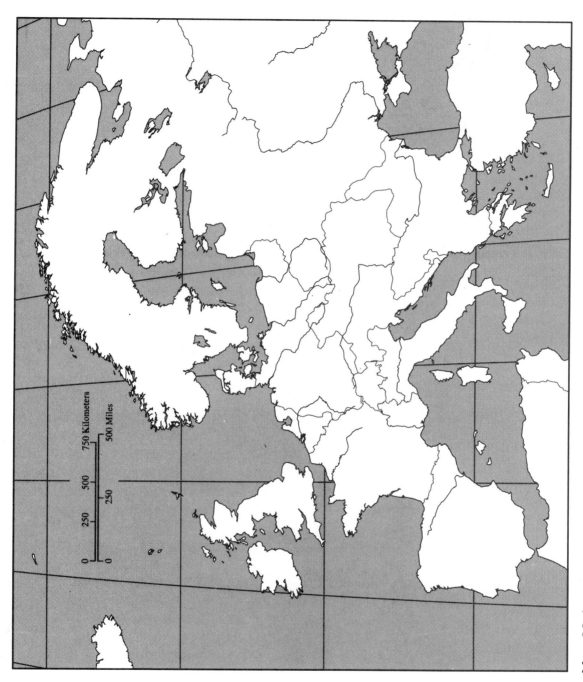

750 Kilometers

500 Miles

500

250

250

250

500

0

0

Map 23.4

Chapter XXV

Map Exercise 8: <u>Africa in 1914</u>

Using various shades of pencil, color and label the following:

1. Algeria
2. Angola
3. Atlantic Ocean
4. Bastuoland
5. Cameroon
6. Congo
7. Egypt
8. Eritrea
9. Ethiopa
10. German East Africa
11. Guinea
12. Indian Ocean
13. Kenya
14. Liberia
15. Libya
16. Madagascar
17. Mediterranean Sean
18. Morocco
19. Mozambique
20. Nigeria
21. Red Sea
22. Rio de Oro
23. Senegal
24. Sierra Leone
25. Somaililand
26. South Africa
27. South West Africa
28. Swaziland
29. Tunia
30. Uganda
31. West Africa

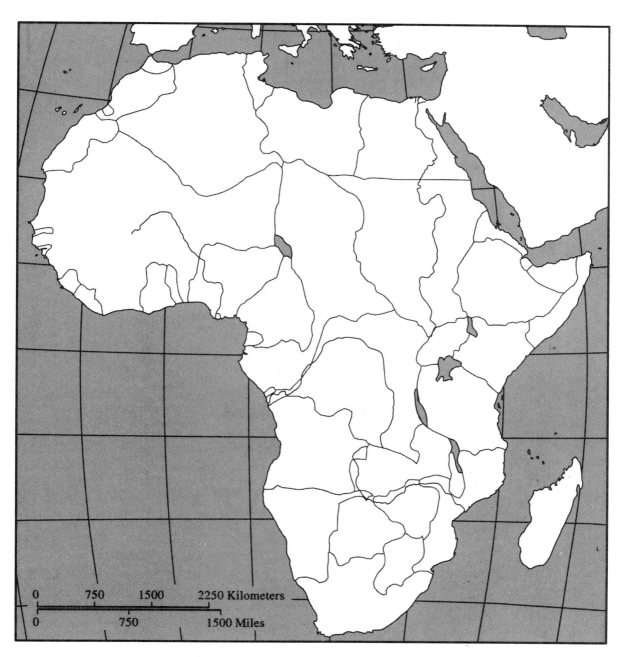

Map 25.2

Chapter XXVI

Map Exercise 9: <u>Europe in 1914</u>

Using various shades of pencil, color and label the following:

1.	North Africa	8.	Italy
2.	Austria-Hungary	9.	Netherlands
3.	Belgium	10.	Ottoman Empire
4.	Britain	11.	Russia
5.	France	12.	Serbia
6.	Germany	13.	Spain
7.	Greece	14.	Switzerland

Pinpoint and label the following:

1.	Aisne River	15.	Marne River
2.	Amiens	16.	Masurian Lakes
3.	Antwerp	17.	Mons
4.	Argonne	18.	Moscow
5.	Berlin	19.	Nancy
6.	Brest-Litovsk	20.	Oise River
7.	Brussels	21.	Paris
8.	Calais	22.	St. Mihiel
9.	Chateau Thierry	23.	Sedan
10.	Cologne	24.	Seine River
11.	Frankfurt	25.	Somme River
12.	Gallipoli	26.	Tannenberg
13.	LeHavre	27.	Versailles
14.	Luxemburg	28.	Vienna

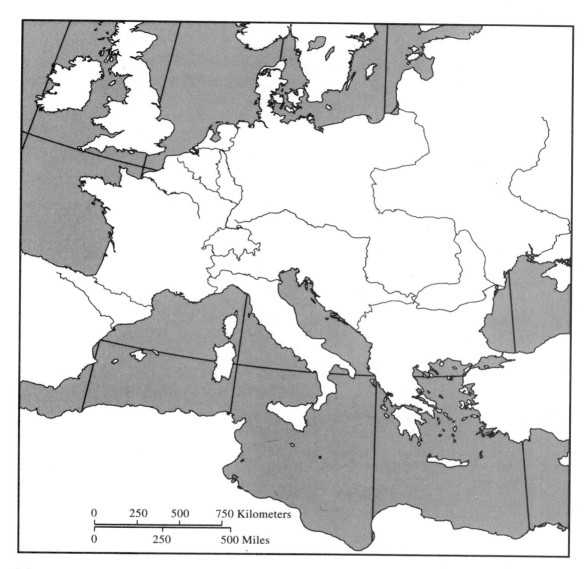

Map 26.1

Chapter XXVIII

Map Exercise 10: <u>WW II in Europe and Africa</u>

Using various shades of pencil, color and label the following:

1. Allied powers: Britain, Portugal, the U.S.S.R., the Middle East, and areas under Allied Control

2. Axis powers: Germany and Itlay

3. Axis satellites and allies

4. Conquests made by Axis 1939-1942

5. Neutral nations

Pinpoint and label the following:

1. Algiers
2. Berlin
3. Casablanca
4. London
5. Moscow
6. Paris
7. Rome
8. Tunis
9. Warsaw

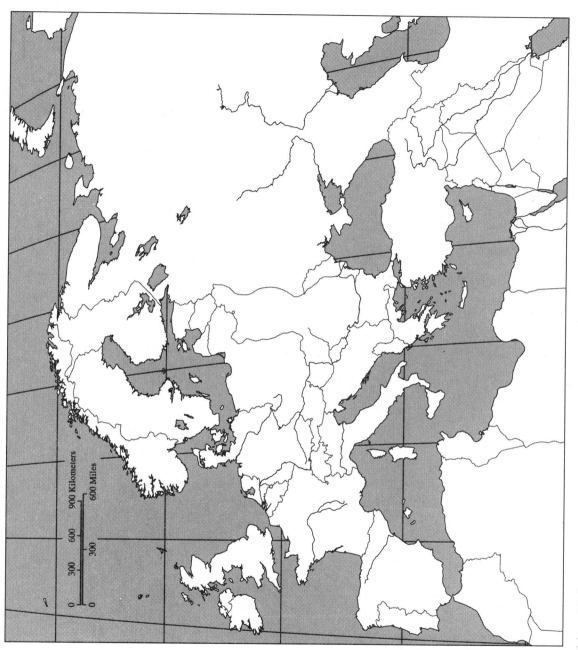

Map 28.2

Chapter XXX

Map Exercise 11: <u>The New Europe</u>

On Map A, label each nation and use different shades of pencil to color each one's affiliations in the Cold War:

1. NATO bloc
2. Warsaw Pact blco
3. Neutral nations
4. Independent nations

On Map B, label each nation and use different shades of pencil to color each one's identity

1. Members of the European Economic Community
2. Former members of the U.S.S.R. now independent
3. Eastern European nations, once in the Soviet bloc, now independent

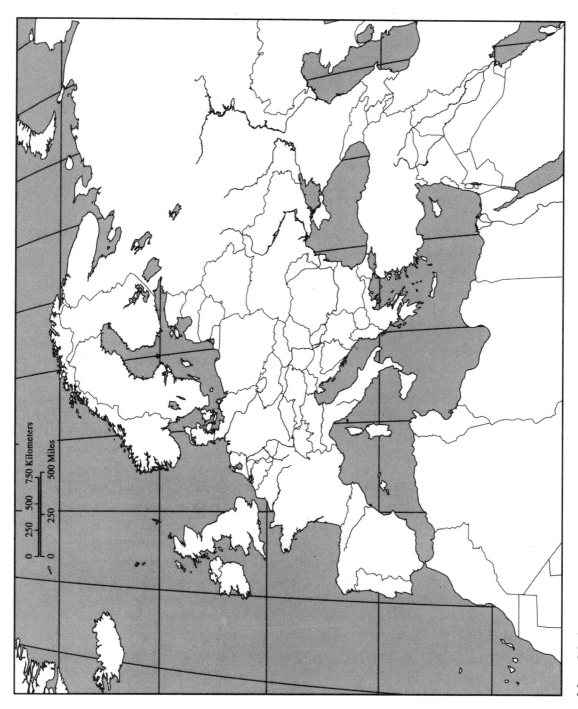

Map 30.1